BRICS and Climate Change

Hussein Solomon · Sanet Solomon · Bashabi Gupta
Editors

BRICS and Climate Change

Balancing National Interests, National Development Goals and Global Environmental Sustainability

Editors
Hussein Solomon
Centre for Gender and Africa Studies
University of the Free State
Bloemfontein, South Africa

Sanet Solomon
Department of Political Sciences
University of South Africa
Pretoria, South Africa

Bashabi Gupta
Department of Geography, Miranda
House
University of Delhi
Delhi, India

ISBN 978-981-97-5531-8   ISBN 978-981-97-5532-5   (eBook)
https://doi.org/10.1007/978-981-97-5532-5

© The Editor(s) (if applicable) and The Author(s), under exclusive license to Springer
Nature Singapore Pte Ltd. 2024

This work is subject to copyright. All rights are solely and exclusively licensed by the
Publisher, whether the whole or part of the material is concerned, specifically the rights
of translation, reprinting, reuse of illustrations, recitation, broadcasting, reproduction on
microfilms or in any other physical way, and transmission or information storage and
retrieval, electronic adaptation, computer software, or by similar or dissimilar methodology
now known or hereafter developed.
The use of general descriptive names, registered names, trademarks, service marks, etc.
in this publication does not imply, even in the absence of a specific statement, that such
names are exempt from the relevant protective laws and regulations and therefore free for
general use.
The publisher, the authors and the editors are safe to assume that the advice and information in this book are believed to be true and accurate at the date of publication. Neither
the publisher nor the authors or the editors give a warranty, expressed or implied, with
respect to the material contained herein or for any errors or omissions that may have been
made. The publisher remains neutral with regard to jurisdictional claims in published maps
and institutional affiliations.

This Palgrave Macmillan imprint is published by the registered company Springer Nature
Singapore Pte Ltd.
The registered company address is: 152 Beach Road, #21-01/04 Gateway East, Singapore
189721, Singapore

If disposing of this product, please recycle the paper.

FOREWORD

With *BRICS and Climate Change: Balancing National Interests, National Development Goals and Global Environmental Sustainability*, the principal authors seek to bridge an important gap in climate response, while highlighting shifts in multilateral polarity which offer cautious optimism that the paltry successes of the existing international order in addressing climate change and other existential threats can be transformed under new configurations of leadership. Indeed, BRICS Plus, and the widening of what has been referred to as the "BRICS circle", offers some hope that promises made at the United Nations and in other international institutions—of a new path of commitments to both climate mitigation and climate finance—could be realized as a matter of urgency.

The authors of this text understand that BRICS Plus represents only one of a number of efforts around the globe to reprioritize regional arrangements as a supplement to global counterparts. Much of this energy, of course, has been focused on economic, trade, investment, and currency arrangements. However, as the authors recognize, there is more than meets the eye here than mere brick-and-mortar living standards. There is also the attempt to forge new focal points of global leadership to, as the authors maintain, "further solidify the strategic importance of BRICS Plus on the international stage".

Such solidifying could well be unsettling to traditional powers that are more comfortable with notions such as the "rules based international order", institutions such as Bretton Woods and the G-20, or even Cold

War-era habits and dynamics which continue to unfold almost daily in the United Nations Security Council. However, countries across the globe, even those who consider themselves to be allies in some measure of the "traditional" powers, have come to distance themselves in either small or large measure from this residual "devil you know" mentality. They continue to witness economic disparities and vast inequalities, global institutions insufficiently committed to levelling the proverbial playing field, officials offering moving testimonies of commitment to climate mitigation and adaptation—which are incarnate neither in sustainable policies nor in adequate climate finance to help countries facing sea level rise—withering crops, and other climate-related threats.

There is little reason to believe that this new iteration of alliance building will abate anytime soon. Where climate change is concerned, however, there are questions as to whether BRICS Plus can avoid replicating what their members have been quick to critique in the existing international order—policy double-standards, resolutions, and other statements disconnected from tangible implementation, words which are performative more than impactful.

Moreover, again relative to climate change, there are questions regarding the ability of the BRICS Plus group and whether its larger circle of influence can ramp up climate finance and action with the needed determination, given that its membership includes several of the largest emitters of greenhouse gases as well as some of the world's major oil and gas producers.

Can such a collection of states address what BRICS Plus member United Arab Emirates during its Security Council presidency in June 2023 referred to as the "existential threat" of climate change with more urgency and effectiveness than the more traditional powers and multilateral institutions? The relative optimism of the principal authors on this matter duly noted, if the BRICS community could, in fact, manage to lead on actionable policies to restrict fossil fuels, substantially reduce emissions, and reverse sea level rising and ocean warming, the leadership which these countries seek among and beyond the "family of nations" would surely be broadly welcome. However, of course, not by all.

As the United Nations prepares for yet another Conference of the Parties (COP), more assertions will surely be made from some familiar quarters that "we have a handle" on climate threats, even as those handles have fallen away long ago. The authors fully grasp the need for a heavy

FOREWORD   vii

push on climate mitigation and adaptation from fresh actors, fresh collaborations, fresh ideas, and renewed commitments to climate finance and reduced emissions. The promises of these annual COP events have, sadly, become increasingly less believable, no matter how many hopeful (if often misleading) statements are uttered.

If the BRICS "circle" is to fulfil its leadership promise, if it is to offer fresh hope on climate risks and resist descending into national or other partisan interests, it will require close and sustained scrutiny from scholars, journalists, and civil society, including, and perhaps especially, from authors such as these. Such scrutiny is increasingly precious in this day and age, due in large measure to the risks which often must be assumed in order to provide it. However, BRICS Plus leadership will surely remain theoretical and self-serving in the absence of nonstate partners who can ask difficult questions and approach new leadership responsibilities and opportunities with fresh eyes.

This work is a most helpful step in that direction.

Dr. Robert Zuber
Executive Director, Global Action
to Prevent War
New York, USA

Dr. Robert Zuber is Director of UN-based Global Action to Prevent War and Armed Conflict where he has directed a small team of researchers, advocates, and policy interns monitoring all facets of the UN's work on security and weapons, gender, sustainable development, and human rights policies. He also serves as consultant, adviser, or board member to a wide variety of non-profit and educational organizations, including Green Map System, the Romero Centre (San Salvador), Global Connections Television, FIACAT (human rights) the Peace Angels Project, and Women in International Security (NY and CA). Based in Harlem, New York, and with degrees in philosophy, theology, psychology, and education from Yale and Columbia Universities, he has written and spoken extensively on peacekeeping, Security Council reform, small arms and arms trade issues, and other human security concerns. He has also organized seminars and conferences in over 30 countries on topics from the relationship of illicit weapons to sustainable development and atrocity crime prevention to the role of civil society in security policy development and the full participation of women and youth in peace policies and processes. He is also a multi-year veteran of courses at NATO School, the Scheller School of Business, and other institutions.

CONTENTS

Introduction Bashabi Gupta	1
Growing in Harmony with Our Cosmic Selves: A Holist Answer to the "No Technical Solution Problem" of Climate Change Bianca Naudé	11
Bridging the Gap: The Brazilian Climate Change Agenda After Bolsonaro Marina Magalhães Barreto Leite da Silva	37
Between Geopolitical Ambition, Energy Nationalism, and Capacity Deficit: Russia's Thorny Relationship with Climate Change Sergey V. Kostelyanets	67
Intersecting Priorities: India's Approach to the Politics of Climate Change—Domestic Development and Global Commitments Bashabi Gupta and Milu Maria Jose	97
China's Evolving Climate Change Strategy: a Dual Role in Mitigation and Adaptation Jana de Kluiver	119

South Africa's Commitment Towards Climate Security and a Just Transition 149
Sanet Solomon

BRICS Plus and Climate Change 165
Hussein Solomon

Saudi Arabia's Climate Change Policy: An Effort towards a Sustainable Future for the Kingdom and the Middle East 183
Md. Muddassir Quamar

India–Africa Cooperation: Joint Engagement in Adaptation to Climate Change 203
Shilpi Ghosh

BRICS Plus and Climate Change: Balancing National Interests, National Development Goals and Environmental Sustainability 233
Hussein Solomon and Sanet Solomon

Index 243

Notes on Contributors

Dr. Marina Magalhães Barreto Leite da Silva is an Assistant Professor at the University of Pernambuco and a Professor at the Brazil–Japan Cultural Institute, both institutions in Brazil. Currently, her research is connected to fields such as Japanese contemporary history and international organizations.

Jana De Kluiver is a PhD student at the University of the Free State. Their research focuses on the political economy of Africa. They have published on topics such as Africa's debt dynamics, China's involvement in African development, and security partnerships in the region. Their work provides valuable insights into the complex intersections of politics, economics, and international relations shaping Africa's trajectory. Their most recent publications include De Kluiver J.C. 2023. "Can China be a More Attractive Security Partner for Africa?" https://issafrica.org/iss-today/can-china-be-a-more-attractive-security-partner-for-africa; De Kluiver J.C. 2023. "Africa's Debt Dilemma: China's Role and Implications for Development." https://issafrica.org/research/policy-brief/africas-debt-dilemma-chinas-role-and-implications-for-development; and De Kluiver J.C. and Neethling T. 2022. "Entering the Dragon's Den: Contemporary Risks and Opportunities of China's Belt and Road Initiative in Africa." *Strategic Review for Southern Africa.* 44(1). https://upjournals.up.ac.za/index.php/strategic_review

xii   NOTES ON CONTRIBUTORS

Shilpi Ghosh is a PhD research scholar at the Centre for African Studies, School of International Studies, Jawaharlal Nehru University, also teaches Political Science at the University of Delhi and contributes to the School of Open Learning. Her doctoral thesis explores the impact of climate change on conflict dynamics, notably focusing on Somalia. She has a keen interest in both traditional and nontraditional security issues in Africa and has published in UGC-listed journals and online platforms.

Prof. Bashabi Gupta works in the Department of Geography, Miranda House, University of Delhi. She is also affiliated with the Department of Geography, Jamia Millia Islamia University, New Delhi. Her research interests include climate change, gender and development, gender in international relations, sustainable livelihoods, cartographic traditions and visual arts, and diaspora studies.

Milu Maria Jose is a Research Associate at the North East Regional Research and Resource Centre (NERRRC), Miranda House, University of Delhi. Her research interests include climate adaptations and policy, translational spaces, and development studies.

Dr. Sergey V. Kostelyanets works at the Institute for African Studies of the Russian Academy of Sciences, Moscow, Russia. His research interests include armed conflicts and conflict resolution in Africa, terrorism, secessionist movements, and relations between Russia, Turkey, Gulf Cooperation Council (GCC) countries, and Africa. His most recent publications include (with Denisova, T.S. 2024) "Terrorism in Nigeria: National Peculiarities and International Linkages. In *Terrorism and political contention: New Perspectives on North Africa and the Sahel Region* (pp. 287–300). Cham: Springer Nature Switzerland; and (2023), "The African Union–United Nations Hybrid Operation in Darfur (UNAMID): Mission Accomplished?" In *Africa and the Formation of the New System of International Relations—Vol. II: Beyond Summit Diplomacy: Cooperation with Africa in the Post-pandemic World* (pp. 301–315). Cham: Springer International Publishing.

Dr. Bianca Naudé is a Senior Lecturer in Political Studies and Governance at the University of the Free State, South Africa. Located in the broad field of international relations theory, her research interests are interdisciplinary in nature and draw on psychoanalysis, philosophy, and anthropology, among other things. She has contributed several scholarly articles and book chapters on African and South African foreign relations, ontological security approaches to topical issues such as terrorism and climate change, colonialism and collective trauma, and emotions in international politics. Her research monograph, *Revisiting State Personhood and World Politics: Identity, Personality, and the IR Subject* (2022), was published in the Routledge Psychoanalytic Political Theory Series and was recently named one of International Affairs' top five books in the category "new thinking in IR theory".

Dr. Md. Muddassir Quamar is an Associate Professor of Middle East Studies in Jawaharlal Nehru University, New Delhi. His areas of interest include politics and society in the Arabian Gulf, Middle East strategic affairs, and India's relations with the Middle East. He is the author of *Education System in Saudi Arabia: Of Change and Reforms* (Palgrave Macmillan, 2021) and Editor of *Politics of Change in Middle East and North Africa since the Arab Spring: A Lost Decade?* (KW and Routledge, 2022).

Prof. Hussein Solomon works at the Centre for Gender and Africa Studies, University of the Free State, South Africa. He is also a Visiting Professor at the Osaka School of International Public Policy, Japan, a Visiting Professor in the Department of History and Political Studies at Nelson Mandela University, a Senior Research Associate of the Jerusalem-based think tank Research on Islam and Muslims in Africa (RIMA), and a Research Fellow at the Security Institute for Governance and Leadership in Africa at Stellenbosch. He is also a member of the Academy of Science of South Africa (ASSAf).

Sanet Solomon is a Political Analyst and Lecturer in the Department of Political Science at the University of South Africa. She is an internationally published author, double cum laude graduate, member of the International Golden Key Honour Society, and PhD candidate in the Centre for Gender and Africa Studies (CGAS) at the University of the Free State. She currently serves as a Council Member of the South African Association of Political Studies (SAAPS), IAPSS Africa Regional Chair, and Deputy Editor-in-Chief of the IAPSS Politikon. She is also a member of the International Political Science Association (IPSA) and British International Studies Association (BISA). She serves as a reviewer for numerous double-blind peer reviewed accredited journals, such as Politeia (UNISA

xiv NOTES ON CONTRIBUTORS

Press Journal), Politikon (Taylor and Francis), and Local Government Studies (Taylor and Francis), Insight on Africa (Sage), and International Studies (Sage). Her research focuses on Africa (particularly South Africa) and the Middle East. Her latest academic publication is a Springer Nature book chapter on the climate-security nexus in Mali.

LIST OF FIGURES

Bridging the Gap: The Brazilian Climate Change Agenda After Bolsonaro

Fig. 1	Deforestation rate—Legal Amazon (INPE 2023)	50
Fig. 2	Deforestation rate—Pantanal (INPE 2023)	51
Fig. 3	Deforestation rate—Cerrado (INPE 2023)	52
Fig. 4	Deforestation rate—Caatinga (INPE 2023)	53
Fig. 5	Deforestation rate—Atlantic Forest (INPE 2023)	53

Intersecting Priorities: India's Approach to the Politics of Climate Change—Domestic Development and Global Commitments

Fig. 1	Per capita CO_2 emissions (*Data Source* Global Carbon Budget [2023], Population-based on various sources [2023], Our World in Data [2023])	103
Fig. 2	Total Energy Supply (TES) by source, India 1990–2021 (*Source* IEA World Energy Balances)	107

LIST OF TABLES

Intersecting Priorities: India's Approach to the Politics of Climate Change—Domestic Development and Global Commitments

Table 1	Estimated direct and indirect jobs in renewable energy worldwide, by industry, 2021–2022 (in thousands)	108
Table 2	BRICS countries' 2020 targets under the Copenhagen Accord vs Actual Performance	110

Introduction

Bashabi Gupta

Climate change is a slow disaster encroaching on various habitats across the globe in a multitude of ways. The ubiquitousness of the climate change phenomenon is undeniable at this point; however, the impact it has and how it is experienced vary according to the geographies of different nations. As the world struggles with the threat of climate change, various nations take centre stage in the global battle against environmental degradation and rising temperatures. Among the key players in this arena are the BRICS nations: Brazil, Russia, India, China, and South Africa, along with the newest addition of Saudi Arabia. These nations, representing different continents, cultures, and stages of economic development, collectively wield significant influence on the world stage and play a crucial role in shaping the future trajectory of global climate policies, as they represent 41% of the global population, approximately 24% of the global GDP, and approximately 16% of global trade (Ministry of External Affairs 2023).

BRICS is an atypical group of developing countries whose global impact is determined by their economic and geopolitical impact as well

B. Gupta (✉)
Department of Geography, Miranda House, University of Delhi, Delhi, India
e-mail: bashabi.gupta@mirandahouse.ac.in

© The Author(s), under exclusive license to Springer Nature Singapore Pte Ltd. 2024
H. Solomon et al. (eds.), *BRICS and Climate Change*,
https://doi.org/10.1007/978-981-97-5532-5_1

1

as their strategic locations. From the lush rainforests of Brazil to the vast steppes of Russia, and from the bustling cities of India and China to the mineral-rich lands of South Africa, each BRICS member brings a unique perspective, priorities, and challenges to the table in the fight against climate change. The power balance across the globe is shifting, with the West-dominated climate governance losing its foothold, and BRICS advancing in their importance in the international climate governance arena. This is a moment of transition that can help to shape the climate change paradigm.

The current global order is profoundly uncertain, which is exacerbated by interconnected challenges spanning economic decisions, climate change, energy resources, and migration. These issues transcend national boundaries and significantly impact collective well-being. Despite their magnitude, practical solutions remain elusive, contributing to a "gridlock", especially in the climate negotiations, hindering global climate governance and exacerbating vulnerabilities.

Within this context, emerging powers, notably the BRICS nations, have emerged as pivotal actors on the global stage, especially for climate governance. Their economic growth fosters internal divergence and reshapes international dynamics, challenging the dominance of Western-centric institutions (Chatin and Gallarotti 2016; Nayyar 2016). If the BRICS nations rationally and suitably integrate into a multipolar context, they could help to improve international climate negotiations and lead the changing global order.

Despite these initiatives, questions linger regarding BRICS' ability to challenge the Western-dominated financial governance embodied by the Washington Consensus (Bagchi 2012). The collective identity of BRICS nations as emerging powers has significantly influenced their approach to climate change. Their perception of developed countries' actions has contributed to forming a collective identity framework within BRICS, especially on climate change, by emphasizing their commitment to engaging responsibly in addressing climate change, aligned with principles such as Common Future and Leaving No One Behind (LNOB) and Common But Differentiated Responsibility (CBDR). The COVID-19 pandemic, as well as the common threat of climate change disasters, has further highlighted the importance of this collective identity and prompted the BRICS nations to focus on inclusive recovery efforts that prioritize the most vulnerable.

INTRODUCTION 3

Looking ahead, this book sets the stage for future research on how BRICS' collective identity, as well as individual nations under the BRICS umbrella, influences joint positions and potential policy coordination on climate governance globally. Furthermore, the book explores BRICS' views on Western practices and institutions, depicting developed nations as the "Other" in their social identity formation. While the BRICS nations are united under a collective identity, tensions and rivalries remain, which lead to the collective identity of the bloc not always translating into seamless cooperation and policy alignment. However, the absence of a military alliance objective among the BRICS nations and the willingness of BRICS states to prioritize collective action over bilateral disputes, particularly on issues such as climate change, indicate deeper collaboration in the future.

Throughout this book, the authors examine the theoretical background, historical context, current policies, and prospects of climate action in each BRICS nation, considering their geopolitical dynamics, economic realities, and environmental concerns. It explores the evolution of climate policies within each country, from early engagement in international climate negotiations to the development of ambitious national strategies to reduce greenhouse gas emissions, promote renewable energy, and enhance climate resilience.

The book probes into whether BRICS, as a leading group among the "emerging powers", represents a challenge to the current global order, which the West has primarily dominated. It explores the growing importance of the BRICS nations in the international arena. It considers whether their rising influence threatens the current international system or offers an opportunity for transition towards a more multipolar world order. Through an analysis of governance structures and soft power dynamics, as well as their role in addressing global issues such as climate change, the book examines the potential for BRICS to shape global governance and contribute to a more equitable and sustainable future.

The introductory chapter, "Growing in harmony with our cosmic selves: A holist answer to the "no technical solution problem" of climate change", by Bianca Naudé, attempts to understand the complexities surrounding climate action within BRICS member states, elucidating the sluggish implementation of decisions attributed to the perceived conflict between economic development and environmental concerns. Advocating for a transformative shift in perspective, it underscores the moral imperative of recognizing nature as an entity with intrinsic value rooted in a collective identity among BRICS nations. The chapter navigates the intricacies of reconciling economic growth with climate resilience by elucidating the failure to meet climate promises and proposing a moral–ethical approach that aligns environmental preservation with national interests. Additionally, it explores ecological theories such as the "Tragedy of the Commons", advocating for a fundamental reevaluation of human values and morality to address pressing global challenges. Drawing from diverse philosophical traditions illuminates the interconnectedness between humans and the environment, suggesting that a holistic approach resonates with the cultural ethos of BRICS member states and offers a promising pathway towards harmonious coexistence with the natural world.

In "South Africa's Approach to Climate-Resilient Development Pathways", Sanet Solomon explores South Africa's unwavering commitment to climate security and "just energy transitions", epitomized by its collaboration with the United States, the United Kingdom, France, and Germany in the Just Energy Transition Partnership (JETP). Despite its heavy reliance on coal for energy, South Africa contends with extreme weather events, water scarcity, and greenhouse gas emissions, prompting a transition towards renewable energy sources that is aligned with the ethos of a "just transition". It elucidates this transition's social and environmental ramifications, underscoring South Africa's steadfast commitment to climate security and the imperative of achieving a just transition. Emphasizing the promotion of sustainable human development, pollution reduction, and environmental enhancement, the chapter examines this shift's multifaceted challenges and opportunities. These include updating energy solutions, climate finance mechanisms, job creation initiatives, and governance reforms to ensure a smooth transition. Furthermore, the chapter examines the nuanced impacts of this transition on various provinces, examining concerns and opportunities arising from the departure from coal reliance. It accentuates the importance of adopting a people-centred approach, prioritizing good health outcomes, quality education, and poverty alleviation, while addressing governance challenges and corruption. Additionally, the chapter provides historical insights into South Africa's energy system, scrutinizing the role of subsidies and the nation's response to climate change. Pertinent issues such as the country's debt-to-GDP ratio, the repercussions of power outages, and recommendations for fiscal management are also discussed. The chapter offers a comprehensive analysis of South Africa's energy transition, delineating the challenges, opportunities, and far-reaching implications for the country's social, economic, and environmental development.

The chapter titled "China's Evolving Climate Change Strategy: A Dual Role in Mitigation and Adaptation" by Jana de Kluiver deeply examines China's historical trajectory and contemporary approach to combatting climate change, meticulously tracing its transformation from a hesitant participant to a critical player in global climate governance. It meticulously explores China's strategic alignment with the United Nations Sustainable Development Goals, its pivotal role in the Paris Summit, and its multifaceted engagement within the Belt and Road Initiative (BRI) and BRICS alliance. The chapter highlights China's significant contributions to both carbon emissions and renewable energy production, highlighting the complexities inherent in balancing economic development with environmental sustainability. Despite commendable strides in renewable energy adoption, challenges persist, particularly in curbing coal power expansion and achieving carbon neutrality. Furthermore, it scrutinizes China's evolving position within global climate negotiations, advocating for more ambitious emissions reduction targets, increased investment in renewable energy, and enhanced transparency in reporting. This comprehensive analysis not only elucidates China's evolving climate policies but also offers invaluable insights into its role as a global climate leader and its challenges in addressing the climate crisis.

The chapter "Between Geopolitical Ambition, Energy Nationalism and Capacity Deficit: Russia's Thorny Relationship with Climate Change" by Sergey Kostelyanets offers a comprehensive analysis of Russia's historical and contemporary stance on climate change, illuminating the evolution of its policies amid intricate geopolitical considerations and economic interests. Tracing Russia's trajectory from pioneering global climate change efforts during the Soviet era to its current climate scepticism, heavily influenced by the oil and gas lobby, the chapter examines the country's commitment to carbon neutrality by 2060 and its reliance on non-Western partners for cooperation in decarbonization endeavours, notably within the BRICS platform. It navigates through Russia's domestic challenges and the dualistic implications of anthropogenic climate change while highlighting its substantial influence on the global climate system as one of the largest emitters of greenhouse gases. The chapter examines Russia's pivotal role in climate change discussions through a historical lens, from its involvement in the Kyoto Protocol to its participation in the Paris Agreement. Ultimately, it presents a detailed and critical overview of Russia's complex relationship with climate change, underscoring the multifaceted interplay of geopolitical, economic, and capacity considerations that shape the country's climate policies.

The chapter by Bashabi Gupta offers a comprehensive analysis of India's multifaceted approach to global climate politics, examining the intricate interplay between its domestic development imperatives and international commitments. It examines India's principled stance in climate negotiations, rooted in notions of equity, historical responsibility, and the polluter pays principle. It also elucidates its role within the BRICS framework and responses to critique, advocating for equitable commitments and financial assistance for developing nations. Moreover, the chapter scrutinizes India's climate policies, including the National Action Plan on Climate Change (NAPCC), highlighting both successes and criticisms, particularly in sectors such as power. It navigates the complexities of ongoing climate negotiations, emphasizing the challenges of differentiating responsibilities, especially among developing nations, and evaluates the achievements and criticisms of collective efforts within groups such as BRICS and BASIC in shaping climate policies that are beneficial to the Global South. In conclusion, the chapter offers a nuanced and analytical overview of India's climate diplomacy, underscoring its pivotal role and acknowledging the hurdles and opportunities it faces in addressing the global climate crisis.

In "Bridging the Gap: The Brazilian Climate Change Agenda After Bolsonaro", Marina Magalhães Barreto Leite da Silva offers a comprehensive analysis of Brazil's climate change policies within the framework of the Bolsonaro administration. The chapter examines Brazil's historical and international positions on climate change, evaluating the recent government's impact on climate policies and emphasizing the pressing need to bridge the resulting policy gap. It outlines the challenges Brazil faces in addressing climate change, particularly under the Bolsonaro administration, and the potential for a revitalized approach under the third presidential term of Luíz Inácio Lula da Silva, highlighting the imperative to rectify setbacks and reassert Brazil's leadership in climate change mitigation. She examines Brazil's historical engagement in international climate negotiations. She scrutinizes the shifts in Brazil's climate policies under Bolsonaro, marked by scepticism towards climate science and relaxation of environmental regulations, resulting in increased deforestation rates and strained relations with environmental organizations. The discussion extends to the prospects under Lula's administration, exploring initial actions, commitments, and challenges, such as curbing deforestation, meeting international climate commitments, and fostering sustainable economic development. The chapter provides a comprehensive analysis of Brazil's approach to climate change, focusing on the period from 2019 to 2022, during the presidency of Jair Bolsonaro, and the subsequent shift in policies under the administration of Luiz Inácio Lula da Silva. Additionally, it stresses the significance of Brazil's role in global climate efforts, particularly within the BRICS nations, and the need to bridge the gap created by the previous administration's environmental policies. The analysis also addresses the historical context of Brazil's environmental policies, the influence of economic activities on environmental surveillance, and the impact of right-wing governance on climate change policymaking, international positioning, and the urgent need for more robust and consistent efforts to address climate change nationally and internationally.

In Dr Md. Muddassir Quamar's chapter, "Saudi Arabia's Climate Change Policy: An Effort Towards a Sustainable Future for the Kingdom and the Middle East", the author meticulously examines Saudi Arabia's multifaceted approach to addressing global warming and climate change, with a particular focus on its Vision 2030 initiatives. The chapter underscores the imperative of adopting a collective and comprehensive strategy to confront the challenges posed by climate change, recognizing the vulnerability of countries and regions due to their geographic location, economic volatility, and high dependence on natural resources. Moreover, the chapter underscores the importance of integrating climate change policies with sustainable development goals, reflecting the global community's acknowledgement of the imperative to address climate change and sustainability issues hand in hand. The chapter explores Saudi Arabia's steadfast commitment to economic diversification, reducing reliance on fossil fuels, and championing a circular carbon economy. However, the chapter also examines the challenges and limitations confronting Saudi Arabia in its climate change policy and action plans, including the delicate balance required for sustaining economic growth in a manner sensitive to climate concerns and the potential adverse impacts of mega developmental projects on local ecologies, especially as an oil-driven economy. The chapter critically analyses Saudi Arabia's endeavours to address climate change, underlining the necessity for a holistic approach that harmonizes economic diversification, sustainable development, and climate change policies. It elucidates the hurdles and constraints faced by the Kingdom in implementing its climate change initiatives, particularly in light of its susceptibility to extreme weather conditions, water shortages, and food insecurity, underscoring the urgency for concerted, concentrated adaptive action.

In her chapter, Shilpi Ghosh provides a comprehensive overview of the collaborative endeavours between Africa and India aimed at addressing the intertwined challenges of climate change and sustainable development. It underlines the imperative of joint efforts to bolster environmental data, enhance digital infrastructure, and foster sustainable practices, recognizing the crucial role of cooperation in transforming agriculture, energy systems, transportation, and water management towards climate resilience and sustainable growth. Both regions are committed to revamping their food and energy systems to mitigate climate impacts and foster sustainable development trajectories. Moreover, the chapter explores the pivotal role of BRICS members, particularly India and South Africa, in championing climate action and advancing energy efficiency measures. It underscores the importance of inclusive, low-emission industrialization and digital transformation as critical pillars for achieving environmental objectives. The chapter highlights the importance of collaborative efforts between Africa and India to combat climate change, preserve land-based ecosystems, and promote sustainable development and the potential for joint initiatives in areas of common interests such as green infrastructure, agroforestry policies, and digital transformation to effectively address environmental challenges.

The final chapter, "BRICS Plus and Climate Change" by Prof. Hussein Solomon, underscores the urgent and far-reaching impact of climate change and the imperative of global consensus and action to address this pressing environmental challenge. It emphasizes the potential role of the expanding BRICS Plus, encompassing Brazil, Russia, India, China, South Africa, and new members such as Saudi Arabia, Egypt, and Ethiopia, in prioritizing climate change as a central concern. While acknowledging the inherent challenges within BRICS Plus, including diverse national interests and geopolitical tensions, it highlights the incremental contributions that BRICS Plus can make towards shaping global consensus and action against climate change. Furthermore, it examines how BRICS Plus could serve as a crucial interlocutor for Africa in international forums, particularly regarding climate change, while also addressing policy disparities and collaborating with the African Union to address climate change on the continent. Ultimately, the chapter stresses the importance of BRICS Plus in advocating for climate justice, facilitating technology transfer, and providing financial support to developing nations, thereby enhancing global efforts to combat climate change.

In the complex global geopolitical landscape, the world struggles with many uncertainties. The challenge of devising actionable solutions to global issues—especially climate change—arises from a multitude of factors, with Western countries' fragmented responses significantly hindering progress. This fragmentation undermines their ability to address global challenges and underscores a growing rejection of the prevailing Western-centric paradigm in global climate governance, paving the way for emerging actors such as the BRICS nations and BRICS plus nations to shape the international order in matters of climate change decision-making.

Despite facing internal political hurdles, the BRICS countries have shown a growing inclination towards enhancing their cooperation, which is evident from their recent summits. The BRICS nations aspire to assume leadership roles in addressing climate change. However, their capacity to translate these aspirations into actionable outcomes remains scrutinized. As scholars ponder over the crises afflicting the Western world, marked by a seeming decline in its central role, questions arise regarding BRICS' potential to fill the resulting power vacuum. Although BRICS' soft power influence remains relatively nascent, the faltering response of Western leadership to transnational issues, particularly climate change, underscores shifting global power dynamics. The prospect of BRICS supplanting Western nations as primary actors in global climate affairs looms large, notwithstanding their reliance on outdated production models contributing to environmental degradation.

BRICS' ability to establish themselves as influential leaders in addressing global climate challenges and prompting transformative changes that alleviate the climate gridlock could significantly bolster their soft power and international standing. The new era presents an opportunity for BRICS to ascend to greater prominence in global climate governance, fuelled by their expanding economic clout and imperative to serve as exemplars. However, despite their economic and institutional influence, BRICS face challenges in achieving political cohesion, necessitating concerted efforts to present credible alternatives and foster unity to realize their potential in shaping future global climate governance systems.

Ultimately, in this book, the authors analyse the role of BRICS as a collective entity in shaping global climate governance, assessing their collaborative efforts, shared interests, and divergent priorities. From joint initiatives to technological cooperation, they assess the extent to which BRICS nations leverage their collective strength to drive meaningful international change. This book aims to provide policymakers, scholars, activists, and concerned citizens with a comprehensive understanding of the climate change landscape within the BRICS nations. The work aims to inspire informed dialogue, foster collaboration, and catalyse action towards a more sustainable and resilient future for all by elucidating the challenges and opportunities inherent in their climate policies.

References

Bagchi, Indrani. 2012. "No Mortar to Hold BRICS Together." *Times of India*, 30 March.

Chatin, Mathilde, and Giulio M. Gallarotti. 2016. "The BRICS and Soft Power: An Introduction." *Journal of Political Power* 9 (3): 335–352. https://doi.org/10.1080/2158379X.2016.1232284.

Ministry of External Affairs. 2023. Brief on BRICS.

Nayyar, Deepak. 2016. "BRICS, Developing Countries and Global Governance." *Third World Quarterly* 37 (4): 575–591. https://doi.org/10.1080/01436597.2015.1116365.

Growing in Harmony with Our Cosmic Selves: A Holist Answer to the "No Technical Solution Problem" of Climate Change

Bianca Naudé

1 INTRODUCTION

The BRICS[1] grouping is increasingly regarded not only as a powerful counterweight to Western dominance in international politics but also as a potential leader in climate action—especially among countries of the developing world (Gu et al. 2018; Dsouza 2022; McLean 2023; Naidoo 2023). Recognizing its role as a global climate actor, BRICS has expressed a commitment to "exploring opportunities for cooperation" to combat climate change and environmental degradation through targeted actions to transition to a green economy (South Africa 2023). BRICS' collaboration on climate action, some scholars now argue, should further be viewed against the backdrop of a collective identity rooted in their shared understanding of morality and responsibility towards the environment (Kıprızlı

---

[1] BRICS, as referred to here, includes Brazil, Russia, India, China, and South Africa. While enlargement of BRICS is duly acknowledged, newly acceded members are not included in this discussion.

B. Naudé (✉)
University of the Free State, Phuthaditjhaba, South Africa
e-mail: NaudeB@ufs.ac.za

© The Author(s), under exclusive license to Springer Nature Singapore Pte Ltd. 2024
H. Solomon et al. (eds.), *BRICS and Climate Change*,
https://doi.org/10.1007/978-981-97-5532-5_2

and Köstem 2022: 281). Indeed, Kıprızlı and Köstem (2022: 290) argue that "[t]he collective identity of BRICS members as emerging powers has shaped their [...] eagerness to act as responsible and constructive stakeholders concerning climate change".

BRICS may speak with one voice on the international climate stage; however, when it comes to implementing discussions regarding climate initiatives, BRICS members are lone actors charged with the design and implementation of domestic policies that will contribute to global climate change targets, and their efforts are marked by significant difficulties. Although Brazil, China, and India have taken measurable steps to combat climate change, it has been suggested that climate action is simply not a priority for Russia (see Nguyen and Khominich 2023: 187). In addition, despite significant collective commitments from BRICS to implement measures to achieve collective climate targets, member states are criticized for their continued (over)reliance on nonrenewable fossil fuels, unsustainable land use and deforestation, and their general climate inertia due to fears that transitions to a green economy are costly and ineffective (see Bhattacharya et al. 2022; Choudhary 2022; Qu 2022; Hale 2023; Tebajjukira 2023). Indeed, no BRICS member has received a "sufficient" rating on their climate actions geared towards reaching the Paris Agreement targets from the Climate Action Tracker Consortium,[2] and consensus appears to be that, on matters relating to climate change, BRICS' "differences trump commonalities" (Downie and Williams 2018: 399).

Reasons for BRICS members' failure to deliver on climate promises appear to be rooted in a view of climate action as an obstacle to achieving national imperatives of economic growth and development, which could be referred to as being in "the national interest". Scholarly literature on China's environmental actions suggests that any climate-related actions by the Chinese government are a direct reaction to the realization that environmental degradation at home has reached such proportions that it threatens the ruling party's claims to power (see, for example, Hofstedt 2010: 72; Shinn 2016: 26). Similarly, the South African response to climate change and environmental degradation is seemingly informed more by fear of the political impact of these phenomena on the current

---

[2] Brazil and South Africa both currently have a rating of "insufficient" for their climate actions, while China, India, and Russia's climate actions are rated "highly insufficient". The Climate Action Tracker can be accessed online here: https://climateactiontracker.org.

government than by an understanding of climate action as a moral and ethical imperative (see South Africa 2022: 2). And, while Brazil and India appear to have a somewhat less reactionary understanding of their obligation to the environment, Russia released an updated "climate doctrine" in 2023, mentioning the "significant, predominantly adverse" effects of climate change on Russian politics and society (*The Moscow Times*, 27 October 2023).

The perception of environmental action as a tool to limit the negative impact of climate change on states is also evident in cooperation on climate action within the BRICS organization. Although cooperation on climate action and the transition to a green economy featured as one of the five themes of the 15th BRICS Summit held in Johannesburg in 2023, wording in the Johannesburg II Declaration issued by BRICS members upon conclusion of the summit refers to the same reactionary approach to climate change as the positions of individual member states previously mentioned:

> We believe that multilateral cooperation is essential to limit the risks stemming from geopolitical and geoeconomic fragmentation and intensify efforts on areas of mutual interest [...] as well as mitigating and adapting to the impact of climate change, education, health as well as pandemic prevention, preparedness and response. (BRICS 2023: 9)

Elsewhere in the document, cooperation in environmental affairs is subordinated to national development priorities, while any climate-related action appears to be contingent on a quid pro quo strategy known as the "common but differentiated responsibilities principle" that underlies BRICS's endorsement for the continued use of fossil fuels to power economic and industrial growth:

> We agree to address the challenges posed by climate change while also ensuring a just, affordable and sustainable transition to a low carbon and low-emission economy in line with the principles of CBDR-RC, *in light of different national circumstances*. We advocate for just equitable and sustainable transitions, *based on nationally defined development priorities*, and we call on developed countries to lead by example and support developing countries towards such transitions. (BRICS 2023: 18; emphasis added)

Demands for assistance from the Global North, and resistance to the implementation of environmental initiatives aimed at reducing carbon emissions, as well as land, water, and air pollution, are predicated on what BRICS see as the Global North's "historic responsibility" for contributing to climate change, and the Global South's ostensible right to follow a traditional development path relying on fossil-fuel-heavy industrialization. The message is that BRICS support international climate action by the Global North, but they definitely want what they consider to be their rightful share of carbon emissions to help them catch up on a development lag without necessarily having to undertake costly climate action themselves.

Reading through the rhetoric, it is clear that—although the BRICS grouping recognizes the importance of climate action aimed at limiting environmental degradation and ensuring the sustainable use of scarce common resources—individual states consider climate action subordinate to, if not wholly incompatible with, their notions of what is in the national interest. While there is hope for BRICS to adopt a leading role as champion of environmental action among developing states, and although BRICS profess a commitment to taking decisive climate action, current evidence suggests that individual notions of the national interest present a significant challenge to realizing collective action against climate change. Within the context of the foregoing, this chapter sets itself the objective of proposing a solution to the question: how can states be compelled to move beyond their thinking of climate action as an obstacle to achieving the national interest of economic growth and development and work towards a collective solution to the problems of climate change and environmental degradation?

Drawing on literature from the field of environmental ethics, the chapter proposes that effective solutions to the "economic growth versus climate health" dilemma can be found in the adoption of a moral–ethical approach to climate action that regards the preservation of the environment not as a threat to achievement of the national interest but as a national interest in itself. This can be achieved through a decentring of international politics to conceive of the social and natural worlds as irrevocably co-constituted, intertwined, and interrelated—adopting, in other words, a holist ontology. While holism and monism are often viewed as "radical" philosophical positions in relation to the dualist metaphysics of mainstream (Western) international relations scholarship, the chapter demonstrates that such metaphysics is not only compatible with BRICS politics and society, but that the collective worldview of BRICS is, in fact, underpinned by the same holist/monist understanding of the world and our place in it.

2 "No Technical Solution Problems" and the Tragedy of the Commons

In his seminal work, "The Tragedy of the Commons", controversial ecologist Garrett Hardin (1968: 1243) argues that, although there is a tendency today to rely on technical solutions to problems encountered in the natural world, some problems, such as overpopulation or the depletion of natural resources in the name of economic development, are "no technical solution problems" that can only be solved by a "change in human values or ideas about morality". This, Hardin (1968: 1243) argues, is because the type of limitless freedom enjoyed in most countries across the world today does not promote the utilitarian conscience that is needed for humans to make the unpopular decisions that are likely to produce sustainable solutions to the resource problem.

Hardin bases his argument on the assumption that our natural world is finite, meaning that there is a limit to the number of resources available for consumption by those who need it. The number of people who need to be supported by these finite resources, on the other hand, is too great and growing at too rapid a pace for the natural world to continue to support their needs. Assuming that humans do not wish to reduce their consumption to almost zero,[3] Hardin (1968: 1243–1244) contends, the human population will need to decrease significantly in order for humanity not to deplete the resources at its disposal. In other words, the rate of procreation will need to be drastically reduced. This is a simple mathematical equation, but its solution is extremely complex. In most states today, the human right to procreate is constitutionally guaranteed, and few countries place any limits on the number

---

[3] Such a drastic reduction, Hardin (1968: 1243) argues, would mean "[n]o gourmet meals, no vacations, no sports, no music, no literature, no art", though I would argue here that the rate at which the global population is increasing would mean that "close to zero consumption" would more than likely now mean barely enough calories to sustain the human body, little to no clothing, no vaccinations or medication, no technology, and so on.

of children an individual can have. The effect is one of exponential population growth, coupled with an increasingly rapid decline in the available natural resources. The laissez-faire philosophy that characterizes modern-day democratic approaches to individual rights, Hardin argues, further entrenches self-interest at the expense of the common good. The result, for Hardin (1968: 1244), is inevitably one of ruin:

> Ruin is the destination toward which all men rush, each pursuing his own best interest in a society that believes in the freedom of the commons. Freedom in a commons brings ruin to all.

Here, morality and ethics enter the picture. Assuming that people are fundamentally good and can set aside their own needs and desires to realize a greater good, why not simply appeal to their conscience to reduce consumption of common resources in such a way that the earth can continue to support the human population? Appeals to conscience about the "right thing to do" are ineffective, Hardin (1968: 1246) argues, since not all people will respond to these pleas. And, locked in competition for a share of essential resources, those who do respond to calls to reduce consumption may be pushed to abandon their good intentions when they see their neighbour ignoring the same appeals. This creates a situation in which those who respond to appeals to the conscience gain an increasingly small share of the commons, while those who do not respond to these appeals gain an increasingly larger share. In other words, "good citizens" are increasingly deprived of access to resources, while exploitative citizens are, in a way, rewarded for their lack of conscience. Over time, those who respond to appeals to the conscience are ostracized completely, leaving only the unconscionable to continue their exploitation of the commons. As Hardin (1968: 1246) remarks, to appeal to the conscience "is to set up a selective system that works toward the elimination of conscience from the [human] race".

One solution to the tragedy of the commons is therefore to impose coercive measures such as sanctions for actions that will lead to the depletion of the commons, and, importantly, government control over population growth. However, these solutions are usually regarded as a loss of freedom to accumulate wealth, loss of access to resources, loss of freedom to determine the size of one's family, and so on; and the loss of certain freedoms is invariably met with opposition from the general public. Yet, as Hardin (1968: 1248) underscores, the loss of certain freedoms in history has paradoxically *increased* freedom. This is the case with laws that restrict, for example, the use of force by the general population to acquire a coveted resource, or laws that protect a person's private property, where the loss of the freedom to use force or take another's property as one's own has actually increased the freedom of those who are now no longer victims of violence or theft. For Hardin (1968: 1248), then, freedom is the recognition of the necessity of restricting certain freedoms.

Hardin's "Tragedy of the Commons", it should be said, is a treatise on overpopulation and environmental degradation in the United States, and mine is not a contribution to debates over the justifiable degree of government intervention in citizens' affairs to effectively combat environmental degradation within a capitalist economic system (see, on this point, McCay 1995: 91–92). This chapter does contend, however, that Hardin's "Tragedy of the Commons" contains some concepts and arguments that are particularly relevant for this volume on BRICS and their response to climate change.

First, Hardin's discussion of individual rights can be extended to the sovereign rights of states to determine economic and trade policy, to decide on the level of industrial pollution they deem acceptable, or to choose the development path they consider most appropriate for their own context. Similar to individuals, states compete for a share of scarce natural resources to grow their wealth, ensure the survival of their citizens, and secure their continued existence. This drive for growth and self-preservation can be likened to the need to procreate, and both of these needs are protected in some way or another by liberal social systems geared towards maximizing individual freedoms. As with people, however, economic growth is irrevocably tied to an unsustainable depletion of natural resources, presenting an economic growth versus environmental health dilemma that requires states to sacrifice certain freedoms. Sacrificing these freedoms, however, will require more than simple appeals to state conscience about the "right thing to do". This chapter aims to propose a way to convince states to accept that the preservation of life will require sacrificing certain freedoms—including those that are currently considered intrinsic features of state sovereignty.

Second, the chapter conceives of the economic development versus environmental health dilemma as a "no technical solution problem", which is, as previously stated, a problem that cannot be solved by a technical or scientific solution but one that requires a shift in the moral or ethical position of an actor in relation to the problem. As long as states continue to view climate change as an obstacle to achieving the national imperative of economic growth rather than a moral or ethical obligation to the common good, global emissions targets and industrial policy aimed at reducing production-related environmental degradation and climate change are not likely to inspire positive responses to environmental problems. It must be said, however, that although several states consider climate action an impediment to achieving their national interest, many do acknowledge their moral and ethical obligation to combat climate change and environmental degradation. Thus, what one is faced with here is the question of how states can be prompted to view climate action not as an obstacle to achieving the national interest but as a national interest in itself. The answer may lie, the chapter contends, in moving away from discussions of climate action as an *obligation* to the environment to see the state's position within it as a symbiotic relationship rather than a hierarchized system.

3   SEEING COMMON RESOURCES IN RELATION TO OURSELVES

Hardin's "Tragedy of the Commons" has received no shortage of criticism from scholars whose work on governance of common resources proves that communities are able to effectively manage the exploitation of finite resources when they are sufficiently incentivized to do so by the threat of extinction as a result of inaction (Frischmann et al. 2019: 216–217). In a retrospective of the "Tragedy of the Commons" some 50 years after its initial publication, Frischmann et al. (2019: 218) highlight two sets of questions that challenge Hardin's essay: the first asks to what extent Hardin's representation of the tragedy corresponds with the lived reality, and the second asks whether Hardin's proposed governance framework exhausts the range of possibilities for effectively managing finite resources.

Responding to the first set of questions, economist Elinor Ostrom (2007: 15283, cited in Frischmann et al. 2019: 218) argues that individuals do not exist in a vacuum, and that they most often choose to engage in communication to find solutions to common problems. For Ostrom, similar to international relations idealists and constructivists, people are motivated to cooperate on issues such as the governance of shared resources by reciprocity, trust, reputation, and relationships more than they are motivated to compete with others by selfish interests, as realists may argue. Second, research by Ostrom et al. (1999), such as the work of international relations liberalists, showed that the institutionalization of cooperation to effectively manage shared resources helps communities overcome issues arising from the unsustainable use of common resources, demonstrating that it is, at the very least, possible to conceive of "bottom-up" solutions to common resource problems that do not require excessive government intervention in the affairs of private citizens (Frischmann et al. 2019: 220–221; see also Ostrom et al. 1999).

In her critique of Hardin's "Tragedy of the Commons", Bonnie J. McCay (1995: 92) argues that effective management of limited natural resources requires a shift in thinking that distinguishes "between the features of the resource and [...] the way people choose to relate to the resource and each other". Similar to Ostrom et al. (1999), McCay (1995: 101) argues that evidence from her research on commercial fishing practices on the East Coast of the United States shows that communities are often able to effectively manage a finite resource cooperatively when they exist in a positive relationship therewith. Instead of regarding resources as things (or possessions) that can be apportioned and regulated, McCay (1995: 92) suggests that solutions to common resource problems should seek to transform the relationships that people maintain with one another as a result of their claims to access resources as well as the relationships that people maintain with resources themselves.

While McCay, similar to Ostrom and others, holds that cooperative management of natural resources is possible, she concedes that the sustainable collaborative management of resources is complex to the point of defection, where resources are migratory or overlap jurisdiction, where multiple communities claim historic rights to the use of a resource, or where governance excludes communities with a historic claim to the right to use a resource (McCay 1995: 102). McCay's solutions to these problems focus on improving state–society relations at both the national and subnational levels, and do not promise much in the way of contributing to this discussion of BRICS climate cooperation. What is interesting for the purposes of this chapter, however, is McCay's suggestion of a mean between strictly prescriptive approaches to solving common resource problems and the laissez-faire approach that Hardin criticizes. Shifting its assumptions about human nature and social cooperation, McCay's (1995: 110) revisionist approach takes into account issues such as "the interplays of conflicting interests, contested and agreed upon meanings and definitions [and] intersections of history, politics, culture, time and space".

To overcome impasses in cooperation on the sustainable management of common resources, McCay (1995: 110–111) argues that one needs to shift one's thinking about actors claiming rights to the use of natural resources as "not just [...] competitive, greedy individuals – which they are and can be in many contexts – but also as social beings capable of and interested in collective action on behalf of the resources and habitats upon which they depend". The language here is interesting: it places human actors in a symbiotic relationship with common resources of which they are not considered to be the owners but rather the custodians. This view is, of course, consistent with legal terminology that defines states as custodians of common resources, charged with the control and management of resources as well as the responsibility to conserve and protect such resources (see, for example, Feris 2012: 10). Custodianship stands in contrast to ownership, which vests an actor with the right to appropriate, exploit, and control as they see fit (Feris 2012: 5). Natural resources, in other words, cannot be considered possessions that states can control and exploit for the benefit of economic growth and development; states are merely custodians, and they have more than just a moral responsibility to conserve and protect these resources (see also Boulangeat et al. 2022: 42).

On the surface, BRICS cooperation on climate issues confirms some of Ostrom's hypotheses: first, it is known that climate cooperation is a standing item on the BRICS agenda, with BRICS leaders regularly meeting to discuss progress on national strategies to combat climate change and environmental degradation, as well as BRICS' common position on climate matters in the international arena (Dsouza 2022: 4). Second, as a regional arrangement acting within the larger international system, BRICS in itself could be seen as a "bottom-up" approach to resource governance in the international system (see, on BRICS in a world of regions, Lagutina 2019). As introductory remarks to this chapter have suggested, however, BRICS' cooperation on climate matters is mostly an ineffective surface narrative without much teeth. Closer inspection of climate-related policies and actions reveals that BRICS member states have been slow to effect any real change, and domestic economic growth initiatives almost invariably replace meaningful climate action at the national level.

Few would argue that BRICS member states do not consider finite resources essential to their survival. If we accept Ostrom's and McCay's evidence that people will work to preserve a resource when they consider it essential to their survival, then BRICS' climate inertia presses us to ask why these states would choose to continue using fossil fuels and producing carbon emissions without any real action to transition to cleaner energy sources, knowing that it is potentially fatal to their own survival. National growth targets would certainly weigh heavily on this equation; however, this chapter suggests that the problem is more philosophical in nature, deriving from a hierarchical ontological position that views nature as subordinate to human activities, desires, and needs. By decentring our gaze to adopt a holist or qualified monist position that endorses a flat ontology, the following sections of this chapter suggest that humanity can move beyond the no technical solution problem of the economic growth versus environmental health dilemma. The answer, it is argued, may well lie in an underexplored observation in Frischmann et al.'s (2019: 220) retrospective survey of critiques on Hardin's "Tragedy of the Commons" that resources "are not purely depletable; as a biological matter, they can reproduce and replenish stocks. The relevant *community* involves more than just [human actors]" (emphasis added). The authors' use of the term community, here, is significant for this contribution to the literature on the governance of collective resources: it pushes us to think of resources not as mere objects but as actors in an interrelated ecosystem of which human actors constitute only one part.

4 THE CASE FOR HOLISM IN GLOBAL CLIMATE THINKING

The dominant metaphysics underpinning most scientific thinking today is what can be referred to as "Cartesian dualism". Dualism conceives of physical matter as entirely separate from mental content and, while philosophical debate usually revolves around the so-called "mind–body problem" of the human and social sciences, a dualist metaphysics tends to dominate thinking on the relationship between human and natural systems that are regarded as distinct and hierarchized, where nature occupies a subordinate position to human beings (see, for example, Boulangeat et al. 2022). A full review of the literature on the mind–body problem in philosophy and the social sciences is not possible here; however, it is useful to briefly summarize the major assumptions of this ontological stance.

French philosopher René Descartes argued that humans are distinct from animals and other objects in the natural world because they are conscious. While objects in the natural world have physical attributes that can be defined in terms of time and space, and while other animals have biological functions that are controlled by a physical brain, human beings have a unique function—consciousness—that cannot be understood in terms of time, space, or physical matter. Consciousness, or some would say "the soul", derives from something or someplace external to the physical world, and it is this unique property of humanness that (at least in Cartesian thinking) places human beings in a category distinct from animals and other objects in the natural world (for a deeper discussion, see Westphal 2016).

The idea of a uniquely human consciousness has, over time, been an essential element in human claims to moral interests that do not extend to the natural world, and in the attribution of rights to exploit nature in the service of these uniquely human moral interests (see McShane 2016: 189). Nonhuman objects have never truly been recognized as having intrinsic value, which Boulangeat et al. (2022: 41) define as "the inherent value of nature and its components [...] independent of human experience"; instead, their value has always been considered either relational, existing in a relationship with human beings such that it contributes to people's identities or their quality of life, or instrumental, as material and non-material contributions to human lives (Boulangeat et al. 2022: 41). And, while it could certainly be claimed that there is growing recognition of nonhuman objects having inherent value that is not tied in any way to human health, happiness, and prosperity, climate action still appears to revolve largely around preserving the natural world in service of human survival. As McShane (2016: 189) argues:

> These days, most ethicists agree that at least some nonhumans have interests that are of direct moral importance. That is to say, there are at least some nonhuman interests that make a moral claim on us. Yet with very few exceptions, both climate ethics and climate policy have operated as though only human interests should be considered in formulating and evaluating climate policy.

Among the most successful responses to the failures of dualist thinking in the social sciences are monist and holist positions that rely on flat ontologies wherein humans are regarded as being embedded in and constituted by the system to which they belong and in which they act, rather than hierarchical ontologies wherein nature is regarded as being external and subordinate to humans. Holism, according to Shane Ralston (2015: 1), "is the notion that all of the elements in a system, whether physical, biological, social, or political, are interconnected and therefore should be appreciated as a whole". Whereas the whole may be considered to exist of individual parts that may vary significantly in their qualities and attributes, the whole cannot be understood through a reductive investigation of these smaller parts. For some holists, importantly, the whole is defined by and understood as the internal relations between its constituent parts (Ralston 2015: 1).

Monism also views the whole as greater than the sum of its parts but regards the whole and its parts as undifferentiated and undetachable (Morganti 2009: 272). It is important to mention here that monist thinking is most often closed, precluding the existence of multiple forms of entities or beliefs—everything is ultimately one (see Ralston 2015: 3). Such a radical holism is difficult to defend when thinking in terms of the human–nature relationship, for although the argument in this chapter has been that humanity *is* nature, it is acknowledged that the impact of human activities on the environment cannot be considered "natural". In arguing for a holist view of the natural world as one system, it is important to differentiate the constituent parts of that system, so that they are not regarded as being the same (see, on this point, Boulangeat et al. 2022: 45–46). Nevertheless, the "thinner" holism adopted in this chapter conceives of human and nature as an irreducible whole, even if the whole can be understood in terms of the relations that its parts (human and nonhuman) maintain with one another, as well as the relationship that these parts maintain with the whole (the natural world) and the impact that the activities of one part can have on the whole (that is, how human activities affect nature).

Here, it may be asked whether a holist ontology is at all compatible with the worldview of the BRICS states. It would be impossible, after all, to compel BRICS states to "buy into" the answer proposed in this chapter to the no technical solution problem of economic growth versus environmental health if its metaphysical underpinning were incompatible with the metaphysical underpinning their own understandings of how the world works. Through a brief look at the philosophies of *Advaita*, *Gongsheng*, *Guanxi*, *Tianxia*, and *Ubuntu*, the final section of this chapter argues that a holist ontology such as the one advanced here is not only

24   B. NAUDÉ

compatible with the worldviews of at least three of the BRICS states, but their guiding philosophies also share the holist metaphysics that this chapter supports.

5   Holism, Monism, or an Irreducible Connectedness

Inspired by decolonial aspirations, the non-Western school of international relations theory has produced an impressive volume of literature on interstate relations from across the non-Western world. Guided by a ubiquitous Confucian worldview (see Hwang 2021: 316), the Chinese School, best known for its relational (*Guanxi*) and *Tianxia* approaches, has established itself as one of the most popular non-Western approaches to understanding global politics, with the Indian school rapidly catching up. And, while it features less prominently in non-Western international relations reading lists, an approach to international relations that draws on the African philosophy of *Ubuntu* has amassed a fair following. While these approaches have important differences that the chapter will not have the occasion to explore, these three approaches distinguish themselves from dominant schools of thought in international relations through their grounding in holist or monist metaphysics. A basic understanding of these three approaches is essential in the consideration of BRICS and climate change, since, as the chapter has argued, it lays a foundation for overcoming the "no technical solution problem" of economic growth versus environmental health grounded in the dominant worldviews that shape the social and political structures of the BRICS member states. It makes it possible, that is, for BRICS to "buy into" the solution, because it is not imposed externally by the Global North; BRICS have ownership of the solution.

Rooted in what Hwang (2021: 316) describes as an "immanent Confucian cosmos", the Chinese School of International Relations has contributed several theories of international politics, three of which carry significance[4] for the present research: the *Tianxia* approach associated with the work of international relations scholar Zhao Tingyang, the relational (*Guanxi*) approach to international relations popularized by

---

[4] It is neither possible to discuss criticism of the Chinese School of international relations here, nor is it likely to contribute much to the present chapter. See, among others, Acharya (2019: 482–489) and Hwang (2021: 317–322).

Yaqing Qin, and the *Gongsheng* School. *Tianxia* is an ancient Chinese concept commonly translated as "All-under-Heaven",[5] which, according to Shahi and Ascione (2015: 324), "rests on a fundamental unity between [the] physical, psychological and political components" of the world (or, perhaps more accurately, the cosmos). In the *Tianxia* view, everything in existence is connected within and derives from a single system[6] to which there is no conceivable "externality". Different parts within the system exist in relation to one another and interact with one another internally, but there are no external relations to speak of, because, quite simply, there is nothing beyond the system itself (Hwang 2021: 315).

Guanxi is an idea embedded in Confucian cosmology that can be understood as "everything being in everything else", where actors exist within a system resembling ripples on a lake—all connected to one another and to the environment (Hwang 2021: 316–317; see also Qin 2007: 329). For Qin (2016), "individuals make decisions based on the degree of intimacy and hierarchical status (superior or inferior) with the totality of the relational context as the background" (Hwang 2021: 317). Here, as in *Tianxia*, we find the notion of different parts that exist within a whole that is not equal to but greater than its constituent parts—a position that Shahi and Ascione (2015: 325) consider a form of "qualified monism" comparable more to a holist ontology than monism. In *Guanxi*, we can make the argument that the environment is expressly included in the whole as an actor in its own right—related to and acting in on the decisions and activities of human individuals with whom it shares an existence. Importantly, Hwang (2021: 317) underscores, the Confucian worldview does not conceive of actors as guided by rationality and self-interest; instead, it regards actors as being "motivated by the need to maintain the continuity of relations within an interrelated society".

The idea of nature and the environment as actors in their own right, different from but equal in intrinsic value to the human actors to whom they are connected and with whom they interact, is perhaps best encapsulated in the neo-Confucian concept of *Gongsheng*, which can be translated

---

[5] A deeper discussion of *Tianxia* is not possible here. Interested readers are instead referred to Shahi and Ascione (2015), Zhao (2019), and Ren (2020).

[6] "System", here, is used interchangeably with "the whole". The term as it is employed here does not invoke comparisons with systems theory, although Shahi and Ascione (2015: 324) draw certain parallels between Chinese *Tianxia* and Western systems theory.

as "nothing exists in isolation" (Wu 2024: 59). Grounded in the "foundational theory of *qi*" and the *minbao wuyu* concept of "universal camaraderie", *Gongsheng* conceives of the world in terms of a "symbiotic interconnectedness of all things" (Wu 2024: 67). In the *Gongsheng* tradition, personal freedoms and rights, such as the right to development and the freedom to choose a development path that is considered appropriate for a nation as discussed here before, are considered secondary to humanity's harmonious coexistence with the planet and its nonhuman inhabitants (Wu 2024: 58). While people exist in competition with one another, and with the needs of nonhuman entities, *Gongsheng* views these tensions as natural and constantly moving towards harmony. The following passage from Zhang Zai's Philosophy of *Qi* (cited in Wu 2024: 59) is instructive:

> The sky is my father and the earth is my mother. I minutely exist, intermingled in their midst. Thus, that which fills up nature I regard as my body, and that which directs nature I consider as my capacity to resonate. All people are my brothers and sisters, and all things are my companions.

As in McCay's notion of a symbiotic relationship between man and nature, *Gongsheng* recognizes that humans depend on nature for their survival. As Genyou Wu (2024: 62) explains, *Gongsheng* appreciates that "even the most microscopic creatures are brimming with life [which is a] qualitative and vital requirement for the survival of living things". Recognizing and respecting all living things as equally entitled to life necessitates in human actors a deep morality, something akin to a "guiding light" (Wu 2024: 65). This guiding light of human morality is essential for the continued survival of nature. Thus, a return to a primitive human state is undesirable; instead, "the light of human civilization should imbue [nature] with the character of human civilization, creating a state of *Gongsheng* characterized by the moral, subjective perception, and self-awareness of all people and things living in harmony" (Wu 2024: 65). How we achieve such harmony is, of course, a question that becomes ever more pressing against the backdrop of climate change.

Relationality as the basis of all existence finds expression beyond Chinese thought in the African philosophy of *Ubuntu*. Among the most popular definitions of the term is Michael O. Eze's interpretation that "a person is a person through other people" (Eze 2010: 190, cited in Graness 2018: 397). Although there is no consensus even among Africans of how exactly *Ubuntu* should be translated, there is agreement that the concept signifies a processual understanding of human interconnectedness within a single system. As Mogobe Ramose (2002: 230–231) explains:

> Just as the environing soil, the root, stem, branches, and leaves together as a one-ness give meaning to our understanding of a tree, so is it with *ubuntu*. The foundation, the soil within which it is anchored, as well as the building, must be seen as one continuous whole-ness [...] to be a human be-ing is to affirm one's humanity by recognizing the humanity of others and, on that basis establish humane relations with them [...] *Ubu-ntu* then not only describes a condition of be-ing, insofar as it is indissolubly linked to *umuntu*, but it is also the recognition of a being becoming and not, we wish to emphasize, be-ing and becoming.

Although *Ubuntu* has been criticized for being anthropocentric, privileging the human species over nonhuman actors (Horsthemke 2015; Galgut 2017), Chibvongodze (2016) argues that the metaphysics underpinning the philosophy of *Ubuntu* relies fundamentally on a human, natural, and spiritual tripartite. Jordan K. Ngubane (1979, cited in Mhlambi 2020: 13) describes this tripartite in his account of the origin of *Ubuntu*:

> All [creation] were manifestations of [Mvelingqangi's] infinite form. Inside [Mvelingqangi's] being was an infinity of specialized forms making up apart of the whole. These were the spirits of living things, some of which had human forms.

Represented by the unique being uMvelinqangi, Sabelo Mhlambi (2020: 13) explains that humans in the *Ubuntu* approach exist both in relation to one another and in relation to other "forms" that constitute the whole, and they accept the interconnectedness of humans, nature, and the spiritual world. Importantly, relationality in the philosophy of *Ubuntu* "is the acceptance of the individuality of others" (Mhlambi 2020: 13). What is evident here is that the concept of "relational personhood" as it is found in *Ubuntu* is very similar to the concept of *Guanxi* in Confucian thought, where a whole that knows no externality is composed of interrelated parts that are recognized as being different but equal in intrinsic value, and that maintaining relationships with one another is shaped by the dynamics and pressures of the irreducible system to which they belong and into which they act.

Ubuntu's uMvelinqangi bears some resemblance to the "single core reality" or the "single hidden connectedness" (Shahi and Ascione 2015: 322, 327) of Brahma, as found in *Advaitic* monism. Rooted in Indian philosophy, *Advaitic* monism conceives of the world and all those that animate and inhabit it as belonging to and acting through a single core reality. In *Advaitic* monism, as in *Confucian* and *Ubuntu* approaches, there is no part–part or part–whole distinction or hierarchy on an ontological level; however, *Advaita* differs from the former in its conception of existence not as being–becoming through relational processes and interactions within the whole, but of being as "'always–already' there" (Shahi and Ascione 2015: 328). If *Tianxia*, as remarked here before, conceives of existence as relational processes resembling ripples on a pond, then *Advaitic* monism regards existence as a perfect state of completeness to which all actors and events belong as a part of a finality that has already been achieved.

Although *Advaitic* monism differs somewhat in its understanding of part–whole relations, it shares with the Chinese School and the African philosophy of *Ubuntu* a view of the universe and its constituents as unbreakably and irreversibly interrelated and interconnected that is radically opposed to Cartesian dualism (Shahi and Ascione 2015: 327). The difference here is, perhaps, only expressed in the degree of porosity between self and all else. Indeed, Shahi and Ascione (2015: 328) argue that there can be no talk in *advaitic* monism of the "self" in relation to outside or other, since there can be no awareness of self outside of its suffusion with the single reality; instead, the self is only a form of consciousness from which it cannot be disentangled:

> Advaita adds the thesis that the self is never an object of consciousness
> [...] in the most rigorous and abstract way, there is no self-knowledge
> in Advaita, if by that is meant knowledge of a self; what is possible is
> knowledge only of the states of consciousness of which the self is a subject.
> (Prasad, cited in Shahi and Ascione 2015: 328)

Here, of course, a valid question to raise would be to what extent the holist/monist theories discussed here form part of the lived experiences of African, Chinese, and Indian communities. Is the assumption that *Advaita*, *Gongsheng*, *Guanxi*, *Tianxia*, or *Ubuntu* translates into the everyday lives of entire societies not a form of theoretical arrogation? And, what of Brazil and Russia in this equation? Is the holism advocated for here at all consistent with the worldviews of these two societies? If generalizability is the gold standard of solid theorizing, how generalizable is the holist approach touted in this chapter? A response comes from the writing of LHM Ling on Daoist Trialectics in international relations.

Responding to Shahi and Ascione's (2015: 322–323) argument that the radical monism of *Advaita* is a superior theoretical position from which to approach the study of international relations than the qualified monism of *Vishistadvaita* and *Tianxia*, Ling (2018: 319–320) cautions that we should "resist falling into the Cartesian trap" of playing monism (*advaita*) off against holist (*vishistadvaita*) and dualist (*dvaita*) metaphysics, since the three branches of thought themselves exist in harmony with one another within a broader system that produces knowledge through its internal tensions and contestations:

> Analytically, each branch of thought could not *be* without the others [...] *advaita-dvaita-vishistadvaita* cross epistemic borders between the divine and the mundane [and between] the body and the mind. All three link the individual with the community, the environment with the cosmopolitical.

Ling's (2018: 323–324) proposal is to think of the interplay between monist, dualist, and holist metaphysics in terms of the Daoist concept of *yin-yang*, where there is a perpetual simultaneous interaction between the ontologically equal and intertwined female *yin* and male *yang* that produces systemic health through the balancing of contending, opposing forces. "Together", Ling (2018: 324) writes, these contending, opposing, intertwined forces "account for continuity *and* change, connections *and* conflicts, masculinity *and* femininity, duality *and* non-duality". The shift that is required in our approach to climate change and the environment, therefore, is not one of paradigms or attitudes but one of *experience*. By removing ourselves from our thinking about others, or the environment, we can move towards relating to things on their own terms and in their own context—as having equal ontological status and value despite our qualitative differences. And it is in this understanding of ourselves as beings *through* nature that we realize that climate action is not an obstacle to our existence—it *is* our existence. To continue to disregard the planet in service of our own needs would be to deny both ourselves and the possibility of our future selves.

The philosophical approaches briefly discussed here contain important nuances that this chapter will not have the occasion to discuss.

30   B. NAUDÉ

What is clear from the foregoing, however, is that there exists in African, Chinese, and Indian thought a strong and celebrated tradition of considering human society to be linked to and embedded within nature and the spiritual world in important ways. These traditions have significant implications for the ways in which BRICS approach climate action, as the concluding remarks to this chapter will highlight.

6   CONCLUSION

Seeking a solution to what the chapter has labelled "climate inertia" on the part of BRICS member states, whose climate initiatives are often critiqued as little more than political rhetoric due to competing national interests that supersede collectively agreed-upon targets, this chapter set itself the task of exploring ways in which these states can move beyond the national interest in their attempts to reconcile the seemingly irreconcilable imperatives of achieving economic development and seriously combatting climate change. An answer to the "no technical solution problem" of economic development versus environmental health, the chapter has argued, lies in moving beyond dualist thinking of the environment as an obstacle to human development in a world "out there" to embrace an understanding of nature as an essential part of an interrelated, interconnected community to which humans belong. Such a position requires shifting our thinking from the dualist view of ourselves as distinct from and hierarchically superior to the wider cosmos in which we ostensibly occupy a central position, to a holist view of ourselves as cohabitants of a system in which all actors, animate and inanimate, possess equal intrinsic value despite significant differences.

The holist position advocated for in this chapter, it has been argued, is consistent with the holist and monist philosophies of *Advaita*, *Gongsheng*, *Guanxi*, *Tianxia*, and *Ubuntu* that enjoy significant support among members of the African, Chinese, and Indian communities. The paradigm shift implied in the adoption of a view of humanity and the climate as irrevocably connected is, therefore, not another incompatible theoretical imposition on BRICS member states—it is already embedded in the everyday lives of their citizens. A holist approach is authentically African, Chinese, and Indian, as is captured in Xi Jinping's opening remarks following the 15th BRICS Summit:

As an African proverb puts it, "If you want to go fast, go alone; if you want to go far, go together". The philosophy of Ubuntu, which believes that "I am because we are", highlights the interdependence and interconnectedness of all peoples. Similarly, harmonious coexistence has been the aspiration of the Chinese nation for thousands of years. (Jinping 2023)

While the chapter has not had the occasion to engage with Brazilian and Russian metaphysics, and although it has not been possible to integrate metaphysical writing from the newly acceded members of the BRICS grouping, Ling's warning that we should avoid falling into the trap of representing dualist, monist, and holist metaphysics as mutually exclusive philosophical positions creates space for an inclusive approach to climate thinking within the context of an enlarged BRICS.

While the chapter has argued that the infusion of a holist understanding of the fundamental interconnectedness between humans and the environment resonates with the worldviews of BRICS members, it should nevertheless be clear that BRICS member states will have to make some difficult and unpopular policy choices to ensure that population growth and economic development do not continue to harm the natural environment. Recognizing that we are mere custodians of the natural world and striving for a positive symbiotic relationship with this part of our universe, BRICS governments will have to carefully consider the policies surrounding fecundity, social welfare, industrial growth, and sustainable economic development. Real climate action will require a fine balancing of the loss of certain entrenched freedoms in favour of gaining the freedom of a secure future. This will require governments to implement "bottom-up" approaches and grassroots (perhaps educational) initiatives to infuse civil society with a more profoundly relational experience of connectedness to the natural environment, such that citizens and citizen organizations themselves develop climate initiatives that will be complementary to government efforts. In a sense, what we are looking to achieve here is to effect a return to our cosmic selves that will allow us to grow into a harmonious future along with the natural environment.

References

Acharya, Amitav. 2019. "From Heaven to Earth: 'Cultural Idealism' and 'Moral Realism' as Chinese Contributions to Global International Relations." *The Chinese Journal of International Politics* 12 (4): 467–494.

AFP. 2023. "Russia's Updated Climate Doctrine Drops Mention of Fossil Fuels." *The Moscow Times*, 27 October. https://www.themoscowtimes.com/2023/10/27/russian-space-boss-warns-iss-equipment-beyond-warranty-a82920.

Bhattacharya, Amar, Homi Kharas, and John W. McArthur. 2022. *Why Developing Country Voices Will Shape the Global Climate Change Agenda*. Brookings Center for Sustainable Development Policy Brief. https://www.brookings.edu/wp-content/uploads/2022/07/Green_Transitions.pdf.

Boulangeat, Isabelle, Sandrine Allain, Emilie Crouzat, Sabine Girard, Séline Granjou, Clara Poirier, Jean F. Ruaul, Yoan Paillet, and Isabelle Arpin. 2022. "From Human-Nature Dualism Towards More Integration in Socio-Ecosystems Studies." In *Exploring Nature's Values Across Landscapes*, edited by Ieva Misiune, Daniel Depellegrin, and Lukas E. Vigl, 37–49. Cham: Springer.

BRICS. 2023. "BRICS and Africa: Partnership for Mutually Accelerated Growth, Sustainable Development and Inclusive Multilateralism." XV BRICS Summit Johannesburg II Declaration. Sandton, 23 August. https://brics2023.gov.za/wp-content/uploads/2023/08/Jhb-II-Declaration-24-August-2023-1.pdf.

Chibvongodze, Danford T. 2016. "Ubuntu Is Not Only About the Human! An Analysis of the Role of African Philosophy and Ethics in Environment Management." *Journal of Human Ecology* 53 (2): 157–166.

Choudhary, Kamya. 2022. "How Is India Tackling Climate Change?" LSE Explainers, 2 November. https://www.lse.ac.uk/granthaminstitute/explainers/how-is-india-tackling-climate-change/.

Downie, Christian, and Marc Williams. 2018. "After the Paris Agreement: What Role for the BRICS in Global Climate Governance?" *Global Policy* 9 (3): 398–407.

Dsouza, Renita. 2022. "A Stocktaking of BRICS Performance in Climate Action." ORF Special Report 182. New Delhi: Observer Research Foundation. https://www.orfonline.org/public/uploads/posts/pdf/20230530171326.pdf.

Elinor, Ostrom. 2007. "A Diagnostic Approach for Going Beyond Panaceas." *Proceedings of the National Academy of Sciences* 104 (39): 15181–15187. https://doi.org/10.1073/pnas.0702288104

Eze, Michael O. 2010. *Intellectual History in Contemporary South Africa*. New York: Palgrave Macmillan.

Feris, Loretta. 2012. "The Public Trust Doctrine and Liability for Historic Water Pollution in South Africa." *Law, Environment, and Development Journal* 8 (1): 1–18.

Frischmann, Brett M., Alain Marciano, and Giovanni Battista Ramello. 2019. "The Tragedy of the Commons After 50 Years." *Journal of Economic Perspectives* 33 (4): 211–228.

Galgut, Elisa. 2017. "Animal Rights and African Ethics: Congruence or Conflict?" *Journal of Animal Ethics* 7 (2): 175–182.

Graness, Anke. 2018. "Ubuntu and the Concept of Cosmopolitanism." *Human Affairs* 28 (4): 395–405.

Gu, Jing, Neil Renwick, and Lan Xue. 2018. "The BRICS and Africa's Search for Green Growth, Clean Energy and Sustainable Development." *Energy Policy* 120: 675–683.

Hale, Erin. 2023. "China Promised Climate Action. Its Emissions Topped US, EU, India Combined." Al Jazeera, 30 August. https://www.aljazeera.com/economy/2023/8/30/chinas-coal-habit-clouds-climate-fight-as-emissions-top-us-eu-combined.

Hardin, Garrett. 1968. "The Tragedy of the Commons." *Science* 162 (3859): 1243–1248.

Hofstedt, Todd. 2010. "China's Water Scarcity and Its Implications for Domestic and International Stability." *Asian Affairs: An American Review* 37: 71–83.

Horsthemke, Kai. 2015. *Animals and African Ethics*. London and New York: Palgrave Macmillan.

Hwang, Yih-Jye. 2021. "Reappraising the Chinese School of International Relations: A Postcolonial Perspective." *Review of International Studies* 47 (3): 311–330.

Jinping, Xi. 2023. "Seeking Development Through Solidarity and Cooperation and Shouldering Our Responsibility for Peace." Remarks by the President of the People's Republic of China at the 15th BRICS Summit, Johannesburg, 23 August. https://www.mfa.gov.cn/eng/zxxx_662805/202308/t20230823_11130928.html.

Kıprızlı, Götuğ, and Köstem, Seçkin. 2022. "Understanding the BRICS Framing of Climate Change: The Role of Collective Identity Formation." *International Journal* 77 (2): 270–291.

Lagutina, Maria L. 2019. "BRICS in a World of Regions." *Third World Thematics: A TWQ Journal* 4 (6): 442–458.

Ling, LHM. 2018. "Heart and Soul for World Politics: Advaita Monism and Daoist Trialectics in IR." *International Relations of the Asia-Pacific* 18 (3): 313–337.

McCay, Bonnie J. 1995. "Common and Private Concerns." *Advances in Human Ecology* 4: 89–116.

McLean, Jordan. 2023. "The Expanded BRICS Can Be a Force to Be Reckoned with in Shaping a New World Energy Order." News24, 25 September. https://www.news24.com/fin24/climate_future/news/analysis-the-expanded-brics-can-be-a-force-to-be-reckoned-with-in-shaping-a-new-world-energy-order-20230925.

McShane, Katie. 2016. "Anthropocentrism in Climate Ethics and Policy." *Midwest Studies in Philosophy* XL: 189–204.

Mhlambi, Sabelo. 2020. "From Rationality to Relationality: Ubuntu as an Ethical and Human Rights Framework for Artificial Intelligence Governance." Carr Center Discussion Paper Issue 2020-009. https://carrcenter.hks.harvard.edu/files/cchr/files/ccdp_2020-009_sabelo_b.pdf.

Morganti, Matteo. 2009. "Ontological Priority, Fundamentality and Monism." *Dialectica* 63 (3): 271–288.

Naidoo, Dhesigan. 2023. "Towards a BRICS Climate Club." *ISS Today*, 24 August. https://issafrica.org/iss-today/towards-a-brics-climate-club.

Ngubane, Jordan K. 1979. *Conflict of Minds*. New York: Books in Focus.

Nguyen, Duc Huu, and Irina P. Khominich. 2023. "The Measurement of Green Economic Quality in the BRICS Countries: Should They Prioritize Financing for Environmental Protection, Economic Growth, or Social Goals?" *Russian Journal of Economics* 9 (2): 183–200.

Ostrom, Elinor, Joanna Burger, Christopher B. Field, Richard B. Norgaard, and David Policansky. 1999. "Revisiting the Commons: Local lessons, Global Challenges." *Science* 284 (5412): 278–282.

Qin, Yaqing. 2007. "Why Is There No Chinese International Relations Theory?" *International Relations of the Asia-Pacific* 7: 313–340.

Qin, Yaqing. 2016. "A Relational Theory of World Politics." *International Studies Review* 18: 33–47.

Qu, Haonan. 2022. "How South Africa Can Advance Reforms to Achieve Its Climate Goals." IMF News, 18 February. https://www.imf.org/en/News/Articles/2022/02/21/cf-how-south-africacan-advance-reforms-to-achieve-its-climate-goals.

Ralston, Shane J. 2015. "Holism." In *The Encyclopedia of Political Thought*. Chichester: Wiley. https://doi.org/10.1002/9781118474396.wbept0477.

Ramose, Mogobe. 2002. "The Philosophy of *Ubuntu* and *Ubuntu* as a Philosophy." In *Philosophy from Africa: A Text with Readings*, edited by Pieter H. Coetzee and Abraham P. J. Roux, 2nd ed., 230–238. Cape Town: Oxford University Press.

Ren, Xiao. 2020. "Grown from Within: Building a Chinese School of International Relations." *The Pacific Review* 33 (3–4): 386–412.

Shahi, Deepshikha, and Gennaro Ascione. 2015. "Rethinking the Absence of Post-western International Relations Theory in India: 'Advaitic Monism' as an Alternative Epistemological Approach." *European Journal of International Relations* 22 (2): 313–334.

Shinn, David H. 2016. "The Environmental Impact of China's Investment in Africa." *Cornell International Law Journal* 49 (1): 25–68.

Republic of South Africa. 2022. "Climate Change Bill B9-2022." Cape Town: South African Parliament. https://www.parliament.gov.za/storage/app/media/Bills/2022/B9_2022_Climate_Change_Bill/B9_2022_Climate_Change_Bill.pdf.

Republic of South Africa. 2023. "BRICS and Africa: Partnership for Mutually Accelerated Growth, Sustainable Development and Inclusive Multilateralism." Pretoria: Department of International Relations and Cooperation. https://brics2023.gov.za/theme-and-priorities/.

Tebajjukira, Damalie. 2023. "The BRICS Summit Should Tackle Climate Change and Energy Security." African Center for Green Economy. https://africancentre.org/the-brics-summit-should-tackle-climate-change-and-energy-security/.

Westphal, Jonathan. 2016. *The Mind-Body Problem*. Cambridge, MA: MIT Press.

Wu, Genyou. 2024. "Introduction on the Ethical "Doctrine of *Gongsheng*" Based on Song-Ming Confucianism's "Unity of Consummate Persons and Things."" In *Across Contexts: A Philosophy of Co-becoming*, edited by Bing Song and Yiwen Zhan, 57–69. Singapore: Palgrave Macmillan.

Zhao, Tingyang. 2019. *Redefining a Philosophy for World Governance*. Translated by Liqing Tao. Singapore and Beijing: Palgrave Macmillan and Foreign Language Teaching and Research Publishing Co.

Bridging the Gap: The Brazilian Climate Change Agenda After Bolsonaro

Marina Magalhães Barreto Leite da Silva

1 INTRODUCTION

Climate change is a pressing global issue that poses significant challenges to the environment, societies, and economies around the world. It refers to long-term changes in temperature patterns, weather conditions, and other aspects of the earth's climate system. The primary driver of climate change is the increase in greenhouse gas emissions resulting from human activities, such as burning fossil fuels, deforestation, and industrial processes. These emissions trap heat in the atmosphere, leading to a rise in global temperatures and disruptive climate events.

The impacts of climate change are far-reaching and diverse. They include rising sea levels, more frequent and severe heatwaves, changes in precipitation patterns, loss of biodiversity, and increased risks to human health and well-being. Addressing climate change requires global cooperation, policy interventions, and sustainable practices to reduce greenhouse gas emissions, adapt to the changing climate, and protect vulnerable ecosystems and communities.

M. M. B. L. da Silva (✉)
University of Pernambuco, Recife, Brazil
e-mail: prof.ninamagal@gmail.com

© The Author(s), under exclusive license to Springer Nature Singapore Pte Ltd. 2024
H. Solomon et al. (eds.), *BRICS and Climate Change*,
https://doi.org/10.1007/978-981-97-5532-5_3

Brazil, as one of the largest countries in the world, holds significant importance within the context of climate change. Its vast territory spans diverse biomes, including the Amazon rainforest, the Pantanal wetlands, the Cerrado savanna, and the Atlantic Forest. These ecosystems play crucial roles in regulating the global climate, providing habitats for countless species, and supporting the livelihoods of local communities.

The Amazon rainforest is often referred to as the "lungs of the Earth" (Mikkola 2021) due to its immense carbon absorption capacity. It serves as a vital carbon sink, absorbing a substantial amount of global greenhouse gas emissions and helping to mitigate climate change. Furthermore, the Amazon region is home to Indigenous communities whose traditional knowledge and sustainable practices contribute to its preservation.

Brazil is also a major agricultural powerhouse, with extensive land use for livestock production and the cultivation of crops such as soybeans and sugarcane (Mueller and Mueller, 2018). In 2016, Embrapa Territorial's assessment indicated that 65,913,738 hectares (7.8%) of the country's land were under cultivation. According to NASA's findings, the cropland area in Brazil was calculated to be 63,994,479 hectares (7.6%) (de Miranda 2018). The management of these agricultural activities and associated deforestation has implications for greenhouse gas emissions, biodiversity loss, and sustainable land use.

Given Brazil's ecological significance, its actions and policies regarding climate change have a profound impact on global climate dynamics and international efforts to combat climate change. Understanding Brazil's approach to climate change mitigation, adaptation, and sustainable development is essential for shaping effective strategies and promoting global collaboration in addressing this urgent global challenge—especially in the light of the recent political crisis and government of the extremist right-wing Jair Messias Bolsonaro, which was a huge setback in Brazilian climate change mitigation policies and commitments.

Therefore, the present chapter aims to address a brief timeline of positions assumed by Brazil in the international arena and analyse the challenges imposed by the previous term of federal government, recognizing the present demand of bridging the gap created by the Bolsonaro administration.

In accordance with the observations made by Brazilian and international researchers, it can be deduced that the Brazilian political landscape has never truly favoured public policies geared towards environmental issues. Even prior to the Bolsonaro government, and despite the significance of the Brazilian territory to the global climate, Brazilian politics never combatted the acceleration of global warming concretely or effectively. During the first two terms of Luíz Inácio Lula da Silva's government, some small steps were taken towards the creation of a more environmentally conscious policy, which, though limited, represented progress. However, it is undeniable that, from 2019 to 2022, Brazil moved in the opposite direction of the policies proposed and adopted to protect the environment.

For instance, during the peak of the COVID-19 pandemic, the statement made by the Minister of the Environment at the time, Ricardo Salles, became widely known. He suggested that the international crisis presented an opportunity to push through policies favourable to unrestricted exploitation of the Amazon and other territories, in terms of both agriculture and mining, effectively "deixando a boiada passar" ("allowing the cattle to pass") before the distraction subsided and people began paying closer attention to government policies (G1 2020).

Therefore, acknowledging the issue concerning the approach taken during the previous presidential term, this chapter also aims to present the changes represented by the new government and the challenges that will be faced to rectify all the retrogressive steps imposed by the previous administration. In addition to carefully observing the current Anthropocene scenario, we need to consider how Brazil can accomplish an economic recovery process and political and financial reengagement with key partners, primarily the BRICS nations, through the implementation of an effective policy regarding climate change.

2 Climate Change Policy in Brazil: A Brief Timeline Until 2018

Brazil has a long history of engagement with climate change issues, marked by a few significant milestones and policy developments. Brazil recognized the importance of addressing environmental challenges, including climate change, as part of its commitment to sustainable development.

Huguenin and Meirelles (2022) conclude that the historical understanding of the evolution of Brazilian public policies regarding the mitigation of the impacts of climate change is fundamental to comprehending that environmental issues are inseparable from social issues.

40   M. M. B. L. DA SILVA

Extreme climatic events are closely tied to the overall political and economic stability of the country.

Despite having lost 25.8% of its coverage in the past 35 years, Brazilian territory maintains 57% of its land covered by native vegetation (MapBiomas 2022). This underscores the significance of environmental protection and the magnitude of the impacts experienced, not only within the national borders but also on a global scale, when this vegetation and biodiversity are compromised.

Throughout the years, the territory suffered several impacts. From 1850 to 1950, Brazil experienced significant deforestation driven by agricultural expansion, primarily for coffee plantations and livestock grazing. These land-use changes contribute to carbon emissions and loss of biodiversity, which caused concern due to the vast biodiversity present within the country's borders.

From the 1970s, the government initiated a more significant participation on debates and decision-making internationally. First, starting with the participation in the United Nations Conference on the Human Environment in Stockholm (1972), which marks a turning point in global environmental awareness and lays the foundation for international cooperation on environmental issues, including climate change. After that, the adoption of a new constitution in 1988 officially defined the environmental protection as a fundamental right and established principles for sustainable development. According to the Constituição da República Federativa do Brasil (1988),

Article 170:
The economic order, based on the valorization of human labor and free enterprise, aims to ensure a dignified existence for all, in accordance with the dictates of social justice, while observing the following principles:
(...)
- environmental protection, including through differentiated treatment based on the environmental impact of products, services, and their production and provision processes
(...)

Article 225:
Everyone has the right to an ecologically balanced environment, which is a common asset of the people and essential to a healthy quality of life. It is the duty of the government and society to defend and preserve it for present and future generations.

However, the country's engagement in global climate negotiations started gaining true momentum in the 1990s, leading to the establishment of key policy frameworks and initiatives. Brazil became a signatory to the Intergovernmental Panel on Climate Change (IPCC), an international body that assesses scientific, technical, and socioeconomic information relevant to understanding climate change, and, two years later, hosted the United Nations Conference on Environment and Development (UNCED), also known as the Earth Summit, in Rio de Janeiro. The summit led to the adoption of the United Nations Framework Convention on Climate Change (UNFCCC), marking a major step in global efforts to address climate change. Moreover, "in 1992, the Ministry of the Environment, Water Resources, and Legal Amazon (MMARHAL) was established, which in 1999 was renamed the Ministry of the Environment (MMA)" (Huguenin and Meirelles 2022: 139). In 1994, Brazil's National Institute for Space Research (INPE) launched the PRODES programme, which uses satellite imagery to monitor deforestation in the Amazon rainforest.

Following the participation in the third meeting of the Conference of the Parties (COP3) and the adoption of the UNFCCC in Kyoto, Japan, Brazil established the Amazon Region Protected Areas (ARPA) Program in 1998, aiming to create a network of protected areas in the Amazon rainforest to promote conservation and combat deforestation.

Huguenin and Meirelles (2022) state that:

> With the turn of the century, in Brazil, during the 2000s, within the government of former President Fernando Henrique Cardoso, there was a period of significant deforestation. (…) In 2004, the Action Plan for the Prevention and Control of Deforestation in the Legal Amazon (PPCDAm) was established by the government of former President Luís Inácio Lula da Silva. (…) The PPCDAm was implemented in different phases and demonstrated a significant reduction in deforestation. (p. 140)

The Amazon Fund was established on 1 August 2008, with the aim of mobilizing resources for projects focused on reducing deforestation, promoting sustainable land use, and supporting the development of local communities in the Amazon region. Another pivotal moment was the creation of the Biodiversity Conservation Institute (ICMBio) in 2009 for control and surveillance aimed at protecting the environment.

In 2009, the Brazilian government also passed the National Policy on Climate Change (PNMC) through legislation. The purpose of this policy was to provide a comprehensive framework for climate change mitigation and adaptation, including targets and actions to reduce greenhouse gas emissions, promote renewable energy, and strengthen climate resilience. The PNMC became a central component of Brazil's climate change policy, outlining specific objectives, strategies, and actions to guide the country's efforts in mitigating and adapting to climate change. The policy established targets for reducing greenhouse gas emissions in key sectors, such as energy, industry, transportation, and agriculture. It also focused on promoting sustainable land-use practices, preserving forests, and enhancing climate resilience (Huguenin and Meirelles 2022).

Another important milestone was the establishment of the Brazilian Panel on Climate Change (PBMC) in 2009, composed of scientists and experts who provide scientific assessments and recommendations to support policy development and decision-making processes.

The year 2012 marked the United Nations Conference on Sustainable Development, popularly known as Rio+20, held in Rio de Janeiro. However, 2012 also represented a setback in environmental protection in Brazil. Changes were made to the Brazilian Forest Code, which revoked previously established rights. In terms of international decisions made during the conference, Brazil also did not exhibit a positive stance, remaining rather conservative and contributing to the lack of definition of the goals outlined in the final document of the Rio+20 (Huguenin and Meirelles 2022).

The COP21 was held in Paris in 2015 and emerged against a backdrop of escalating climate change concerns, such as the alarming rise in the planet's atmospheric temperature or the increase in sea levels caused by polar ice melting. In total, 196 countries, including Brazil, recognized the pressing need to address this global threat comprehensively during the conference and came together with the shared goal of curbing the devastating impacts of climate change. The so-called Paris Agreement was a ground-breaking accord that aimed to limit global warming to well below 2 °C above preindustrial levels, which signified a global commitment to drastic emissions reductions and climate resilience. Brazil's participation was significant due to its status as one of the world's largest greenhouse gas emitters and its extensive Amazon rainforest, a vital carbon sink. Brazil submitted its Nationally Determined Contribution (NDC), outlining its commitment to reducing deforestation and curbing emissions from various sectors, setting the audacious target of achieving zero deforestation in the Amazon by 2030. Brazil has taken the lead among nations categorized as "developing" by being the first to pledge a reduction in greenhouse gas emissions, setting a goal to achieve a 43% reduction by 2030 (Huguenin and Meirelles 2022: 141).

President Dilma Rousseff's government presented few distinct decisions from her predecessor, whereas the real political shift began with her impeachment and the commencement of Michel Temer's administration. Many of the policies adopted during the 13 years of the Workers' Party's governance were abandoned, marking a clear change in direction towards a more far-right-oriented governance.

It is also important to acknowledge that, when it comes to Brazilian participation in the international decision-making process and the formulation of legislation, very little has been implemented. The agrarian nature of the economy has consistently carried significant influence in terms of domestic policy and environmental surveillance. This was one of the most significant influences on environmental policy and the way in which the Brazilian government approached climate change over the years, especially from 2019 to 2022. Nascimento and Torres (2022) emphasize that, starting with the reestablishment of democracy, and continuing until Jair Bolsonaro's presidency, Brazil's approach displayed varying degrees of responsiveness to environmental and climate change concerns, fluctuating over time (p. 415).

3   GOVERNMENT'S APPROACH
TO CLIMATE CHANGE FROM 2019 TO 2022

The election of Jair Messias Bolsonaro in 2018 did not necessarily signify a shocking ideological shift, as Brazil followed the international trend of right-wing-leaning governments. Taking a cue from the election of Donald Trump in the United States, the discourse of a patriotic anti-corruption hero captured the hearts and minds of the middle class and the business community. The primary idea was to establish an extreme contrast to the social policies adopted by previous governments, which were blamed as the main drivers of the escalating economic crisis.

As mentioned by Marquardt et al. (2022), "under the motto Brazil above everything, God above everyone, Bolsonaro promised to recover the economy, value the family, fight corruption, and tackle crime. Against this background, Bolsonaro's presidential campaign and politics also trans-formed and eroded Brazilian climate change policies" (p. 788).

Over the years, the government's stance on climate change has evolved, reflecting a combination of environmental preservation, economic development, and political considerations. However, while previous administrations emphasized Brazil's commitment to sustainable development and global climate change mitigation efforts, Bolsonaro's government's approach has brought some shifts in political priorities. Among the 13 candidates for the Brazilian presidency, only Bolsonaro did not officially present proposals for environmental policies and measures to mitigate the impacts of climate change (Marquardt et al. 2022: 788). This directly influenced the political stance adopted during the government that came to power in 2018.

Under Bolsonaro's administration, there has been a greater emphasis on economic growth and reducing bureaucratic hurdles to attract investments. However, concerns have been raised about the impact of certain policies and statements on environmental protection and climate change action; "the anti-environment and anti-indigenous government of President Jair Bolsonaro (2019–2022) partially dismantled environmental governance" (Pereira 2022: 5).

Huguenin and Meirelles (2022) state that:

> During President Jair Bolsonaro's administration, the former Minister of the Environment, Ricardo Salles, implemented several administrative actions related to the issue of climate change. Among these actions was the withdrawal of Brazil as the host country for COP-25. Subsequent attacks on the scientific community and environmental institutions, such as the National Institute for Space Research (INPE), which is involved in monitoring the Amazon rainforest, only underscored how climate denialism has also become a political agenda of the current government. This stance aims to deregulate environmental laws established throughout Brazilian history and demonstrates a lack of commitment to international agreements. (p. 141)

The Bolsonaro administration's stance on climate change has been the subject of significant debate, both nationally and internationally, since taking office in January 2019. The government has adopted an approach that differs substantially from previous administrations regarding environmental policy and climate change. This position is characterized by scepticism towards climate science, a reduction in environmental oversight, an increase in deforestation rates in the Amazon rainforest, and a perceived antagonism towards environmental NGOs and activists.

One of the key features of this approach has been scepticism about climate change itself. President Bolsonaro has questioned the scientific consensus on global warming and climate change, suggesting that the concerns are exaggerated; "during a public campaign speech, Bolsonaro portrayed the PA [Paris Agreement] as a communist and 'globalist' trap, that would undermine Brazil's 'national sovereignty' over 136 million hectares of the Amazon" (Marquardt et al. 2022: 789). Even before assuming the presidency of Brazil, Bolsonaro already announced his intention to withdraw from the Paris Agreement and invest in an expansion of the economic exploitation of Brazil's so-called natural treasures. Through the unrestricted use of false information, often referred to as "fake news", and the dissemination of an antiscience discourse that characterized his government, the international community grew concerned about the path Brazil was taking, given its prominence among developing countries.

Additionally, Bolsonaro's administration has implemented policies that have led to a significant increase in deforestation in the Amazon rainforest. This includes measures that have relaxed environmental regulations, reduced funding for environmental agencies, and created a climate of reduced enforcement of environmental laws. This has resulted in a notable rise in deforestation rates in the Amazon, which is a matter of global concern due to the forest's role as a critical carbon sink.

In 2019, during the first year of his administration, the Minister of the Environment, Ricardo Salles, dismantled a series of environmental protection mechanisms throughout his tenure in office, in addition to reducing the federal government's investment in the national climate change programme by 95% (Mariz 2019). The Secretariat for Climate Change and Forests was also abolished as one of Salles's initial measures in office (Marquardt et al. 2022: 790).

One of the institutions most adversely affected during the Bolsonaro administration was the Brazilian Institute of the Environment and Renewable Natural Resources (IBAMA). Established in 1989, IBAMA is the agency responsible for overseeing and preserving Brazil's natural resources. It is the inspectors of this institution who are tasked with monitoring, fining, and deterring predatory exploitation within environmental protection areas, known as APAs. The government systematically undermined the authority of both IBAMA and ICMBio, hindering the imposition of fines and the confiscation of equipment used in actions classified by the constitution as environmental crimes. The dismantling of regulatory institutions led to extreme levels of deforestation and the destruction of wildlife in Brazil's primary biomes. Data from both public and private agencies indicated a significant increase in affected areas during the years of the Bolsonaro administration. As of March 2022, only 2.17% of the deforestation alerts issued received the appropriate response and oversight, while more than 97% of these alerts were disregarded (Dantas 2022).

The increase in deforestation in the Amazon led to significant protests, especially by European governments, and resulted in the suspension of donations to the Amazon Fund. The cessation of donations to the Amazon Fund has prompted a significant shift in the Bolsonaro government's approach to the issue of deforestation in the Amazon rainforest. Established in 2008, the Amazon Fund was a critical source of international financing aimed at supporting projects focused on reducing deforestation rates and promoting sustainable development in the region. It received contributions from various international donors, with Norway and Germany being prominent contributors.

However, tensions had been brewing between the Bolsonaro administration and donor countries, largely due to concerns about the Brazilian government's environmental policies and its approach to the Amazon rainforest. These tensions culminated in the suspension of donations in 2019 and the subsequent cessation of contributions to the fund. This abrupt halt in financial support had several notable effects on Brazil's stance regarding deforestation.

An official report prepared by the Office of the Union Controllership (CGU) highlighted that the management of the Ministry of the Environment under the Bolsonaro government jeopardized the continuity of the Amazon Fund and other environmental policies; much of this is attributed to the poor management of then-Minister Ricardo Salles (Peixoto 2022a, b).

From the cessation of contributions, the Brazilian government faced increased financial pressure to address deforestation and environmental preservation in the absence of international funding. The Amazon Fund has played a crucial role in financing projects aimed at curbing deforestation and fostering sustainable development practices. The loss of these funds forced the government to seek alternative sources of financing to support its environmental agenda.

At the same time, the cessation of donations prompted a reevaluation of environmental policies. While the Bolsonaro administration had initially advocated for reduced environmental regulations and prioritized economic development in the Amazon, the funding interruption necessitated a reassessment of these policies. The international scrutiny and diplomatic tensions surrounding the funding issue compelled the government to reconsider its approach to both domestic and international concerns.

There was a noticeable shift in rhetoric. President Bolsonaro, who had previously downplayed concerns about deforestation and criticized environmental nongovernmental organizations (NGOs), faced increased pressure to acknowledge and address deforestation more seriously. Public statements began to reflect a greater recognition of the need to combat illegal logging, wildfires, and deforestation activities in the Amazon.

Furthermore, the cessation of funding led the Brazilian government to seek new partnerships and initiatives aimed at supporting environmental conservation and combatting deforestation. This included discussions with private sector entities and other countries interested in addressing deforestation issues in the Amazon. The situation underscored the significance of international diplomacy in addressing deforestation. The Bolsonaro administration engaged in diplomatic efforts to mend relations with donor countries and attract international support for its environmental initiatives. These diplomatic efforts were considered critical in garnering international assistance and addressing deforestation concerns effectively.

The government has also taken a confrontational stance towards environmental NGOs and activists, often accusing them of undermining Brazil's interests abroad. This has created a challenging environment for civil society organizations working on environmental and climate issues. The most severe incident within the challenging scenario in which environmental organizations and activists found themselves was the murder of the journalist Dom Phillips and the Indigenous activist Bruno Pereira. Both were killed on 5 June 2022 by a group of people accused of engaging in illegal fishing in rivers within the Vale do Javari region, near the border between Brazil and Peru.

More recently, as reported by France Presse (2023),

investigators argue that Dom Phillips, 57, and Bruno Pereira, 41, were killed by a group of illegal fishermen, possibly in response to the indigenous activist's work against environmental crimes in the region. The double murder gained international attention and exposed the prevailing violence in the world's largest tropical rainforest, where environmental destruction continues unabated.

Despite these policies and rhetoric, the government has made commitments to reduce greenhouse gas emissions, particularly within the context of deforestation. However, the effectiveness of these commitments has been questioned due to the inconsistency between the government's actions and its stated goals. In 2021, the administration announced its intention to withdraw from the Paris Agreement but later reversed this decision, signalling a degree of uncertainty and inconsistency in Brazil's climate policy. However, Bolsonaro's Vice-President, Hamilton Mourão, became concerned about the international repercussions of Brazil's poor environmental management and established a Crisis Cabinet for Amazon-related matters. Mourão even announced an ambitious plan to achieve zero deforestation by 2028. Bolsonaro has moderated his controversial language as he aims to restore Brazil's damaged environmental reputation on the global stage and project a more responsible approach to stewardship (Biller 2021).

In summary, the Bolsonaro administration's approach to climate change is marked by scepticism, relaxation of environmental regulations, increased deforestation, and confrontations with environmental organizations. These policies have raised concerns about Brazil's commitment to addressing climate change, despite the country's significant role in global efforts to combat the climate crisis.

Just two weeks before the end of President Bolsonaro's term, the federal government issued a measure that allowed for the extraction of timber in Indigenous lands, which raised concerns among experts as the document opened the door to significant environmental impacts and increased deforestation in these protected areas (Peixoto 2022a, b). That was a final act of aggression by Bolsonaro's government against environmental protection policies and efforts to combat climate change.

4 Four Years of Setbacks

During the Bolsonaro administration, Brazil faced significant environmental challenges in various critical biomes, including the Amazon rainforest, Pantanal, Cerrado, Caatinga, and Atlantic Forest. By the end of 2022, INPE released a technical report with data on deforestation in Brazil until the end of 2021. The given information covered most of the critical environmental moments during the Bolsonaro term.

Under President Bolsonaro's leadership, there was a substantial increase in deforestation rates in the Brazilian Amazon, with data from INPE revealing significant expansion in cleared land and deforested areas, linked to activities such as logging, agriculture, and mining. Images taken by satellites showed vast areas of destruction due to illegal exploitation and criminal wildfires.

As mentioned by INPE (2021),

> The estimated value was 13,235 km^2 of clear-cutting in the period from August 1, 2020, to July 31, 2021. This figure represents an increase of 21.97% compared to the deforestation rate reported by PRODES 2020, which was 10,851 km^2 for the nine states of the ALB (Legal Amazon Basin). This estimate is the result of the Legal Amazon Satellite Deforestation Monitoring Project (PRODES). (p. 1)

The national agency's estimate materialized in a significant increase in deforested areas in the region known as the Legal Amazon. The Legal Amazon corresponds to approximately 59% of Brazilian territory, encompassing eight states—Acre, Amapá, Amazonas, Mato Grosso, Pará, Rondônia, Roraima, and Tocantins—as well as part of the state of Maranhão, totalling an area of five million km^2. Prior efforts to reduce deforestation in this region were undermined by a marked increase from 2019 to 2022.

According to data provided by PRODES, an area of 45,612 km^2 in the Legal Amazon was deforested over these four years. Compared to figures from previous administrations, particularly from 2009 onwards, there was an annual increase of approximately 3000 km^2. See Fig. 1 (INPE 2023).

The Pantanal, one of the world's largest tropical wetlands, covering an area of 250,000 km^2, also faced severe challenges during this period. Intentional wildfires, primarily for land clearance, devastated extensive areas of this ecosystem, threatening biodiversity and significantly increasing greenhouse gas emissions.

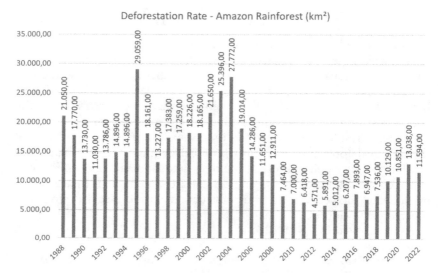

Fig. 1 Deforestation rate—Legal Amazon (INPE 2023)

In September 2020, the situation in the Pantanal reached one of its most critical moments, with scientific confirmation that approximately 23% of the biome had already been burnt, marking a 200% increase in illegal fires between 2019 and 2020. The Bolsonaro administration attempted to discredit the presented scientific data and significantly reduced the funding allocated for firefighting efforts. Much of the firefighting and wildlife rescue work was carried out by volunteer brigades. Vice-President Mourão even conducted an overflight of one of the affected areas, claiming that it was not fire damage but rather a rocky terrain. This incident was yet another episode of the dissemination of false information (Haje 2020).

According to data provided by PRODES, the Pantanal area was reduced by 2806 km^2 from 2019 to 2022. Compared to figures from previous administrations, particularly from 2007 onwards, there was an annual increase of around 200 km^2. See Fig. 2 (INPE 2023). Despite not representing a significant difference, what characterized the period of setbacks was a complete disregard for combatting this deforestation process.

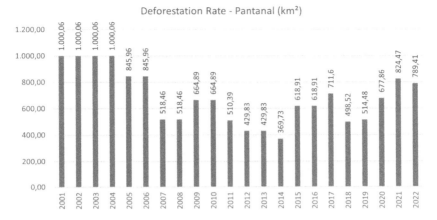

Fig. 2 Deforestation rate—Pantanal (INPE 2023)

Cerrado is a Brazilian biome rich in resources and biodiversity, located in the central region of the country, covering approximately 2 million km². One of its main characteristics is that it is a type of savanna, subject to natural wildfires due to the dry climate but with a remarkable capacity for regeneration. However, over the years, the Cerrado has experienced continued deforestation and conversion to agricultural land. This biome plays a crucial role in Brazil's water supply system and carbon sequestration, making the loss of Cerrado habitats a risk to both local and global environmental systems.

From 2019 to 2022, the biome also endured neglect under the Bolsonaro administration. As an area primed for agricultural expansion, notably in soybean and grain production, environmental protection in the Cerrado gave way to favouring agribusiness throughout Bolsonaro's tenure. This mirrored what transpired in the Pantanal, with insufficient efforts dedicated to fire control and monitoring the expansion of agricultural lands. An area of approximately 33,445 km² was lost during this period. See Fig. 3 (INPE 2023).

The Caatinga biome, on the other hand, spans approximately 734,000 km² and is an exclusively Brazilian biome not found anywhere else in the world (Leal et al. 2003). As a semi-arid biome in northeastern Brazil, the area confronted issues related to land degradation, desertification, and unsustainable land-use practices, posing a threat to its unique flora and

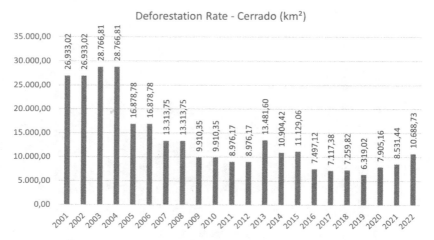

Fig. 3 Deforestation rate—Cerrado (INPE 2023)

fauna. Compared to the other Brazilian biomes, it was likely the least affected in terms of area loss, but it was not immune to the reduction in environmental oversight.

According to data provided by PRODES, the Caatinga area was reduced by 8818 km² from 2019 to 2022. Compared to figures from previous administrations, there was not a significant difference. See Fig. 4 (INPE 2023).

The Atlantic Forest biome, one of the world's most threatened biodiversity hotspots, continued to experience deforestation and habitat fragmentation, with profound ecological consequences. Data from PRODES showed that the forest coverage lost from 2019 to 2022 was similar to the period before Bolsonaro's administration. See Fig. 5 (INPE 2023).

However, the reduction in the authority of environmental oversight agencies resulted in an increase in environmental crimes being committed without the imposition of fines. According to the NGO "SOS Mata Atlântica" (2020),

> the Bolsonaro government advised environmental agencies (Ibama, ICMBio, and the Institute of Botanical Gardens) to disregard the Atlantic Forest Law (Law No. 11,428/2006) and apply more lenient rules outlined in the Forest Code (Law No. 12,651/2012) for areas deemed consolidated in the Atlantic Forest regions. In practice, these areas are those with

Fig. 4 Deforestation rate—Caatinga (INPE 2023)

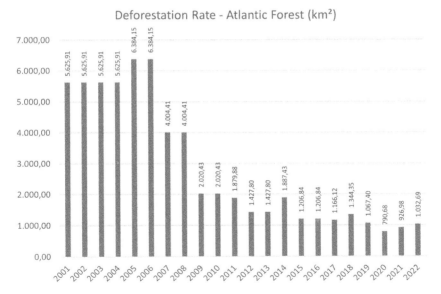

Fig. 5 Deforestation rate—Atlantic Forest (INPE 2023)

economic activities that were exploiting lands before 2008. With this directive, they will no longer be required to restore areas considered irregular and illegal under the Atlantic Forest Law.

These environmental challenges in Brazil's diverse biomes attracted international attention and prompted diplomatic tensions. The Bolsonaro administration's approach, often perceived as prioritizing economic development over environmental conservation, faced criticism and scrutiny. The stance on climate change also reflected in Brazil's international positioning, marking a departure from traditional Brazilian diplomatic practices.

5 Addressing Climate Change Internationally: Brazilian Commitments, Collaborative Efforts, and BRICS

Brazil has played a significant role in international climate change negotiations, contributing to global efforts to address this pressing challenge. As a major developing country with vast natural resources and diverse ecosystems, Brazil's participation and engagement in these negotiations have been crucial. Nevertheless, the last four years have also had a significant impact on Brazil's international image and main partnerships.

Back in the 1990s, leading up to the Earth Summit in Rio de Janeiro in 1992, Brazil was a prominent participant in the UNFCCC negotiations. The summit resulted in the adoption of the UNFCCC, which marked the beginning of global efforts to address climate change. During this period, Brazil focused on crucial issues such as the preservation of forests and the principle of "common but differentiated responsibilities" (CBDR), which acknowledges different responsibilities for developed and developing countries regarding climate action. Brazil played a leading role in advocating for the inclusion of forests in climate discussions and for the creation of mechanisms such as the Clean Development Mechanism (CDM) under the Kyoto Protocol.

The UNFCCC negotiations, which serve as the foundation for international climate action, are one of the main arenas of Brazilian participation. The country has been vocal in advocating for the interests of developing nations, highlighting the need for differentiated responsibilities and respective capabilities in addressing climate change.

Throughout the Kyoto Protocol era, spanning from 2002 to 2012, Brazil ratified the protocol in 2002. However, as a developing country, Brazil was not subject to emission reduction targets. Nevertheless, the country implemented various policies aimed at reducing emissions, particularly within the context of deforestation in the Amazon and the expansion of biofuels.

Following the Kyoto Protocol (United Nations 1997), Brazil made voluntary commitments to reduce deforestation and greenhouse gas emissions. In 2015, Brazil played a key role in the negotiations that led to the Paris Agreement. The country committed to reducing emissions by 37% below 2005 levels by 2025 and submitted its NDC. Brazil's involvement in international climate negotiations during this period was marked by the delicate balance between environmental protection and economic development (BNDES 2023).

Brazil's NDC includes ambitious targets to combat climate change. In addition to the proposal to reduce emissions by 37% by 2025, Brazil also committed to zero illegal deforestation by 2030, aiming to restore 12 million hectares of forests. Additionally, the NDC promotes renewable energy, with a goal of achieving 45% of total energy consumption from renewable sources by 2030 (BNDES 2023). Sustainable agriculture practices, adaptation strategies, and international cooperation are key components of Brazil's climate action plan.

During the lead-up to the Copenhagen Climate Conference in 2009, Brazil was part of the BASIC group (Brazil, South Africa, India, and China), seeking to coordinate positions on climate issues. The BASIC group emerged within the same context as the BRICS (Brazil, Russia, India, China, and South Africa) group and the IBSA (India, Brazil, and South Africa) alliance, bridging the gap left by developed countries and creating ties that would strengthen countries in the Southern Hemisphere both economically and strategically. As mentioned by Narayanan (2019), "there is no palpable difference in these expressions of multilateralism. They could be interpreted as multilateral 'groupings' striving to go beyond the straitjacket of existing institutions". These alliances were also part of Brazil's stance regarding the issue of climate change.

Rinaldi et al. (2016) state that:

since the BRICS' first summit in 2009, the climate issue was considered an important theme on their agenda. Related to energy efficiency, they declare prepared to promote conversations to deal with climate changes in bases of the CBDR principle, considering the need to combine measures to protect the environment with actions toward their goals of socioeconomic development. (p. 4)

However, the period following 2019, with the election of Bolsonaro, brought significant changes to Brazil's climate international stance. The government shifted its focus towards prioritizing economic development over environmental protection, which led to concerns about deforestation and weakened environmental enforcement. Brazil faced international criticism for its policies, and this period marked a challenging phase in the country's international climate relations—leaving behind international policy challenges for the third Lula government as well.

6 LULA 3.0

On 1 January 2023, the third presidential term of Luíz Inácio Lula da Silva (Lula) began. According to de Lima (2023), Lula 3.0's government represented, in the words of the president-elect in October 2022, a resurgence of Brazil's "active and assertive" foreign policy and a strong position towards climate change. This marked a return to the international relations practices that predated the disaster represented by the stances and policies adopted during the Bolsonaro government.

The 2022 presidential election was a pivotal moment in the country's political landscape. It featured a closely contested race between the incumbent president, Jair Bolsonaro, and former president, Lula. The election revolved around key issues such as the COVID-19 pandemic response, the economy, environmental protection, crime, and social programmes. In the end, Lula emerged as the victor, marking a significant shift in Brazilian politics. His win signalled a return to left-wing governance after years of far-right leadership under Bolsonaro. Lula's campaign focused on social equality, poverty reduction, and a more inclusive approach to economic policies.

As defined by de Lima (2023):

With Jair Bolsonaro's electoral defeat and in the face of such destruction and dismantling of the state and public policies, the term "revogaço" (big revocation) has definitively entered the Brazilian political lexicon. The actions of the Transition Office, between Lula da Silva's victory and his inauguration on January 1, 2023, underscored the new government's commitment to eradicating the cursed legacy and signaling a fresh start for Brazil.

This election had substantial implications for Brazil's future direction. It suggested a potential shift in policy priorities, emphasizing social programmes, and environmental protection. However, it also presented challenges, as the new government needed to address economic struggles and navigate a politically divided landscape. The election reflected the complex dynamics of Brazilian politics and the desire for change among many citizens. The incoming government faced the task of addressing pressing issues while attempting to unite the nation under its leadership.

In the first 100 days of the Lula administration, it became evident that significant changes were underway. Much like what was being demonstrated during the inauguration ceremony when a diverse group of citizens ascended the government palace alongside the newly elected president and symbolically invested Lula as the new president of Brazil, the new government made efforts to build a representative, inclusive, and transformative administration. In an unprecedented achievement, ministries were filled in a gender-balanced manner, new departments were established, and social policies were once again implemented and reinforced.

The reinstatement of Marina Silva as the Minister of the Environment was one of the most significant decisions in the current government's stance on environmental protection and climate change mitigation policies. Following the process of overturning the misguided decisions of the Bolsonaro era, environmental oversight institutions were strengthened, and initiatives that had been abandoned in the past four years were resumed.

The situation inherited by the Lula government was considered by experts to be a scenario of devastation, with restrictions on operations and a prohibition on imposing fines. In February 2023, the Ministry of the Environment launched the reinvigoration of the IBAMA and the restoration of its enforcement potential. Bechara (2023) asserts that Marina Silva's ministry used images of the support provided to the Yanomami Indigenous People, who recently faced a severe humanitarian crisis, to joyfully announce, "IBAMA is back!" IBAMA revoked the previous government's decision to block the imposition of fines, which had already accumulated a total of R$29 billion in charges, in another demonstration of a return to stricter environmental protection policies (Peixoto 2023).

Recently, during the opening of the United Nations General Assembly, President Lula provided further details of Brazil's position on specific policies. Following the track established during the XV BRICS Summit in

South Africa, the speech reinforced the international stance taken by the current government. Brazil resumed South–South negotiations, with a focus on strengthening ties with BRICS partners and setting new parameters for alliances with other countries, especially European and the United States.

Lula (2023) emphasizes that:

> acting against climate change involves thinking about tomorrow and facing historical inequalities. Rich countries grew based on a model with high rates of climate-damaging gas emissions. The climate emergency makes it urgent to correct course and implement what has already been agreed. There is no other reason why we speak of common but differentiated responsibilities. It is the vulnerable populations in the Global South who are most affected by the loss and damage caused by climate change. The richest 10% of the world's population are responsible for almost half of all carbon released into the atmosphere. We, developing countries, do not want to repeat this model. In Brazil, we have already proven once and will prove again that a socially fair and environmentally sustainable model is possible.

The Lula administration, in line with its campaign promises, faces the formidable challenge of rectifying the errors of the previous government. While it has already achieved some results during the first months of its administration, finding concrete solutions to bridge the gap created over the past four years and advance genuine climate change mitigation policies remains imperative.

7 How Can Brazil Bridge the Gap?

The third government of Luiz Inácio Lula da Silva faces formidable challenges in rejuvenating Brazil's climate change mitigation and adaptation efforts. These challenges encompass a wide spectrum and necessitate a comprehensive and harmonized approach. As of 2023, Brazil's climate policies are expected to undergo a reorientation. The government has emphasized its commitment to combat deforestation, meet its NDC targets, and strengthen its position in international climate negotiations. The future role of the country in these negotiations will likely revolve around balancing environmental protection with economic development, particularly in critical sectors such as agriculture, forestry, and energy.

Foremost among these challenges is the pressing issue of deforestation, particularly in the Amazon rainforest. During the previous years, deforestation rates escalated dramatically, raising profound concerns about biodiversity loss and heightened greenhouse gas emissions. In stark contrast to the preceding Bolsonaro administration, Lula's government must prioritize robust environmental enforcement, strengthen protected areas, and endorse sustainable land-use practices to curtail deforestation.

Moreover, Brazil's international commitments loom large on the agenda. As a signatory to the Paris Agreement, Brazil is anticipated to play a substantial role in global climate change mitigation. Rebuilding Brazil's international credibility and demonstrating a firm commitment to achieving climate targets are paramount. This entails maintaining ambitious emission reduction goals, implementing renewable energy strategies, and engaging constructively in international climate negotiations.

Balancing climate action with economic development stands out as another pivotal challenge. Lula's administration must strike a delicate equilibrium by formulating policies that foster sustainable economic growth while concurrently mitigating carbon emissions. Investments in green technologies, renewable energy sources, and sustainable agricultural practices are imperative to align economic development with climate objectives.

Respecting the rights of Indigenous communities and safeguarding their territories emerge as critical components of climate change mitigation. Acknowledging Indigenous knowledge and involving these communities in environmental conservation efforts can significantly contribute to combatting deforestation and preserving critical ecosystems.

Transitioning towards cleaner energy sources is central to Brazil's climate goals. The government must actively promote renewable energy projects, such as wind and solar power, to reduce the nation's dependence on fossil fuels. Additionally, advancing electric mobility and implementing energy-efficient initiatives are indispensable for emissions reduction.

Climate resilience is also of paramount importance. Brazil must invest in resilient infrastructure to withstand extreme weather events, refine water management strategies, and enhance agricultural practices to ensure food security in the face of changing climate conditions.

Public awareness and education constitute crucial aspects of climate action. Lula's government can make strides in this regard by spearheading educational campaigns that inform citizens of the significance of climate action and encourage sustainable practices at the individual and community levels.

Finally, diplomacy and collaboration on the international stage are vital. Brazil should actively seek partnerships with other nations, take a proactive role in climate summits, and engage in collaborative efforts to research and develop climate solutions.

In contrast to the preceding Bolsonaro administration, which faced international criticism for its environmental policies and record on deforestation, the third government of Lula da Silva appears poised to adopt a more progressive stance on climate change. The extent to which these challenges are met will determine Brazil's standing as a leader in climate change mitigation and adaptation on the global stage.

During the initial remarks at the United Nations General Assembly (UNGA) in September 2023, Lula reaffirmed Brazil's commitment to mitigating the impact of climate change. Continuing the stance briefly interrupted during the previous administration, the current government has resumed the historical position of Brazilian diplomacy. Consistent with his statements in previous meetings held throughout the year, including the BRICS summit in Johannesburg, Lula emphasized the importance of environmental protection and proactive climate crisis mitigation, with a focus on the common good.

In his speech, Lula (2023) states that:

> acting against climate change involves thinking about tomorrow and facing historical inequalities. Rich countries grew based on a model with high rates of climate-damaging gas emissions. The climate emergency makes it urgent to correct course and implement what has already been agreed. There is no other reason why we speak of common but differentiated responsibilities. It is the vulnerable populations in the Global South who are most affected by the loss and damage caused by climate change. The richest 10% of the world's population are responsible for almost half of all carbon released into the atmosphere. We, developing countries, do not want to repeat this model. In Brazil, we have already proven once and will prove again that a socially fair and environmentally sustainable model is possible.

8 Conclusion

In conclusion, climate change is a critical global issue with far-reaching impacts on the environment, societies, and economies worldwide. Human activities, particularly the emission of greenhouse gases, are the primary drivers of climate change, leading to rising global temperatures and disruptive weather patterns.

Brazil, as one of the world's largest countries with diverse biomes, plays a crucial role in addressing this challenge. Given its ecological significance, Brazil's policies on climate change have a profound influence on global climate dynamics. However, recent political developments in Brazil, exemplified by the government of Jair Messias Bolsonaro, have posed significant setbacks to climate change mitigation efforts. The government's approach, characterized by a disregard for environmental protection, threatens the progress made in previous years.

In this way, the third Lula administration inherited a dire legacy in terms of environmental policies, with disorganized institutions, an increase in deforestation, and dismantled oversight. To restore Brazil's image of leadership and reinstate environmental protection, the new administration needs to bridge the gap left by the previous government. Lula has internationally undertaken the commitment to fight against the climate crisis, walking hand in hand with his partners. One of the fundamental aspects of this resurgence lies in the reapproach with BRICS and the reestablishment of South–South ties.

Now, almost a year after the start of the Lula 3.0 government, the reestablishment of fundamental policies concerning climate change and the restructuring of environmental oversight and protection agencies have become evident.

As we navigate the Anthropocene era and work towards economic recovery, political reengagement, and climate-conscious policies, Brazil's role in international climate efforts, especially within the BRICS nations, becomes increasingly crucial. It is imperative to bridge the gap created by the previous administration and steer Brazil towards a more sustainable and climate-resilient future.

References

Arruda Filho, Marcos Tavares de, Pedro Roberto Jacobi, Zenaida Lauda-Rodriguez, and Beatriz Milz. 2022. "Brazil and Its Disarranged Climate Policy Towards COP 27." *Ambiente & Sociedade* 25: 1–8.

Bailão, André S. 2022. "Imagining Nations and Producing Climate-Change Knowledge in Brazil." In *The Anthropocene of Weather and Climate: Ethnographic Contributions to the Climate Change Debate*, edited by P. Sillitoe, 271–293. Berghahn Books.

Bechara, V. 2023. "Desmoralizado na gestão Bolsonaro, o Ibama mostra força renovada." *Revista Veja.* https://veja.abril.com.br/brasil/desmoralizado-na-gestao-bolsonaro-o-ibama-mostra-forca-renovada.

Biller, D. 2021. "Brazil to Seek Zero Deforestation by 2028, up from 2030." PBSO News Hour. https://www.pbs.org/newshour/world/brazil-to-seek-zero-deforestation-by-2028-up-from-2030.

BNDES. 2023. "Painel NDC – Nossa contribuição para as metas de redução de emissões do Brasil." https://www.bndes.gov.br/wps/portal/site/home/desenvolvimento-sustentavel/resultados/emissoes-evitadas.

Bolsonaro, Jair. 2018. "Agencia Brasil." Facebook (live). https://agenciabrasil.ebc.com.br/politica/noticia/2018-12/bolsonaro-diz-que-pode-sair-fora-do-acordo-de-paris.

Casarões, Guilherme, and Daniel Flemes. 2019. "Brazil First, Climate Last: Bolsonaro's Foreign Policy. GIGA Focus Lateinamerika", 5. Hamburg: GIGA German Institute of Global and Area Studies – Leibniz-Institut für Globale und Regionale Studien, Institut für Lateinamerika-Studien. https://nbn-resolving.org/urn:nbn:de:0168-ssoar-64011-4.

Dantas, C. 2022. "97% dos alertas de desmatamento no Brasil emitidos desde 2019 não foram fiscalizados, aponta levantamento." G1 – Meio Ambiente. https://g1.globo.com/meio-ambiente/noticia/2022/05/03/97percent-dos-alertas-de-desmatamento-no-brasil-emitidos-desde-2019-nao-foram-fiscalizados-aponta-levantamento.ghtml.

de Lima, Maria Regina Soares. 2023. "A dialética da política externa de Lula 3.0." *CEBRI-Revista* 2 (5): 79–95.

de Miranda, Evaristo Eduardo. 2018. "Áreas Cultivadas no Brasil e no Mundo." *Agroanalysis* 38 (2): 25–27.

Falkner, Robert, and Barry Buzan, eds. 2022. *Great Powers, Climate Change, and Global Environmental Responsibilities*. Oxford University Press.

France Presse. 2023. "Fotos de Bruno e Dom feitas antes do assassinato na Amazônia são reveladas." https://g1.globo.com/am/amazonas/noticia/2023/06/02/fotos-de-bruno-e-dom-feitas-antes-do-assassinato-na-amazonia-sao-reveladas.ghtml.

G1. 2020. "Ministro do Meio Ambiente defende passar 'a boiada' e 'mudar' regras enquanto atenção da mídia está voltada para a Covid-19." https://g1.globo.com/politica/noticia/2020/05/22/ministro-do-meio-ambiente-def ende-passar-a-boiada-e-mudar-regramento-e-simplificar-normas.ghtml.

Haje, L. 2020. "Inpe confirma aumento de quase 200% em queimadas no Pantanal entre 2019 e 2020. Câmara do Deputados – Meio Ambiente e Energia." https://www.camara.leg.br/noticias/696913-inpe-confirma-aum ento-de-quase-200-em-queimadas-no-pantanal-entre-2019-e-2020/.

Huguenin, L., and R. M. S. de Meirelles. 2022. "Do período colonial à COP26: Breve resgate histórico sobre as mudanças climáticas relacionadas ao uso da terra no Brasil." *Revista Brasileira De Educação Ambiental (RevBEA)* 17 (5): 132–149.

INPE. 2021. "Estimativa de desmatamento por corte raso na Amazônia Legal para 2021 é de 13.235 km2. São José dos Campos," 27 October.

INPE. 2022. "Nota Técnica Terrabrasilis." Brasília, 14 December.

INPE. 2023. "TerraBrasilis." https://terrabrasilis.dpi.inpe.br/app/dashboard/deforestation/biomes/.

Jacobi, Pedro Roberto, and Marcos Tavares de Arruda Filho. 2021. "O Brasil na COP: histórico, crise e perspectivas para o future" [Brazil at the COP: History, Crisis, and Perspectives for the Future]. Histórico, Crise e Perspectivas para o Futuro. https://www.clacso.org/boletin-2-cambio-ambiental-glo bal-metabolismo-social-local-gobernanza-y-alternativas/.

Leal, Inara Roberta, Marcelo Tabarelli, and José Maria Cardoso da Silva, eds. 2003. "Ecologia e conservação da caatinga." Editora Universitária UFPE.

Lula. 2023. "Speech by President Luiz Inácio Lula da Silva at the opening of the 78th UN General Assembly." *Planalto.* https://www.gov.br/planalto/en/follow-the-government/speeches/speech-by-president-luiz-inacio-lula-da-silva-at-the-opening-of-the-78th-un-general-assembly.

Maciel, Tadeu Morato. 2023. "Avanços e desafios da Política Externa brasileira após 100 dias de governo Lula." *Boletim do LEPEB – UFF* 1 (1): 20–24.

MapBiomas. 2022. "Statistics." https://brasil.mapbiomas.org/en/estatisticas/.

Mariz, R. 2019. "Ministério do Meio Ambiente bloqueia 95% da verba para o clima." O Globo. https://oglobo.globo.com/brasil/ministerio-do-meio-amb iente-bloqueia-95-da-verba-para-clima-23646502.

Marquardt, Jens, M., Cecilia Oliveira, and Markus Lederer. 2022. "Same, Same but Different? How Democratically Elected Right-Wing Populists Shape Climate Change Policymaking." *Environmental Politics* 31 (5): 777–800.

Matos Nascimento, V., and Ferreira Torres, M. 2022. "O Brasil no Regime Internacional sobre a Mudança do Clima: uma análise sobre o governo Bolsonaro." *Brazilian Journal of International Relations* 11 (3): 406–430.

Mendes, Priscylla Dayse Almeida Gonçalves, Ana Cláudia de Almeida, Gabriela Litre, Saulo Rodrigues Filho, Carlos Hiroo Saito, Nelson Eduardo Bernal

Dávalos, Larisa Ho Bech Gaivizzo, Diego Pereira Lindoso, Rafael Moraes Reis, and Júlia Lopes Ferreira. 2022. "Public Policies and Adaptation to Climate Change: Three Case Studies in the Brazilian Semi-Arid Region." *Sustainability in Debate* 13 (3): 209–245.

Mikkola, Heimo, ed. 2021. *Ecosystem and Biodiversity of Amazonia*. BoD – Books on Demand.

Morato Maciel, T. 2023. "Avanços e desafios da Política Externa brasileira após 100 dias de governo Lula." *Orbis - Boletim Trimestral Do LEPEB/UFF* 1 (1): 20–24.

Mueller, C.C., and Mueller, B. 2018. "From Backwardness to Global Agricultural Powerhouse: The Transition of Brazilian Agriculture." In *Agricultural Development in the World Periphery. Palgrave Studies in Economic History*, edited by Vicente Pinilla and Henry Willebald, 389–412. Cham: Palgrave Macmillan.

Narayanan, R. 2019. "Tazir Asked: What Is the Fundamental Difference Between IBSA, BRICS and BASIC?" Manohar Parrikar Institute for Defense Studies and Analyses. https://www.idsa.in/idsanews/difference-between-ibsa-brics-and-basic.

Nunes, Matheus Simões. 2022. "O Brasil no Acordo de Paris sobre mudanças climáticas: Energia • Decolonialidade • Decrescimento. Editora Dialética."

Peixoto, R. 2022. "Fundo Amazônia: Entenda o que é a iniciativa abandonada por Bolsonaro e que tem R$3,2 bilhões paralisados." G1 – Meio Ambiente. https://g1.globo.com/meio-ambiente/noticia/2022/11/03/fundo-amazonia-entenda-o-que-e-a-iniciativa-abandonada-por-bolsonaro-e-que-tem-r-32-bilhoes-paralisados.ghtml.

Peixoto, R. 2022. "No fim do mandato, Bolsonaro libera exploração de madeira em terras indígenas, inclusive por não indígenas." G1 – Meio Ambiente. https://g1.globo.com/meio-ambiente/noticia/2022/12/16/no-fim-do-mandato-bolsonaro-libera-exploracao-de-madeira-em-terras-indigenas-inclusive-por-nao-indigenas.ghtml.

Peixoto, R. 2023. "Ibama anula despacho do governo Bolsonaro que barrava cobranças de R$29 bi em multas ambientais." G1 – Meio Ambiente. https://g1.globo.com/meio-ambiente/noticia/2023/03/25/ibama-anula-despacho-do-governo-bolsonaro-que-barrava-cobranca-de-r-29-bi-em-multas-ambientais.ghtml.

Pereira, Joana Castro. 2022. "As políticas amazónicas do Brasil (2019–2022) e a necessidade de uma mudança transformadora." *Relações Internacionais* 76: 5–15.

Rinaldi, A.L., and P. N. Martuscelli 2016. "The BRICS on Climate Change Global Governance." *Meridiano* 47 (17): e17020. https://doi.org/10.20889/M47e17020.

Silva, A.L.R., and R. Holleben 2022. "De Lula a Bolsonaro: rupturas e continuidades discursivas na política externa brasileira para os BRICS (2003–2020)." *Monções: Revista de Relações Internacionais da UFGD* 11 (22): 200–226.

Soares de Lima, M. R. 2023. "A dialética da política externa de Lula 3.0." *CEBRI-Revista: Brazilian Journal of International Affairs* 5: 79–95.

SOS Mata Atlântica. 2020. "Governo Bolsonaro estimula crimes ambientais na Mata Atlântica. Notícias." https://www.sosma.org.br/noticias/governo-bol sonaro-estimula-crimes-ambientais-na-mata-atlantica/.

United Nations. 1997. "Kyoto Protocol to the United Nations Framework Convention on Climate Change, Conference of the Parties on Its Third Session." FCCC/CP/1997/L.7/Add.1, 10 December.

Between Geopolitical Ambition, Energy Nationalism, and Capacity Deficit: Russia's Thorny Relationship with Climate Change

Sergey V. Kostelyanets

1 INTRODUCTION

The earth's climate system is characterized not just by dynamic changes but by cyclicity on the scale of hundreds of millions of years. We now find ourselves in a period of dramatic climate change, which has often been referred to as global warming. Climatologists across the world mostly agree that, first, the temperatures of the atmosphere, geosphere, and hydrosphere are all increasing; second, the driver of the increase is a change in the gas composition of the atmosphere in terms of carbon-, phosphorus-, and nitrogen-containing gases that make up the greenhouse layer, along with dust and water particles; and, third, the change in the gas composition occurs due to the extraction of conserved carbon from the depths of the planet in the form of fossil fuels and its release into the atmosphere. The latter is an almost exclusively anthropogenic factor,

---

S. V. Kostelyanets (✉)
Institute for African Studies of the Russian Academy of Sciences, Moscow, Russia
e-mail: sergey.kostelyanyets@gmail.com

HSE University, Moscow, Russia

© The Author(s), under exclusive license to Springer Nature Singapore Pte Ltd. 2024
H. Solomon et al. (eds.), *BRICS and Climate Change*,
https://doi.org/10.1007/978-981-97-5532-5_4

68   S. V. KOSTELYANETS

which allows us to refer to this phenomenon as anthropogenic climate change (ACC).

Due to its sheer size and geographic diversity, Russia faces a particularly difficult set of challenges posed by ACC but also exerts a significant influence on the climate of the rest of the world. In terms of the domestic challenges, the country has been witnessing a substantial increase in the frequency and scale of natural disasters, adverse changes in the productivity of agriculture, forestry, and fisheries, and infrastructure damages due to the degradation of permafrost, etc. On the other hand, the most pronounced positive implications of ACC have included the longer growing season and easier navigation along the Northern Sea Route, the latter being critical for the development of Russia's Arctic regions. In particular, in 2023, the Russian Federal Service for Hydrometeorology and Environmental Monitoring (Roshydromet) reported that the average annual temperature increase in Russia from 1976 to 2022 amounted to 0.49 °C per decade, with the greatest increases observed on the Taymyr Peninsula in Russia's Far North (+1.1 °C per decade). Correspondingly, the length of the growing season has been increasing throughout the country but most rapidly in Southern Russia (+6 days per decade since 1976). In the Russian Arctic, the area occupied by sea ice at the end of the summer season (in September) from the mid-1990s to the mid-2000s decreased from more than 1,200,000 km^2 to approximately 200,000 km^2 and has been fluctuating below this value ever since. In 2016, scientists observed the minimum historical record of 26,000 km^2, which made naval and maritime passage along Russia's northern shores that season practically unobstructed (Roshydromet 2023).

On the other hand, being the largest country on the planet, with an area of over 17.3 million km^2 (within internationally recognized borders—just under 17.1 million km^2), spanning 11 time zones and four climate zones (polar, subpolar, temperate, and subtropical), and possessing a large share of global reserves of fossil fuels (the world's largest proven gas reserves, the second largest coal reserves, and the eighth-largest oil reserves) (EIA 2023), Russia occupies a key position in the global climate system. As a major producer and consumer of fossil fuels, Russia unsurprisingly is one of the largest emitters of greenhouse gases (in the fourth place after China, the United States, and India) and was responsible for 4.8% of global greenhouse gas emissions in 2022 (European Commission 2023). Perhaps, the key peculiarity about Russia's greenhouse gas emissions has been their dramatic decrease since 1990.

While annual global greenhouse gas emissions grew in 1990–2021 by almost 60%, Russia's total annual emissions over the same period fell by nearly 32% (without accounting for land use, land-use change, and forestry—LULUCF), with most of the drop taking place between 1991 and 1993 due to the post-Soviet economic meltdown (UNFCCC 2024).

The country also heavily relies on revenues from oil and gas exports, which in 2021 constituted 45% of the federal budget revenue, thus facilitating greenhouse gas emissions in other countries. Furthermore, as global temperatures rise, we may witness the release of hundreds of billions of tonnes of greenhouse gases stored in Russia's permafrost—permanently frozen ground that covers 65% of the country's landmass. At the same time, Russia is home to the largest area of forest in the world—almost 8 million km^2, approximately a fifth of the world's forest cover, second only to the Amazon rainforest in terms of carbon sequestration (Carbon Brief 2022). Russia's renewable water resources rank second in the world, and the country also boasts the largest technical potential for renewable energy on the planet, including hydro, solar, wind, bio, tidal, and geothermal energy. To sum up, Russia is set to remain among the countries that are leading anthropogenic contributors to global warming, but it also possesses enormous natural and other resources that could be employed to mitigate the ensuing negative effects.

2 The USSR and the Challenge of Global Warming: From Discovery to Leadership

Russian (then Soviet) science stood at the root of the recognition of ACC as a major global challenge. In the form of a working hypothesis, the process of global warming was first described by the Soviet climatologist Mikhail Budyko in 1971—at a time when climate researchers around the world almost unanimously believed that the warming that had been observed in the nineteenth century was to be succeeded by an era of global cooling. Budyko presented a new theory of global warming at a conference in Leningrad (now St. Petersburg), where he not only accurately predicted and substantiated the continuation of global warming but also explained that this global process was an inevitable result of human economic activity. In 1972, Budyko published a brochure titled "Man's Impact on Climate", where he claimed that a substantial rise in air temperature would occur within 100 years and lead to the complete melting of the Arctic Ocean's ice cover by 2050. Budyko's forecasts for the period 1970–2019 have since been corroborated by modern observations (Lapenis 2020).

Budyko's idea that global warming would be driven by anthropogenic factors was first rejected by the international scientific community; however, with time, it prompted massive new research across the world, which by the late 1980s facilitated broad consensus regarding humans' contribution to climate change and, among other things, led to the adoption of the groundbreaking United Nations Framework Convention on Climate Change (UNFCCC) at the 1992 United Nations Conference on Environment and Development in Rio (also known as the Earth Summit), which reflected the transfer of knowledge on the global warming issue from theory to practice (Safonov 2021).

In the late 1970s and 1980s, the USSR came to play an important role as a champion of the global warming agenda, actively promoting various bilateral efforts to research climate change and develop corresponding initiatives. As a matter of fact, the USSR had already been an energetic supporter of the international ecological effort, for instance, of the 1971 Ramsar Convention on Wetlands, which had become the first of the modern global nature conservation conventions (Matthews 1993), and even though, for political reasons, Moscow boycotted some related events, e.g. the 1972 Stockholm Conference on the Human Environment, the new ecological challenge fell on fertile soil. Amid the continuing Cold War and new tensions arising from the Soviet incursion in Afghanistan (1979–1989), Soviet–American collaboration in the field of climate change proved to be exceptionally immune to geopolitical rivalry, pointing to the importance that the two superpowers attached to the issue. Within the framework of the 1972 Agreement on Cooperation in the Field of Environmental Protection between the United States and the Union of Soviet Socialist Republics, Moscow and Washington carried out regular joint symposia (1976–1979) followed by expert meetings of the US–Soviet working group on climate (since 1981), discussing empirical data related to climate change and the problems of forecasting future climate (Budyko and MacCracken 1987).

Another important platform that brought together representatives of the Western and Eastern blocs was the International Institute for Applied System Analysis, which was founded in 1972 in Vienna, Austria. There, scientists from the USSR and several other socialist countries joined their counterparts from the United States, Japan, and Western Europe in researching climate change and its anthropogenic drivers (Rindzeviciute

2016). At the first World Climate Conference, held in Geneva in February 1979, Soviet scientists supported the declaration that called for intensifying global cooperation in further research and mitigation of climate change that specifically focused on the human impact on the global climate system. In 1986, the Soviet Union hosted two major international events dedicated to the topic of climate change: the seventh session of the United Nations Brundtland Commission on Environment and Development and an International Symposium on Climate and Human Health, the latter conducted jointly by the World Meteorological Organization, World Health Organization, and United Nations Environment Program (Beuerle 2023). The United Nations Brundtland Commission, which operated in 1983–1987, was tasked with formulating long-term environmental strategies within the framework of the sustainable development approach to social and economic planning, while the Symposium on Climate and Human Health covered topics related to the potential impacts of a large-scale climatic change on human health (Kalkstein 1990).

Beuerle (2023) suggests that it was the Intergovernmental Panel on Climate Change (IPCC), an intergovernmental body of the United Nations established in 1988 to advance scientific knowledge about ACC, that prompted the true engagement of the Soviet government with the climate change agenda. In fact, one of the three IPCC working groups—focused on the social and economic effects of climate change—was chaired by the Head of the State Committee for Hydrometeorology and Environmental Monitoring of the USSR (Goskomhydromet), Yuri Izrael. Later, the IPCC became the focal international body that was responsible for reporting on climate change trends and coordinating the activities of all major scientific teams engaged in climate research. In the late 1980s, Moscow started thorough preparations for the 1992 Earth Summit, intending to play a role that would be in line with its status as one of the two superpowers and a major greenhouse gas emitter. A high-ranking Soviet delegation of over 250 representatives led by Soviet President Mikhail Gorbachev was to take part in the event (Beuerle 2023). In general, the Soviet Union acknowledged the anthropogenic nature of climate change and acted accordingly.

3 CLIMATE CHANGE POLICY DURING THE FIRST YELTSIN TERM: GOING BY INERTIA

In the early 1990s, Russia attempted to take over the Soviet Union's position as one of the leading voices on climate change. However, the Russian delegation that attended the Earth Summit totalled just 11 people and was headed by Vice-President Alexander Rutskoy; the first Russian President Boris Yeltsin (1991–1999) stayed at home. In comparison, the United States sent 200 delegates with George W. Bush at the helm (Beuerle 2023). At the Summit, Russia joined the UNFCCC, where it was included in the Annex I along with other developed countries, albeit marked as a transition economy. The UNFCCC's supreme decision-making body, the Conference of the Parties (COP), has been meeting annually ever since to assess progress with ACC. In Rio, Russia also signed the Convention on Biological Diversity.

In 1994, Moscow was among the first countries to ratify the UNFCCC. Russia also started implementing international guidelines developed by the IPCC with regard to taking GHG inventory. Five Russian regions were chosen as pilot areas for this project, which was funded by the World Wildlife Fund and US Environmental Protection Agency (WWF 2002).

In general, in 1990–1996, Russia's climate policy was characterized by the development of basic environmental institutions. Moscow's aspirations to leadership in the global warming agenda, which had been inherited from the USSR, were undercut by domestic economic difficulties and political instability, the geopolitical retreat from Eastern Europe and the Global South, and generally unassertive foreign policy. Evidently, Russia possessed no financial, technological, or even political capacity to lead the global climate agenda, as the Soviet Union had planned to, and largely proceeded by inertia. In 1996, with great difficulty, Yeltsin was reelected for his second term as the president of Russia. The climate agenda was nowhere near the top of his priorities, as Russia was losing the First Chechen War (1994–1996), and the Communist Party, his principal political opponent, had become the largest faction in the Russian Parliament in 1995.

4 THE LATE YELTSIN YEARS AND RUSSIA'S CLIMATE DILEMMA

The debates over the Kyoto Protocol marked a certain watershed for Moscow's climate policy, with an incremental rise of climate scepticism starting to occur. While participants of the UNFCCC did not undertake any specific commitments to limit greenhouse gas emissions, the Kyoto Protocol was intended to fill this void and impose concrete obligations on its signatory parties. Initially, Russia demonstrated much scepticism and sided with OPEC countries in rejecting the setting of quantitative limits on greenhouse gas emissions within the protocol. Russia's oil and gas tycoons who had privatized the Soviet energy industry started exerting increasing influence on the country's climate policy. To appease Russia and some other hesitant parties, the protocol eventually came to include an emission-trading mechanism and also set 1990 as the base year for the calculation of emissions, which enabled Moscow to both foster national industry—which had suffered a major hit during the radical economic reforms of the early 1990s (the so-called shock therapy), unintentionally decreasing emissions drastically—and, supposedly, also gain proceeds from selling emission quotas at the global market. The main goal of Kyoto became to reduce greenhouse gas emissions in the world by at least 5% between 2008 and 2012—a relatively modest target that was a compromise from 15% proposed by the European Union. The European Union and EU candidate countries would reduce their emissions by an average of 8%, the United States by 7%, Japan and Canada by 6%, and Russia and Ukraine would pledge not to exceed their 1990 emissions, while developing countries such as China and India would make no concrete commitment. Andonova (2013) noted that, under the protocol, Russia achieved the most favourable terms of all industrialized states by far.

Since 1997, the domestic focus shifted towards the discussion of costs and benefits of the implementation of the Kyoto Protocol. Russia was nowhere near taking its full quota of emissions: in 1998, its GDP hit the floor at about 60% of the 1990 level, and greenhouse gas emissions fell accordingly by over 30%. Some studies put the potential benefit for Russia from selling emission quotas at up to $34 billion annually (Victor et al. 2001: 263). Besides pointing to the potential financial gain, the proponents of the protocol argued that, first, Russia within its framework would develop energy-saving and eco-friendly technologies, and, second, that it would be advisable for Moscow to remain part of the climate change debate to influence the development of the rules of the game. Moreover, as carbon exchanges had already been established in the United States and United Kingdom, it would be unfortunate for Russia to forego the opportunities they offered.

There were, however, many climate sceptics who opposed the signing of the protocol, questioned climate science, and claimed that Russia's economic development would be restricted by the ratification of Kyoto. The sceptics argued that, first, there was no solid scientific proof that global warming was caused by carbon dioxide emissions; second, joining the protocol would be detrimental to economic growth because it would divert investment to the construction of treatment facilities; and third, the adoption of the protocol would facilitate the reduction in prices for hydrocarbons, which were the most important item of Russian export (Averchenkova 2022: 170). Eventually, in 1999, the Yeltsin administration signed the Kyoto Protocol, though Russia did not ratify it until years later under the next president. In his speech at the Federal Assembly in 1999 (TASS 2015), Yeltsin addressed the issue:

> Entering a new era, we must part with the old view of nature as our "workshop". Its resources are not endless. We need new rules of human behavior on Earth: to protect the natural environment means to protect life itself on Earth. The economic policy of the state must finally begin to take environmental restrictions seriously.

5 "The Economic Stranglehold of Kyoto": Putin's Era of Climate Scepticism

At the end of 1999, in a surprise address to the nation, Yeltsin announced his resignation as president of Russia and named Vladimir Putin (then prime minister) the acting president until elections. Putin was soon victorious in the presidential elections in March 2000 and focused on economic recovery, job creation, and the reintegration of Chechnya. From the very beginning of his presidency, Putin demonstrated scepticism regarding humanity's ability to halt climate change and claimed that Russia could actually benefit from global warming. The more sceptical attitude Russia adopted towards global warming was primarily dictated by concerns about restrictions on the national economy, particularly extractive industries. In 2003, Putin hosted the World Climate

Change Conference, where he stated the following in his opening speech (President of Russia 2003):

> Limits should not be allowed to be placed on economic growth and social development (...) In Russia, you can often hear, either in joke or seriously, that Russia is a northern country. If it was two or three degrees warmer, this would be no big deal. Maybe it would even be a good thing – we would spend less money or fur coats and other warm items. Specialists on agriculture say: the grain harvest is increasing here, and it will continue to increase, thank God.

In early 2004, the Russian Academy of Sciences (RAS) started fulfilling the government's order to provide an expert opinion on the feasibility of Russia's accession to the protocol. Academicians were supposed to decide whether the Kyoto Protocol was scientifically sound and whether it met Russia's objectives of economic development. The answers to both questions were found to be negative. The first paragraph of the resulting document read that the protocol had no scientific basis. The academicians further highlighted that climate warming (no matter what caused it) would only benefit Russia—"the coldest country in the world"—as it could help reduce heating and transport costs and increase the country's biomass. Yuri Izrael, who was the director of the Institute of Global Climate and Ecology under the RAS and the Roshydromet at the time, argued (HSE 2004):

> Businessmen and the officials who support them talk about quota trading, but everyone has forgotten about the climate. The implementation of the Kyoto Protocol will lead to a reduction in greenhouse gas emissions by only 0.3%, since it involves countries that account for only a third of CO_2 emissions. Large greenhouse gas emitters such as China, India and Saudi Arabia refrained from ratifying the document.

Izrael was not only a leading critic of climate change, saying in 2007 that "the panic over the global warming is totally unjustified", but also the most influential scientific advisor to Putin (Andonova 2013). As relations with Washington and London began to sour in 2003 against the backdrop of the Iraq War and Western offers of asylum for Putin's critics, some pundits went as far as to suggest that the Kyoto Protocol was contrived by the West to put an economic stranglehold on Russia (Nezavisimaya Gazeta 2003).

Curiously, the fate of the entire protocol depended on Russia. By 2004, it had been signed by 121 countries, but its entry into force was conditional on the ratification by states that accounted for at least 55% of global greenhouse gas emissions in 1990. The United States, which in 1990 produced 35% of the world's carbon dioxide emissions, refused to ratify the protocol, deciding that compliance with its obligations was too expensive. By ratifying Kyoto, Russia, the second largest emitter of greenhouse gas in 1990 with a share of 17% of the global emissions, would have made the treaty binding for the participating nations (ESA 2004).

The key proponents of the ratification in the government were the Foreign Ministry and the Ministry of Industry and Energy of the Russian Federation. The Foreign Ministry suggested the establishment of a joint Russo–European trust fund to finance projects in Russia aimed at curbing greenhouse gas emissions, while the Ministry of Industry and Energy identified 70 projects that could attract "hydrocarbon investment" amounting to €850 million. The Ministry of Industry and Energy also intended to direct new investment flows to the utilization of associated petroleum gas and the reduction of losses incurred during the transportation of methane gas (HSE 2004).

In October 2004, Moscow ratified the Kyoto Protocol, despite the criticism of economists and Russia's scientific community. One of the motivations for the ratification might have been to gain income from selling carbon credits. However, the price of carbon credits in the global market subsequently fell dramatically, greatly frustrating the Russian government (NRDC 2015). On the other hand, Russia's bargaining leverage at Kyoto, which was compounded by the differences between the European Union and the United States, might have earned it something else politically or economically. One version is that there was a deal between Russia and the European Union, whereby Brussels greenlit Moscow's membership to the World Trade Organization (WTO) in exchange for the ratification of the protocol (Andonova 2013), even though the entry to the WTO only occurred in 2011. Importantly, as Averchenkova (2022) notes, ratification of the protocol did not result in any major shift in Russia's climate change policy. To illustrate Moscow's continued scepticism towards the voluntary reduction of greenhouse gas emissions, one may recall the G8 Summit in Germany in 2007, where six leading industrialized nations— EU countries, Japan, and Canada—agreed at least to halve global CO_2 emissions by 2050, while Russia and the United States abstained from this commitment.

In general, Putin's first two presidential terms (2000–2008) were characterized by the resurgence of economic and especially energy "nationalism" and corresponding state interventionism, which trumped any global leadership aspirations that may have lingered, including in the sphere of climate change mitigation. The government re-established or consolidated its control over the largest Soviet-era oil and gas enterprises, thus starting to take their interests even closer to the heart, and bargained hard for any climate concessions. Domestic implementation of the climate-related agenda in this period was kept to a minimum, with the adoption of only two noteworthy pieces of legislation: the 2001 Program for Energy Efficient Economy, aimed at the reduction of the energy intensity of the economy by 13.4% over 5 years and by 26% over 10 years, and the 2003 Rules of Using Thermal Performance of Buildings, which encouraged the construction of energy-efficient buildings.

6 The Medvedev Interregnum: A Quest for Sustainable Modernization

The problem of climate change was given more attention during the period of the so-called political tandem—the presidency of Dmitry Medvedev and the premiership of Vladimir Putin (2008–2012). Averchenkova (2022) argues that, by that time, the oil and gas model of rapid economic development had exhausted itself, which necessitated a modernization drive that could only be enabled by Western technologies and equipment. In June 2008, Medvedev issued a decree "on some measures to improve the energy and environmental efficiency of the Russian economy", which provided for a 40% reduction in the energy intensity of GDP by 2020 from 2007 levels. In November 2009, Medvedev signed the federal law "on saving energy and increasing energy efficiency", which established basic principles to regulate energy consumption and provided for various amendments to existing legislation to enforce energy-saving rules. In December 2009, a day before the end of the COP15 in Copenhagen, Denmark, Moscow adopted its first climate doctrine in a symbolic move. Despite its bold rhetoric, the new doctrine reiterated the approach to climate change that dominated Putin's first and second presidential terms: the focus was placed on improving energy efficiency and minimizing the possible consequences of global warming rather than on reducing emissions (Hydrometcenter of Russia 2009). Golub and Shenin (2023) note that Russia's strategy under the

2009 doctrine was to adapt to climate changes rather than to prevent them.

Russia's climate scepticism narrative was still largely rooted in the interests of extractive industries. Medvedev's closest aide, Arkady Dvorkovich, publicly declared that if COP15 participants in Copenhagen followed the path of restrictions, this would constitute a kind of tax on Russia's energy sector. Indeed, the economic growth that occurred in Russia in the 2000s was largely driven by the oil and gas sector, so the latter's interests were to be respected. The concerns were further augmented by geopolitical and geoeconomic considerations. The factor of the untapped riches of the Arctic was playing an increasing role in Russia's climate policy. In his 2010 address to the Security Council of Russia, Medvedev (TASS 2015) argued that:

> Climate changes may give rise not only to physical changes and changes in the natural environment, but also to interstate contradictions that are associated with the search and production of energy resources, the use of sea transport routes, biological resources, and the shortage of water and food resources. Already today, circumpolar countries are taking active steps to expand their research, economic and even military presence in the Arctic zone. At the same time, unfortunately, there are attempts to limit Russia's access to the exploration and development of Arctic fields, which, of course, is unacceptable from a legal point of view and unfair due to the geographical location and the very history of our country.

During his visit to the Arctic in 2010, Prime Minister Putin once again demonstrated his sceptical attitude when he said that he was still waiting for an answer regarding whether global climate change was the result of human activity or whether it is "the earth living its own life and breathing". As anthropogenic factors could not be responsible for climate change, instead of trying to prevent warming, wasting precious resources, and slowing down economic growth, humans should adapt to change, Putin continued (Korsunskaya 2010). In 2010–2011, Russia along with Japan and Canada refused to support the second phase of the Kyoto commitments, citing the lack of obligation of the other largest polluters—the United States and China—to reduce their emissions.

Overall, the push for economic modernization and greater energy efficiency, which characterized Medvedev's 2008–2012 tenure, did not result in a breakthrough in Russia's environmental policies but contributed to the expansion of climate legislation and the institutionalization of the climate agenda across ministries and other government agencies. On the other hand, in the absence of concerted pressure from the West, which itself was divided over the Kyoto Protocol, or financial and political incentives, Moscow expectedly refused to endorse the extension of the protocol.

7 PUTIN 2.0: A SHOT AT "SOVEREIGN DECARBONIZATION"

In 2012, Putin returned to the presidency, while Medvedev became the head of his government in what some pundits dubbed "the Kremlin castling". The Kremlin's priorities shifted noticeably, with the new focus on building "sovereign democracy" to respond to external threats (such as colour revolutions) and suppressing local non-systemic opposition, some of which had been greatly disappointed with "liberal" Medvedev's decision not to run for the second term in 2012 and responded with protests in December 2011. The modernization rhetoric and a "spring-like thaw in relations with (…) the West" (Waugh 2012) that had been promoted by Medvedev were largely cast aside. Averchenkova (2022) notes that the decarbonization drive that had gained some momentum under the previous administration exhausted itself as, first, President Putin prioritized developing energy exports as an instrument of geopolitical competition, and, second, the Medvedev government had to channel resources and attention towards the preparation of the 2014 Sochi Olympics, which cost over $50 billion.

Putin's first noticeable move regarding climate change during his third term was the issuance of the 2013 Decree "On Greenhouse Gas Emission Reduction". The decree set a target for Russia's greenhouse gas emissions: in 2020, they were not supposed to exceed 75% of the 1990 level. This target was, however, criticized by experts, because the 2012 level of emissions in Russia stood at 68.2% of the 1990 level, so reaching 75% would have actually constituted an increase in greenhouse gas emissions rather than a reduction (Korppoo and Kokorin 2017). Indeed, Russia's strategy continued to enable economic growth unimpeded by the climate agenda, while paying lip service to the reduction of greenhouse gas emissions.

In 2014, Russia adopted the State Program on Energy Efficiency and Energy Development, which updated and replaced Medvedev's 2009 legislation on energy efficiency. The 2014 programme, which aimed at, among other things, the reduction of "anthropogenic impacts of the

80   S. V. KOSTELYANETS

energy sector on the environment", kept the target of a 40% decrease of the energy intensity of the GDP by 2020, but embarrassingly lowered the target for the share of renewable energy sources from 4.5 to 2.5%. It also envisaged the mass installation of smart meters (18.9% by 2020) and raising public awareness of energy conservation and efficiency (Climate Change Laws 2014).

During the lead-up to the COP21 in Paris in 2015, which was to convene to establish a legally binding mechanism to limit "the increase in the global average temperature to well below 2°C above preindustrial levels" (UNFCCC 2015), Putin surprised Western experts by a change of tone, offering what they called a "platter of climate-friendly platitudes" (Fleur 2015). At the United Nations General Assembly in September 2015, Putin (President of Russia 2015a) stated:

> It is in our interest to ensure that the coming UN Climate Change Conference that will take place in Paris in December this year should deliver some feasible results. As part of our national contribution, we plan to limit greenhouse gas emissions to 70–75 percent of the 1990 levels by the year 2030.

At the COP21 opening in November 2015, Putin (President of Russia 2015b) emphasized that:

> Climate change is one of the most serious challenges humanity faces today. Hurricanes, floods, droughts and other extreme weather phenomena caused by global warming are causing ever-greater economic losses and destroying our familiar and traditional environment. (...) Russia is taking active measures to address global warming. (...) We have more than fulfilled our obligations under the Kyoto Protocol: from 1991 to 2012, not only did Russia have no increase in greenhouse gas emissions; it substantially reduced its emissions over this time. This has saved the equivalent of around 40 billion tons of carbon dioxide gas from entering the atmosphere. For comparison, (... total emissions by all countries in 2012 came to 46 billion tons. In other words, Russia's efforts have made it possible to slow down global warming by nearly a year. (...) Over this same time, Russia's GDP nearly doubled. This shows that it is entirely possible to put the focus on economic growth while at the same time looking after the environment. (...) We support the new agreement's long-term goal: to keep global warming within an increase of two degrees Celsius to the end of this century.

After these speeches, some experts even went as far as to claim that Putin, despite all his past talk about the benefits of "spending less on fur coats", was, in fact, not sceptical about the gravity of climate change but instead demonstrated caution in view of the reserved positions of other top emitters—the United States, China, and India. They also commended Putin's government for its actions to date, including the development of a framework for monitoring and reporting greenhouse gas emissions and drafting a law allowing their regulation (NRDC 2015).

Indeed, in April 2016, Russia signed the Paris Agreement along with other 174 parties. However, in November 2016, the government approved the Plan for the Implementation of a Set of Measures to Improve the State Regulation of Greenhouse Gas Emissions and Prepare for Ratification of the Paris Agreement, which set the deadline for the preparation of a report on the advisability of ratifying the agreement to the first quarter of 2019. This effectively meant that the ratification of the Paris Agreement by Russia would be postponed to no earlier than 2019. Admittedly, the document also set out an unprecedented roadmap of legislation and programmes to be developed to facilitate the implementation of the Paris Agreement in Russia, including a plan for state regulation of greenhouse gas emissions (to be drafted by December 2017), a national plan for adaptation to adverse climate change (December 2018), a federal law on state regulation of greenhouse gas emissions (June 2019), a presidential decree on 2030 greenhouse gas emission targets (December 2019), an action plan for reaching the greenhouse gas emission targets (March 2020), and a long-term low greenhouse gas emissions development strategy until 2050 (June 2020) (Climate Change Laws 2016). In 2018, Russia also donated funds to the IPCC and endorsed the initiative to establish the Green Climate Fund aimed at assisting developing countries in adaptation and mitigation practices to counter climate change.

Nevertheless, the experts who commended Putin and his government have been proven wrong as the Russian president continued to issue ambiguous statements regarding climate change. At the 2018 Russian Energy Week International Forum, Putin (Kozlovsky 2019) argued that:

Indeed, we are apparently observing global warming, but the reasons for this warming are unclear, because there is still no answer. The so-called anthropogenic emissions are likely not the main cause of this warming. These could be changes of a global nature, cosmic changes, some shifts invisible to us in the galaxy, and that's it, we don't even understand what's happening.

In 2019, Putin's spokesman, Dmitry Peskov, unequivocally confirmed that Putin did not agree with the causes of global warming corroborated in the Paris Agreement. Nevertheless, Putin did not want to appear to be an outlier in climate terms, and, in September 2019, Russia became one of the last countries to ratify the agreement. Putin instructed the government to meet the national commitment made in the framework of the Paris Agreement, as long as this did not impede economic growth. In December 2019, the government adopted the National Action Plan for the First Phase of Adaptation to Climate Change, which defined the "economic and social measures implemented by federal and regional executive bodies in order to reduce the vulnerability of the Russian population, economy and natural objects to the effects of climate change" (Climate Change Laws 2020). This was probably the last climate-related move of Medvedev, who retired as prime minister in January 2020. It should be noted that the Medvedev government implemented all planned steps towards the implementation of the Paris Agreement, often ahead of the roadmap's schedule.

Golub and Shenin (2023) note that the first steps of Prime Minister Mikhail Mishustin and his cabinet disappointed Western observers. In 2020, the government drafted the "Strategy of Socio-economic Development of the Russian Federation with Low Greenhouse Gas Emissions Until 2050", which Safonov (2021) described as a de facto "voluntary emissions reporting act" and which envisioned "a rise (not decline) in carbon emission targets (...) by up to 80 percent in 2050". Next, in June 2020, came the adoption of the Energy Strategy to 2035, which was aimed at increasing domestic oil and gas production, processing, and exportation in another sign of prioritization of economic development over environmental concerns.

In accordance with the NDC submitted within the framework of the Paris Agreement, Putin issued a Decree "On Reducing Greenhouse Gas Emissions" in November 2020, which provided for 30% reduction in emissions by 2030 in comparison with 1990. In fact, however, Russia's emissions in 2020 were still lower than the 2030 target, thus enabling it to actually increase greenhouse gas emissions over the following decade. Furthermore, Russia calculated its reduction in emissions by taking into account the absorption capacity of Russian forests, which was neither provided for in the Paris Agreement nor recommended by the IPCC (Climate Score Card 2021).

In 2012–2020, the climate agenda in Russia was increasingly viewed through the prism of competition with the West, which was catalysed by the events in Ukraine. The choice seemed to be an extremely difficult one: the implementation of the Paris Agreement was expected to decrease Russia's annual economic growth by up to 0.3% (Makarov et al. 2018), but opting out of the agreement would unavoidably lead to the introduction of tariff and possibly nontariff trade barriers by the largest trading partner (the European Union) as well as other industrialized nations, which would entail even greater economic losses. In general, market power would likely shift to the consumers of energy (Makarov et al. 2018), which would serve a major blow to Russia's geopolitical standing in the world. As geopolitical tensions between Russia and the West gradually started to limit foreign investment and technological innovation, Moscow searched for a special path towards decreasing greenhouse gas emissions, which would allow it to keep developing and exporting fossil fuels, including in the Arctic, while shedding the image of a climate pariah; we may call this path "sovereign decarbonization" to mimic the model of "sovereign democracy" that Russia had been developing politically.

8 RUSSIA ON THE PATH TOWARDS CARBON NEUTRALITY: THE DOMESTIC AND GLOBAL CONTEXTS

Some experts called Moscow's interest in climate change until 2021 desultory (Hill 2021). In our opinion, however, in 2000–2021, Russia implemented predictable and consistent policies, which boiled down to the recognition of the grave threat of global warming, simultaneous scepticism about its anthropogenic nature, and accession to the most relevant international treaties while having no real intention to demonstrate the actual reduction of existing greenhouse gas emissions. Indeed, the real focus was placed on the development of low-carbon sources of power—hydro, nuclear, and natural gas—and on preserving and strengthening the absorptive capacity of forests and wetlands. These policies were driven mostly by the realization that the exports of carbon-intensive products were likely to be discriminated in the foreseeable future. In parallel, as Golub and Shenin (2023) note, Moscow was actively taking advantage of climate change in the spheres of agriculture, resource extraction in the Arctic, and the development of shipping infrastructure along the Northern Sea Route.

The Kremlin's cynical yet pragmatic approach to climate change was facilitated first by domestic public opinion and, second, by the favourable international environment. The Russian public did not consider climate change to be a major threat, with the country consistently ranking well below the median in terms of the share of people concerned with global warming, confident in its anthropogenic nature, or finding it personally important (Fagan and Huang 2019; Leiserowitz et al. 2021), thus giving Putin and Medvedev a free hand to carry out climate change policymaking and allowing extractive industries (both Russian and foreign) to lobby the government without regard for climate activists.

As for the international scene, it should be emphasized that the inconsistent policies of the United States—the largest greenhouse gas emitter on the planet—enabled Moscow to find easy excuses for its own duplicity. American journalists even called Russian and US policies on climate change "uncomfortably alike" (Brown 2022), which was especially visible under the last two Republican administrations in the White House. In 2001, the Bush administration refused to implement the Kyoto Protocol, while Donald Trump withdrew from the Paris Agreement in 2017. In 2018, Trump said about climate change that "I don't think it's a hoax. I think there's probably a difference. But I don't know that it's manmade" (ITVX 2018). While the present book is not intended to analyse the US climate change policy, these striking similarities between the positions of Washington and Moscow must be highlighted, which may be explained by the influence of the oil and gas lobbies (incidentally, the key sponsors of both the Republican Party and Russia's budget) in the two countries.

The return of the Democrats to the White House, however, has turned the table. President Joe Biden signed an executive action to rejoin the Paris Agreement just hours after his inauguration on 20 January 2021. The Biden administration went even further and started insisting that the Paris Agreement was obsolete because the global climate was destabilizing at an increasing pace, so emergency measures had to be taken in the sphere of the reduction of carbon emissions. Biden also set a new ambitious national contribution to the reduction of global emissions within the framework of the Paris Agreement—50–52% from 2005 levels by 2030. More importantly for Russia, however, the United States and European Union started discussions about the imposition of carbon-based tariffs on steel, aluminium, and other industrial imports. By the end of 2022, the European Union developed a system of border tariffs based on carbon emissions caused by manufacturing, known as the Carbon Border Adjustment Mechanism (CBAM), which required importers to begin reporting the embedded emissions in 2023 and paying tariffs in 2026. According to some estimates, Russia's losses from the implementation of CBAM would amount to $5 billion annually (Bashmakov 2022); expected similar US measures would further augment the losses. Thus, the pessimistic forecasts from the past years started to materialize.

In view of the mounting pressure from Washington and Brussels, and the growing risks for Russian exports, Putin changed his climate rhetoric in 2021. In his address to the Federal Assembly in April 2021, Putin set a new goal of keeping Russia's total greenhouse gas emissions over the following 30 years below the EU level. At the virtual Leaders Summit on Climate the same month, Putin claimed that Moscow was "genuinely interested in stepping up international cooperation (…) to search for effective solutions to climate change" (President of Russia 2021a). In July 2021, Putin signed the Law "On Limiting Greenhouse Gas Emissions", which established the legal framework for mandatory carbon reporting by the most polluting companies (to commence in 2023) and a national market for carbon offsets that could be generated through the voluntary implementation of climate projects. In September 2021, the government started work on a system of carbon tariffs analogous of the CBAM. The same month Prime Minister Mishustin announced the preparation of a plan aimed at the reduction of the consumption of fossil fuels and the development of alternative energy sources. In October 2021, the government finally adopted the Strategy of Socio-economic Development of the Russian Federation with Low Greenhouse Gas Emissions Until 2050. Sakhalin Island in the Far East was also chosen for a pilot programme to limit greenhouse gas emissions and achieve carbon neutrality at the regional level by 31 December 2025. Suddenly, the agenda of energy transition and decarbonization captured the official and media discourse.

At the G20 Summit in October 2021, Putin emphasized that a new programme adopted in Russia would "make an important contribution to our achieving carbon neutrality by 2060 at the latest" (President of Russia 2021b). The latter suggestion even took experts by surprise (Mastepanov 2022). Finally, in November 2021 at the COP26, Russia presented a new climate and energy policy, which came as a drastic change from the former passive stance and centred on Moscow's acceptance of carbon neutrality as an imperative of sustainable development. Indeed, Russia also put forward a set of conditions, which included the recognition of nuclear and hydroelectric power sources as "green"; the integration of the carbon absorption capacity of forests into the equation for carbon neutrality; and a revision of the rules of international carbon trading. Moscow's overall energy and climate change policies still constituted a particular path of "sovereign decarbonization", i.e. a focus on increasing exports of natural gas and hydrogen and augmenting the absorption capacity of forests and other natural carbon sinks. For instance, the absorption capacity of Russian forests in 2020–2050 was to more than double and reach 1.2 million metric tonnes of carbon dioxide (Sokolova 2022). All in all, as Trenin (2021) notes, in 2021 Russia finally seemed to start taking climate-related issues seriously, even if under pressure from the key powers—the United States, the European Union, and China—all of whom pledged carbon neutrality.

9   Climate Change Landscape in Russia After 24 February 2022 and the Rise of BRICS

The start of a special military operation in Ukraine on 24 February 2022, and the subsequent waves of Western economic sanctions against Moscow, had a major impact on Russia's decarbonization agenda. On the one hand, the sanctions constituted a serious external shock. The largest market for Russian fossil fuels—the European Union—made a political decision to phase out energy imports from Russia by 2030. By 2024, Russia already lost over two-thirds of Europe's natural gas market. Several natural gas pipelines connecting Russia with the European Union were deliberately sabotaged, while other transnational gas and oil pipelines became hostage to politicking and extortion by transit countries in Eastern Europe. Furthermore, most of the decarbonization-related equipment and technologies that Russia planned to use to increase energy efficiency and lower emissions in line with its international commitments originated from the European Union, the United States, or Japan, which imposed comprehensive trade sanctions that made no exception for this category of products. Joint projects with the European Union in the field of decarbonization were cancelled. Many Western companies also withdrew from Russia, which led to a decrease in low-carbon investment in the country, difficulties with servicing Western equipment previously purchased by Russian companies, and lower potential demand for carbon credits. For example, the withdrawal of the Finnish company Fortum postponed plans to build wind farms in the country. EU certification of emissions trading in Russia became improbable, disincentivizing Russia from aligning with CBAM standards.

On the other hand, Paris Agreement sceptics emerged in Russia. Politicians, officials, businessmen, and scientists argued that, in view of the geopolitical tensions and the sanctions war, Moscow's participation in the climate accord was impractical. In addition, the Russian energy sector had to refocus on developing new export infrastructure to replace the European direction, which required major additional expenditure. By 2024, many experts agreed that Western sanctions had failed to achieve their aims, i.e. hadn't lead to Russia's economic collapse, weakened its military industrial potential, or forced Moscow to change its foreign policy. Yet much public funding was channelled towards mitigating the impact of the sanctions and the war effort, thus unavoidably limiting the availability of climate financing in the country. Consequently, some climate initiatives were postponed. For instance, the achievement of carbon neutrality on Sakhalin was rescheduled for 2028, and Russian car producers were allowed to abide by lower pollution control standards than they had had to prior to 2022. Despite the circumstances, Russia officially upheld its commitments to carbon neutrality. In June 2022, First Deputy Minister of Economic Development, Ilya Torosov, stated (TASS, 2022):

> We remain within the framework of our climate strategy; the goals and objectives set out in it, outlined by the President of the country, remain the same. Because we understand that this is our domestic agenda, our ecology, there is a public demand for it, and it is an important aspect of socio-economic policy. We understand that low-carbon technologies are a factor of long-term competitiveness, and we must not fall out even as market conditions change.

In October 2022, Putin confirmed that achieving carbon neutrality remains in Russia's interest. According to experts, maintaining its position at the global climate policy table in practical terms would allow Russia, first, to demand exemptions from sanctions for decarbonization-related goods and, second, have another channel open for dialogue with the West (Mitsui 2022). Yet, sanctions were taking their toll: at the COP27 in Egypt in November 2022, Russian scientists presented a forecast that, due to Western restrictions Russia, would reduce its emissions by only half of what had been planned by 2050. They also calculated that Russia's dependence on imported decarbonization-related equipment and technologies was 55% in the oil sector, 45% in the coal sector, and 31% in the power sector (ESG Congress 2023). Indeed, in Egypt, the Russian delegation pressed hard for the lifting of sanctions related to the development of low-carbon technologies but to no avail. However, at the COP27, Moscow managed to add low-carbon emission sources such as nuclear and hydropower to the list of renewable energy sources.

In February 2023, the government announced that it would revise the 2021 Strategy of Socio-economic Development due to the limited access to Western decarbonization technologies. Deputy Minister Torosov also envisioned the replacement of Western "green" investors with Chinese, Indian, and Arab ones and other measures to decrease the impact of sanctions on Russia's energy transition. Russia would also need to prioritize the compliance of its greenhouse gas emissions verification system with Asian rather than European standards (Kommersant 2023).

In October 2023, ahead of the COP28, Putin signed the new climate doctrine into law, intended to replace the previous doctrine issued in 2009 and elaborate on the practical implementation of key principles and mechanisms of Moscow's climate change mitigation policies. The new doctrine highlighted the imperative of achieving carbon neutrality in Russia by 2060. Fundamentally, the 2023 doctrine bluntly acknowledged "the influence of human activity on the climate ..., which leads to significant, mainly unfavorable consequences for humans and the environment" (Government of Russia 2023), while the 2009 doctrine only cautiously recognized "the ability of anthropogenic factors to have an impact on the climate" (Hydrometcenter of Russia 2009).

The adoption of the climate doctrine at the time of the fierce armed conflict in Ukraine and the new Cold War unfolding between Russia and the West, the latter accompanied with the attempts to isolate and exclude the Russian Federation from all possible international dialogue platforms and formats, testified to the importance that Moscow continued to attach to the UNFCCC framework, not least in view of the fact that the climate agenda had become an intrinsic element of international economic relations not only with the West but also with the rest of the world.

At the COP28 in Dubai in November–December 2023, Russia confirmed its previous decarbonization commitments and, after much deliberation, also gained the support of other parties in adopting an exception for fuels with a low-carbon footprint that facilitate the transit to carbon neutrality, with the final COP28 agreement recognizing that "transitional fuels can play a role in facilitating the energy transition while ensuring energy security" (UNFCCC 2023), thus de facto endorsing Moscow's plans to continue developing natural gas and nuclear power generation alongside renewable energy sources. In Dubai, Russia also joined the Declaration on Sustainable Agriculture, Resilient Food Systems, and Climate Action (but refrained from participating in a dozen of other initiatives and pledges), while one of the largest Russian oil companies, Lukoil, signed the Oil & Gas Decarbonization Charter, which brought together 50 energy companies representing more than 40% of global oil production that pledged to become carbon neutral by 2050 (Kokorin 2024).

Given the new geopolitical environment, Russia has gradually turned its gaze towards China and the Global South, with BRICS becoming the key multilateral non-Western platform for political dialogue and, increasingly, economic cooperation. By expanding its membership in 2023 to nine countries (Egypt, Ethiopia, Iran, and the United Arab Emirates in addition to Brazil, Russia, India, China, South Africa), the intergovernmental organization has further raised its global standing vis-à-vis G7 and became vitally important for Russia's effort to bypass Western sanctions and counter its political propaganda. The climate agenda has also been successfully integrated in the architecture of BRICS, with the first BRICS High-level Meeting on Climate Change taking place in May 2022. Since then, Russia has been actively promoting with its BRICS partners the development of uniform standards for carbon absorption projects, the formation of a BRICS market for carbon credits trading, and mutual decarbonization-related investment. In 2024, Russia assumed the chairmanship of BRICS and put the climate theme high on the agenda of the organization (Izvestiya 2023).

However, Russia increasingly seems to be a reluctant passenger on the climate agenda train. In the 2024 federal budget, several state environmental programmes have been sequestered by 12%–50% (The Moscow Times, 2023). The objective of implementing low-carbon technologies has been supplanted under the influence of sanctions by an all-encompassing one of "technological sovereignization", but unlike "sovereign decarbonization", which implied Russia's agency in climate change policymaking amid continued importation of Western technologies and equipment, the new goal demands an unprecedented effort to substitute imports by developing fundamental science, stimulating demand for innovation, and securing large-scale investment in research

and development. The prospects of Russia's "technological sovereignization" in the sphere of decarbonization, as some experts note, are quite
dim (Bashmakov 2023).

10 CONCLUSION

When considered altogether, the Soviet Union/Russia's climate change
policy from the 1970s until now has fundamentally been determined by
the often-conflicting frameworks of geopolitical ambition, the capacity to
act, and the national economic interest, while the actual global warming
considerations have taken a back seat. The USSR strove to beat the
West at just about everything, so it could not forego an issue with
such wide international resonance as climate change, not least because
it had been discovered and investigated by Soviet scientists. Moscow had
the resources to act on climate change, and it did so almost in unison
with Washington and other Western capitals, despite the evident threat
to its carbon-intensive economy. As Russia became the successor to the
USSR in the 1990s, former Soviet functionaries largely remained in power
and attempted to continue "superpower business" as usual, though the
post-Soviet economic implosion deprived them of the capacity to lead
on climate change, while the national economy clung to the lifeline of
Western loans. What they attempted to "sell" to the world community as
a contribution to climate change mitigation was the unsolicited reduction
in greenhouse gas emissions as a result of an undiluted economic decline,
which worked only to a limited degree. In the second half of the 1990s,
the country's climate policy was increasingly influenced by the interests
of the dynamic oil and gas sector. Moscow's initial hesitation regarding
the Kyoto Protocol and its alignment with OPEC demonstrated a break
with the Soviet geopolitical ambition of leadership on ACC and a shift
towards pragmatism and economic nationalism, which became especially
vivid under President Putin in the early 2000s.

Russia's rapid economic growth in the 2000s was driven not as much
by Putin's economic reforms but by growing energy prices, which further
elevated the voice of the oil and gas industry. Putin himself openly
demonstrated scepticism about the anthropogenic nature of climate
change, which his predecessors had never done. The era of Putin's climate
scepticism was essentially ushered in by the nationalization of major
oil and gas assets and the rising contribution of the energy industry
to Russia's national income and foreign earnings, and it was facilitated

by differences among leading Western nations. Decarbonization-related geopolitical ambitions had been long shelved, while the realization that carbon exchanges would not generate billions of dollars for Moscow undermined the factor of the national economic interest. Medvedev's tenure exposed Russia's increasing capacity to act on ACC, which had been enabled by impressive economic development as well as the necessity to implement the climate agenda due to the limits to extensive growth and the growing demand for Western technologies and investment, yet brought little genuine change, not least because the looming competition in the Arctic invoked quite different geopolitical imperatives.

Putin's return to the Kremlin was accompanied by the adoption of a more passive stance on the climate agenda. The geopolitical ambition was now to expand energy exports, develop the Arctic, and host the Sochi Olympics. Until 2021, Russia was doing the minimum to meet its climate change obligations, evidently hoping that Western powers would keep bickering about the path towards carbon neutrality, leaving room for Moscow to manoeuvre. In 2021, however, the United States and the European Union swiftly agreed to develop barriers for carbon-intensive imports, suddenly making climate agenda a key priority for Russia. Indeed, that year Moscow pledged to achieve carbon neutrality and adopted corresponding legislation, which was a major breakthrough. Essentially, in 2021, Moscow simultaneously possessed both the national economic interest and the capacity to act on ACC in a conducive geopolitical environment, which held much promise for the climate agenda. In 2022, the overall situation changed dramatically, as a sanctions war with the West greatly undermined Russia's capacity and readiness to implement climate change agenda. The national economic interest, framed by energy nationalism, however, now dictates the imminent need for the adoption of climate change mitigation measures, in particular a greenhouse gas emissions verification system, to protect Russian exporters, while the realities of current geopolitics raise the value of every platform for dialogue with the West or the Global South, including the UNFCCC and BRICS. Hence, the Russian "reluctant passenger" is unlikely to leave the climate agenda train that is now only accelerating; however, unless the sanctions on decarbonization-related technologies and equipment are lifted, Russia's contribution to international climate efforts would remain underwhelming for years to come, with considerable ecological consequences for the entire planet.

Acknowledgment This article is prepared in the framework of the project of the Russian Science Foundation, No 24-18-00650.

REFERENCES

Andonova, Liliana B. 2013. "The Climate Regime and Domestic Politics: The Case of Russia." In *The Politics of Climate Change*, edited by P.G. Harris, 29–50. Routledge.

Averchenkova, Alina. 2022. "Great Power Ambitions and National Interest in Russia's Climate Change Policy." In *Great Powers, Climate Change, and Global Environmental Responsibilities*, edited by Robert Falkner and Barry Buzan, 164–186, Oxford: Oxford University Press.

Bashmakov, Igor A. 2022. "CBAM and Russian Export." *Voprosy Ekonomiki* 1: 90–109.

Bashmakov, Igor A. 2023. "Nizkouglerodnye tekhnologii v Rossii: Nyneshnii status i perspektivy" [Low Carbon Technologies in Russia: Current Status and Views], Seminar Presentation, 11 July. https://www.imemo.ru/files/File/ru/seminars/EnergyDialogue/2023/Bashmakov.pdf.

Beuerle, Benjamin. 2023. "From Continuity to Change: Soviet and Russian Government Attitudes on Climate Change (1989–2009)." *Climatic Change* 176 (4): 36.

Brown, Kate. 2022. "On Climate Change, Russia and the U.S. are Uncomfortably Alike." *Washington Post*, 27 May. https://www.washingtonpost.com/outlook/2022/05/27/climate-change-russia-us-are-uncomfortably-alike.

Budyko, Mikhail I., and Michael C. MacCracken. 1987. "US-USSR Meeting of Experts on Causes of Recent Climate Change." *Bulletin of the American Meteorological Society* 68 (3): 237–243.

Carbon Brief. 2022. "The Carbon Brief Profile: Russia." https://www.carbonbrief.org/the-carbon-brief-profile-russia.

Climate Change Laws. 2014. "State Program on Energy Efficiency and Energy Development." https://climate-laws.org/document/state-program-on-energy-efficiency-and-energy-development-approved-by-government-decree-no-321_35d5?l=russia&o=20.

Climate Change Laws. 2016. "Decree 2344-r Approving the Plan for the Implementation of a set of Measures to Improve the State Regulation of Greenhouse Gas Emissions and Prepare for Ratification of the Paris Agreement." https://climate-laws.org/document/decree-2344-r-approving-the-plan-for-the-implementation-of-a-set-of-measures-to-improve-the-state-regulation-of-greenhouse-gas-emissions-and-prepare-for-ratification-of-the-paris-agreement_0036?l=russia&o=10.

Climate Change Laws. 2020. "National Action Plan for the First Phase of Adaptation to Climate Change, approved by Order of December 25, 2019 No. 3183-r." https://climate-laws.org/document/national-action-plan-for-the-first-phase-of-adaptation-to-climate-change-approved-by-order-of-december-25-2019-no-3183-r_2882?l=russia&o=10.

Climate Score Card. 2021. "Russia Has Set an Ambitious Goal for Reducing Emissions by 2030." https://www.climatescorecard.org/2021/07/russia-has-set-an-ambitious-goal-for-reducing-emissions-by-2030/#_ftn3.

EIA. 2023. "Russia." https://www.eia.gov/international/analysis/country/RUS.

ESA. 2004. "Russian Duma Ratifies Kyoto Protocol." https://www.esa.int/Applications/Observing_the_Earth/Russian_Duma_ratifies_Kyoto_protocol.

ESG Congress. 2023. "2022 United Nations Climate Change Conference (COP27)." https://esgcongress.com/ru/cop27.

European Commission. 2023. "GHG Emissions of All World Countries." https://edgar.jrc.ec.europa.eu/report_2023.

Fagan, Moira, and Huang, Christine. 2019. "A Look at How People Around the World View Climate Change." Pew Research Center, 18 April. https://www.pewresearch.org/short-reads/2019/04/18/a-look-at-how-people-around-the-world-view-climate-change.

Fleur, Nicholas St. 2015. "The Road to a Paris Climate Deal." *The New York Times*, 1 December. https://www.nytimes.com/interactive/projects/cp/climate/2015-paris-climate-talks/vladimir-putin-climate-change-pledges-russia.

Golub, Yuri G., and Sergey Yu Shenin. 2023. "Global Warming: Russia's Approaches and the West's Reaction." *Izvestiya of Saratov University. History. International Relations* 23 (2): 238–243.

Government of Russia. 2023. "Climate Doctrine of Russia." http://publication.pravo.gov.ru/document/0001202310260009.

Hill, Ian. 2021. "Is Russia Finally Getting Serious on Climate Change?" *The Interpreter*, 1 November. https://www.lowyinstitute.org/the-interpreter/russia-finally-getting-serious-climate-change.

HSE. 2004. "Ekspertnye mneniya: Minpromenergo i RAN razoshlis' v rekomendatsiyakh Putinu po Kiotskomu protokolu" [Expert opinions: The Ministry of Industry and Energy and the Russian Academy of Sciences disagreed on recommendations to Putin on the Kyoto Protocol]. Accessed https://iq.hse.ru/news/177736823.html.

Hydrometcenter of Russia. 2009. "Climate Doctrine of Russia." https://meteoinfo.ru/climatedoctrine.

ITVX. 2018. "Trump: Climate Change Not a Hoax, but I Don't Know that it's Manmade." https://www.itv.com/news/2018-10-15/trump-climate-change-not-a-hoax-but-i-dont-know-that-its-manmade.

Izvestiya. 2023. "V RFPI rasskazali ob initsiativakh Rossii v prirodno-klimaticheskikh proektakh" [RDIF Spoke About Russia's Initiatives in Climate Change Projects], 5 December. https://iz.ru/1615463/2023-12-05/v-rfpi-rasskazali-ob-initciativakh-rossii-v-prirodno-klimaticheskikh-proektakh.

Kalkstein, Laurence S. 1990. "Climate Change and Public Health: What do we Know and Where Are We Going." *Environmental Impact Assessment Review* 10, no. 4: 383–392.

Kokorin, Alexey. 2024. "COP-28 in Dubai: Highlights of the Forum." Klimaticheskaya platforma. https://climate-change.moscow/article/ks-28-v-dubae-osnovnye-itogi-foruma.

Kommersant. 2023. "Strategiya nizkouglerodnogo razvitiya budet peresmotrena iz-za sanktsii" [Low Carbon Development Strategy will be Revised due to Sanctions], 19 February 2023. https://www.kommersant.ru/doc/5839349.

Korppoo, Anna, and Kokorin, Alexey. 2017. "Russia's 2020 GHG Emissions Target: Emission Trends and Implementation." *Climate Policy* 17 (2): 113–130.

Korsunskaya, Darya. 2010. "Putin Ponders Climate Change in Arctic Russia." Reuters, 23 August 2010. https://www.reuters.com/article/us-russia-climate-putin-idUSTRE67M3G920100823.

Kozlovsky, Sergey. 2019. "Rossiya soglasilas' borot'sya s global'nym potepleniem, khot' Putin v nego ne verit. Chto ee zastavilo?" [Russia has Agreed to Fight Global Warming, Even Though Putin Doesn't Believe in it. What made her?]. BBC, 8 October. https://www.bbc.com/russian/features-49953830.

Lapenis, Andrei. 2020. "50-Year-Old Global Warming Forecast That Still Holds Up." *Eos* 101: 1–10.

Leiserowitz, A., J. Carman, N. Buttermore, X. Wang, S. Rosenthal, J. Marlon, and K. Mulcahy. 2021. "International Public Opinion on Climate Change." New Haven, CT: Yale Program on Climate Change Communication and Facebook Data for Good. https://climatecommunication.yale.edu/wp-content/uploads/2021/06/international-climate-opinion-february-2021d.pdf.

Makarov, Igor A., Chen, Henry, and Paltsev, Sergey V. 2018. "Impacts of Paris Agreement on Russian Economy." *Voprosy Ekonomiki* 4: 76–94.

Mastepanov, Alexey. 2022. "Russia on the Way to Carbon Neutrality." *Energeticheskaya politika* 1: 94–103.

Matthews, G.V.T. 1993. "The Ramsar Convention on Wetlands: Its History and Development." Gland: Ramsar Convention Bureau. https://globalpact.informea.org/sites/default/files/documents/Matthews-history.pdf.

Mitsui. 2022. "Russia's Climate Change Strategy after the Invasion of Ukraine: No Change in Targets, but Decarbonization Stalls." https://www.mitsui.com/mgssi/en/report/detail/__icsFiles/afieldfile/2023/02/07/2212e_kitade_e.pdf.

Nezavisimaya Gazeta. 2003. "Kiotskii protokol – ekonomicheskaya udavka dlya Rossii" [The Kyoto Protocol is an Economic Stranglehold for Russia]. https://www.ng.ru/regions/2003-12-15/9_climate.html.

NRDC. 2015. "The Putin Puzzle." https://www.nrdc.org/stories/putin-puzzle.

President of Russia. 2003. "Opening Address at the International Conference on Climate Change." http://en.kremlin.ru/events/president/transcripts/22132.

President of Russia. 2015a. "70th session of the UN General Assembly." http://en.kremlin.ru/events/president/news/50385.

President of Russia. 2015b. "Conference of the Parties to the UN Framework Convention on Climate Change." http://en.kremlin.ru/events/president/transcripts/50812.

President of Russia. 2021a. "Leaders Summit on Climate." http://en.kremlin.ru/events/president/news/65425.

President of Russia. 2021b. "G20 Summit Second Session." http://www.en.kremlin.ru/events/president/transcripts/67044.

Rindzeviciute, Egle. 2016. "The Power of Systems: How Policy Sciences Opened Up the Cold War World." London/Ithaca: Cornell University Press.

Roshydromet. 2023. "A report on Climate Features on the Territory of the Russian Federation in 2022." https://meteoinfo.ru/images/media/climate/rus-clim-annual-report.pdf.

"Russia to Slash Funding for Air Quality, Environment Projects in 2024 Budget." *The Moscow Times*, 20 October 2023. https://www.themoscowtimes.com/2023/10/20/russia-to-slash-funding-for-air-quality-environment-projects-in-2024-budget-a82826.

Safonov, Georgy. 2021. "Back to the Future? Russia's Climate Policy Evolution." https://www.csis.org/analysis/back-future-russias-climate-policy-evolution.

Sokolova, Natalya. 2022. "Russian Climate Policy in a Changing Geopolitical Environment." *Klimaticheskaya Platforma*. https://climate-change.moscow/article/rossiyskaya-klimaticheskaya-politika-v-usloviyah-izmeneniya-geopoliticheskoy-obstanovki.

TASS. 2015. "Chto govorili lidery Rossii ob izmenenii klimata" [What Russian Leaders said About Climate Change]. https://tass.ru/info/2444358.

TASS. 2022. "Il'ya Torosov: Rossiya ne budet snizhat' ambitsioznost' planov po klimatu, eto zapros obshchestva" [Ilya Torosov: Russia will not Decrease the Ambition of Climate Plans, this is a Request from Society]. https://tass.ru/interviews/14976985.

Trenin, Dmitry. 2021. "After COP26: Russia's Path to the Global Green Future." Carnegie Endowment. https://carnegiemoscow.org/commentary/85789.

UNFCCC. 2015. "Paris Agreement." https://unfccc.int/sites/default/files/eng lish_paris_agreement.pdf.

UNFCCC. 2023. "First Global Stocktake." https://unfccc.int/sites/default/files/resource/cma2023_L17_adv.pdf.

UNFCCC. 2024. "Greenhouse Gas Inventory Data." https://di.unfccc.int/det ailed_data_by_party.

Victor, David G., Nebojša Nakićenović and Nadejda Victor. 2001, "The Kyoto Protocol Emission Allocations: Windfall Surpluses for Russia and Ukraine." *Climatic Change* 49 (3): 263–277.

Waugh, Paul. 2012. "Medvedev: Links to West will Thaw, Just Like Spring." *The Standard*, 13 April. https://www.standard.co.uk/hp/front/medvedev-links-to-west-will-thaw-just-like-spring-6919302.html.

WWF. 2002. "Teper' umeyut schitat v Rossii" [Now They Know how to Count in Russia]. https://web.archive.org/web/20220201142039/https://wwf.ru/resources/news/arkhiv/teper-umeyut-schitat-i-v-rossii.

Intersecting Priorities: India's Approach to the Politics of Climate Change—Domestic Development and Global Commitments

Bashabi Gupta and Milu Maria Jose

1 INTRODUCTION

India, as a historically low-emissions, fast-growing, and developing nation, grapples with unique and arduous challenges in addressing the climate crisis. While India has the lowest per capita greenhouse gas emissions globally, it is also the world's third-largest emitter of greenhouse gases after China and the United States, contributing 7.06% of total greenhouse gas emissions (Dubash 2021; Gupta et al. 2022). This creates a challenge for those tasked with making international climate agreements that simultaneously address the bulk of global emissions and consider the development needs of the nation. India is among the most vulnerable countries to climate change, making it essential for the nation to reach a meaningful outcome from climate negotiations (Mohanty and Wadhawan 2021; Gupta et al. 2022; Swami et al. 2018). The Indian government

---

B. Gupta (✉)
Department of Geography, Miranda House, University of Delhi, Delhi, India
e-mail: bashabi.gupta@mirandahouse.ac.in

M. M. Jose
North East Regional Research and Resource Centre, Miranda House,
University of Delhi, Delhi, India

© The Author(s), under exclusive license to Springer Nature
Singapore Pte Ltd. 2024
H. Solomon et al. (eds.), *BRICS and Climate Change*,
https://doi.org/10.1007/978-981-97-5532-5_5

needs to weigh its aspirations to be an international dealmaker against other domestic priorities of achieving social and economic development and reducing poverty.

Within the global landscape, India's positioning is multifaceted: it ranks the lowest within the BRICS nations in the Human Development Index Report 2023, and its primary sources of carbon emissions are from the energy sectors (34%), industrial production (28%), and agriculture (17.8%) (Gupta et al. 2022). The emissions levels reflect India's development goals and economic aspirations and have developed from its historical background. India's engagement in climate politics is rooted in historical milestones, notably initiated by former Prime Minister Indira Gandhi's United Nations Conference on Human Development speech in 1972 (Gandhi 1972). Gandhi held developed nations accountable for global environmental issues, setting the stage for India's interest in climate discourse. The Rio Earth Summit 1992 further underscored the agenda of "climate justice", cementing India's global negotiating foundation in the climate change discourse (Dubash 2013, 2021).

India's role in climate governance evolved notably over time. From initial reluctance to cooperate, India showcased flexibility at the 2009 Copenhagen Climate Summit, offering voluntary reductions in carbon emissions and subsequent adjustments in domestic climate policies. The nation made further commitments, pledging at the Paris Agreement in 2015 to curtail greenhouse gas emissions by 33–35% by 2030, with Prime Minister Narendra Modi reaffirming these efforts at COP26 in Glasgow in 2021, with five nectar elements (*Panchamrit*) of India's climate action that aims for net-zero emissions by 2070 and 50% of its energy requirements from renewable energy by 2030 (Ministry of Environment Forest and Climate Change 2022a, 2022b).

This chapter examines the nuanced dynamics behind India's shifting climate policy. The focus here lies on domestic preferences as a driving force behind India's decision-making within international climate governance. This paper centres on the pivotal role of India as a political actor engaged in parallel domestic and international negotiations. The study leans into the elucidation of India's decision-making processes through the lens of domestic preferences.

2 HISTORICAL EVOLUTION OF INDIA'S CLIMATE POLICY

India's climate policy is intricately woven with fundamental principles that underpin its stance and negotiation strategies on the global stage. Three key principles—equity, historical responsibility, and the polluter pays ideology—form the bedrock of India's approach to climate policy, significantly influencing its decisions and negotiation strategies in international forums.

2.1 India's Climate Diplomacy in the International Policy Arena

In the landscape of global climate change endeavours, India emerges as a critical player, owing to its emission rates, economic position, and position as the leader of the developing countries (Vihma 2011). India's approach has undergone significant evolution, mirroring the transformative shifts observed in international climate politics. Initially entwined within its energy consumption and economic development policies, India's strategy to address climate change has transitioned into a distinct and proactive endeavour encompassing multifaceted mitigation and adaptation measures (Dubash 2013; Vihma 2011). The evolution of India's domestic climate policy reflects a dynamic journey marked by a strategic alignment between developmental aspirations and environmental stewardship (Atteridge et al. 2012; Blankespoor et al. 2014; Sengupta 2019).

Over the past two decades, India's approach to climate change has transcended from a defensive and cautious stance to one that actively emphasizes global leadership and participation in climate-related negotiations and initiatives. Rooted in principles of equity, historical responsibility, and the polluter pays ideology, India's stance in international negotiations will persist until a transition to voluntary carbon emissions reduction becomes feasible (Vihma 2011). India's journey in crafting and implementing climate policy has been characterized by a series of pivotal moments that have significantly shaped its approach to addressing climate change on the global stage (Atteridge et al. 2012; Nirupama 2020; Sengupta 2019).

India's engagement in international climate negotiations is rooted in historical milestones, notably initiated by former Prime Minister Indira Gandhi's United Nations Conference on the Human Environment speech in 1972: "On the one hand the rich look askance at our continuing poverty – on the other, they warn us against their own methods. We do not wish to impoverish the environment any further and yet we cannot for a moment forget the grim poverty of large numbers of people. Are not poverty and need the greatest polluters?" Gandhi held developed nations accountable for global environmental issues, setting the stage for India's interest in climate discourse (Gandhi 1972).

In 1991, India put forth a proposal at the Intergovernmental Negotiating Committee centred on the equity principle—the cornerstone of India's Climate Policy—which advocated for equal rights to the earth's atmosphere for all individuals. This proposal urged developed countries to reduce emissions and bear the additional costs of mitigation and adaptation efforts in developing and underdeveloped nations as they are historically responsible for the emissions. This stance gained significant backing from other developing countries. The Rio Earth Summit in 1992 further underscored the agenda of "climate justice", cementing India's negotiating foundation in the climate change discourse globally (Dubash 2021; World Commission on Environment and Development 1992).

Commencing in 1992 with the signing of the United Nations Framework Convention on Climate Change, India set its foundations in international climate cooperation. This initial commitment marked India's formal entry to the global dialogue on climate action, establishing a framework for its participation in subsequent multilateral agreements and discussions (Dubash et al. 2013).

However, there were efforts from many to reshape the fundamental structure of the UNFCCC, from COP1 in 1995 when Germany proposed that more advanced developing nations take on mitigation commitments to COP3 by introducing an article on voluntary commitments. India opposed the idea of voluntary commitments, arguing that it would establish a new party category not outlined in the convention. The article was eventually discarded.

Before the Kyoto Protocol was signed, the United States refused to accept mandatory emission caps until nations such as India and China did the same, laying the groundwork for the Copenhagen Accord in 2009, which was criticized for its lack of transparency and weak consensus. In 2001, the United States officially withdrew from the Kyoto Protocol, citing flaws damaging to its economy and exempting developing countries from full participation (Gupta et al. 2015). Under pressure to adopt commitments, the ratification of the Kyoto Protocol in 2002, coupled with the hosting of the United Nations Climate Conference (COP8), showcased India's active engagement and willingness to take on a more prominent role in shaping global climate initiatives. These actions underscored India's recognition of the urgency of climate change and its commitment to being part of the solution (Sengupta 2019).

Subsequently, India proposed nationally appropriate mitigation actions supported by technology, finance, and capacity-building at COP13 in Bali, Indonesia. A significant shift in India's stance emerged ahead of COP15, considering emission cuts without guarantees of funds and technology. This change sparked controversy in India, prompting parliamentary debates and demands for clarification. Despite signalling flexibility, India affirmed three non-negotiables: refusal of legally binding emission cuts, setting a peaking year, and international review of mitigation actions without international support (Gupta et al. 2015).

In 2008, India declared its National Action Plan on Climate Change and outlined a comprehensive framework for combatting climate change through eight national missions. It showed India's intent to address climate challenges across various sectors of its economy (Department of Science & Technology, 2020). In 2009, India voluntarily announced its target to reduce CO_2 emissions by 30–35% of GDP intensity by 2025, using 2005 as the base year (Dasgupta 2011). This emphasized India's determination to reduce its greenhouse gas emissions while balancing its economic growth goals.

The inclusion of "climate justice" in the UNFCCC constitution in 2015 was a notable milestone that reflected India's emphasis on fairness and equity in climate negotiations (Gupta et al. 2015). This term underscored the importance of considering historical responsibilities and the varying capacities of nations in addressing climate change. India further solidified its global leadership in climate action with the launch of the International Solar Alliance in 2016, uniting 121 countries to promote solar energy adoption. This initiative exemplified India's commitment to promoting renewable energy on a global scale and fostering international collaboration in clean energy solutions (PAGE 2023; World Bank 2016). Moreover, events such as the 16th International Energy Forum Ministerial Meet in 2018 reiterated India's increasing significance in global energy discussions. This event showcased India's evolving climate policy landscape, highlighting its proactive engagement in international dialogues concerning energy and climate issues.

In August 2022, India reaffirmed its commitment to combatting climate change by updating its Nationally Determined Contributions

(NDC). The revised targets include a 45% reduction in emissions intensity of GDP by 2030 compared to 2005 levels, a goal to achieve nearly 50% of electricity capacity from non-fossil fuel sources by 2030 through technology transfer and international financial support, and a push for sustainable living through a "LIFE" movement, emphasizing traditional conservation values. This NDC update aligns with India's broader objective of achieving net-zero emissions by 2070, supported by the submission of a separate document outlining India's long-term low-carbon development strategy to the UNFCCC secretariat in November 2022 (Ministry of Environment Forest and Climate Change 2022b; World Bank 2016).

The National Action Plan on Climate Change (NAPCC) encompasses missions focused on solar energy, energy efficiency, water conservation, sustainable agriculture, Himalayan ecosystems, sustainable habitats, healthcare, afforestation, and knowledge for climate adaptation. Specific efforts include the National Solar Mission, which plays a pivotal role in advancing sustainable growth and bolstering India's energy security. Measures such as allowing 100% Foreign Direct Investment (FDI) in renewable energy, waiving Inter-State Transmission System (ISTS) charges for solar and wind power, setting Renewable Purchase Obligation (RPO) targets, establishing Ultra Mega Renewable Energy Parks, and implementing various schemes such as PM-KUSUM and Solar Rooftop Phase II reflect India's proactive approach in promoting renewable power (IRENA and ILO 2023; Ministry of Environment Forest and Climate Change 2022b; World Bank 2016). Additionally, steps such as creating green energy corridors, formulating standards for solar devices, facilitating investments, setting bidding guidelines, enacting rules for promoting renewable energy, and ensuring prompt payment to renewable energy generators through regulatory measures showcase the nation's comprehensive strategy towards fostering renewable energy utilization (Department of Science & Technology 2020; IRENA & ILO 2023; PAGE 2023).

3   India's Climate Policies and Domestic Demands

India's climate narrative is intricately entwined with its domestic demands, wherein the formulation of climate policies harmonizes with critical national priorities such as poverty reduction, economic development, and the pursuit of sustainable development goals. India's approach to climate change is filled with complexities, challenges, and potential pathways towards sustainable development that extend far beyond national borders. India's approach to climate change politics reflects a delicate balance between domestic imperatives and global responsibilities (Fig. 1).

India has long championed the "common but differentiated responsibility" principle, advocating for per capita carbon emissions as a global climate responsibility measure during UNFCCC negotiations (Dubash 2021). India argued that its minimal contribution to cumulative greenhouse gas emissions absolved it from significant responsibility. The disparity in per capita emissions between developed and developing nations was central to India's stance, aiming to balance economic growth, poverty reduction, and climate resilience.

At the domestic level, India's early climate policy was perceived as a diplomatic issue, handled by the Ministry of External Affairs and the Department of Science and Technology, rather than a development priority. Parliamentary engagement and formal institutionalization

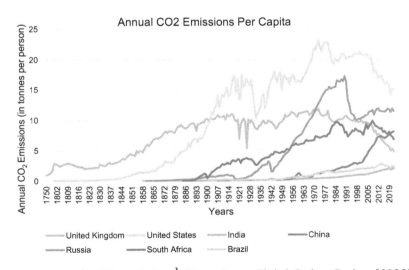

Fig. 1 Per capita CO_2 emissions[1] (*Data Source* Global Carbon Budget [2023], Population-based on various sources [2023], Our World in Data [2023])

---

[1] Carbon dioxide (CO_2) emissions from fossil fuels and industry. Land-use change is not included.

of climate policies were minimal despite India being the world's largest democracy. However, evolving climate vulnerabilities, the need for green infrastructure, and enhancing adaptive capacities are prompting a shift in India's climate policy trajectory. These emerging factors are driving India towards redefining its climate policy landscape (Dubash 2021; Wang et al. 2013).

Until the mid-1990s, the common belief was that the development of the nation and climate change mitigation measures were in conflict with each other. However, in recent years, research has shown that mitigation and development go hand in hand, which led to the rise in popularity of the co-benefits approach (Stahlke 2023). India has progressed significantly from the idea that mitigation measures are threatening economic growth to adopting the co-benefits approach. However, the idea of "differentiated responsibilities" and of securing the right to emit equal amounts as the industrialized countries are deeply rooted within the psyche of the nation.

India's climate policy in the early decades was majorly influenced by the idea that mitigation impedes economic growth and the nation's progress. Thus, the initial policy until the early 2010s was made while national goals of development and poverty reduction were weighted against mitigation measures (Atteridge et al. 2012). This was reflected in the National Environmental Plan of 2006 (Government of India 2006), and mitigation was a threat to development and the pace of development.

India's domestic policy saw a change, reflecting the idea of co-benefits as well as the international scenario and the National Action Plan on Climate Change (NAPCC) was adopted in 2008 (Dubash 2013). The climate debate and its principles became a national topic of debate, while globally India was low in per capita emissions, and nationally the ideas of equity became debated as the economic divide within the nation widened. As the nation increasingly faced extreme climate-related events where the poor and marginalized became the targets, the debate moved towards the distributional justice of climate benefits (Dubash 2013).

The nation became increasingly aware of the vulnerability and danger that climate change posed to its economic growth, and mitigation became an opportunity to achieve the developmental goals, especially with the popularity of multidimensional poverty measures. Thus, just becoming economically stronger was not sufficient—clean water, air, and a good environment became the goals. In addition, the mounting international pressure to maintain positive cooperation became paramount to India's policy change.

NAPCC aligned with United Nations framework conventions, aimed to combat global and domestic challenges by safeguarding vulnerable sections of society and regions susceptible to climate change impacts. Comprising eight sub-missions, including the National Solar Mission (NSM), National Mission for Enhanced Energy Efficiency (NMEEE), and National Mission on Sustainable Habitat (NMSH), among others, this strategic framework outlined diverse approaches aimed at fortifying ecological sustainability within India's developmental trajectory. They focused on both mitigation and adaptation strategies. The initial three missions targeted mitigation, and the subsequent five (excluding the National Mission on Strategic Knowledge for Climate Change) addressed adaptation (Department of Science & Technology 2020; Government of India 2022; Ministry of Environment Forest and Climate Change 2022b; Nirupama 2020).

The scrutiny of the missions' achievements reveals a mixed picture. Some missions, such as the National Mission for Enhanced Energy Efficiency and the National Mission for Sustaining the Himalayan Ecosystem, displayed negligible accomplishments. The missions were critiqued for the undemocratic decision-making practices and limited expert engagement in development and implementation. It was criticized for its excessive focus areas with little to no in-depth solutions for climate vulnerabilities, particularly for marginalized and vulnerable communities. The insufficient coordination between institutions, inadequate financial management mechanisms, and skewed state-wise financial allocations across missions, leading to disparity in resource distribution, were also critiqued.

The state-level climate action plans also faced similar critiques. Instances such as West Bengal's climate action plan were developed without consulting vulnerable local communities and lacked strategic advice and specific budget allocations for critical areas such as biodiversity and ecosystem management in regions such as Uttarakhand. States with heavy agricultural dependence, such as Uttar Pradesh and Gujarat, received disproportionately minimal budget allocations for agricultural development, despite significant agricultural workforces (Chettri 2017; Ghosh and Ghosal 2021; Rattani 2018).

Energy use is at the heart of India's pollution and climate change problems, as the present energy sources have direct and extensive implications for the economy and the lives of millions in India's rapidly urbanizing population. India accounts for nearly one-quarter of the global energy demand growth to 2040, according to International Energy Agency (IEA), more than any other country over the same period. While the high energy demand is a key factor in enhancing economic prosperity, the same would entail significant negative environmental impacts in the near future, as India will become the largest contributor to global CO_2 emissions growth (International Energy Agency 2023).

Given the complex nature of clean energy transitions, coherent policy packages are needed to deliver the necessary rate of change across the entire energy system. Energy-related air pollutants and CO_2 emissions arise from the same sources. Thus, if well-designed, energy policies that seek to address air pollution or climate change can deliver important co-benefits for other targets (International Energy Agency 2022).

A pivotal milestone emerged in 2001 with the enactment of the Energy Conservation Act, a legislative move that underwent significant augmentation in August 2022. India was one of the few countries that passed the Energy Conservation Act in 2001 (Mohan 2017; Nirupama 2020). This legislative update stands as a testament to India's evolving priorities, emphasizing a pivotal shift towards non-fossil fuel sources for energy needs (International Energy Agency 2022). Notably, it expanded the Energy Conservation Building Code (ECBC) to encompass larger office and residential buildings, signalling a proactive stance in addressing energy consumption patterns in the built environment, while setting specific benchmarks for energy use in transportation sectors such as ships and vehicles.

While India has had several energy efficiency and renewable energy expansion policies in effect, it has no plan to phase out coal. The 2018 National Electricity Plan envisages net additions of 46 GW between 2022 and 2027. This is evident in Fig. 2, as coal and oil are the two largest energy sources in India, with wind, solar, and other renewables holding the smallest share. In the long term, the share of coal in power generation is likely to decrease due to the economic competitiveness of renewables and difficulties in financing and insuring new coal power plants.

Here, timing and technological choices are crucial for making measures such as renewables deployment, enhanced emissions standards, energy efficiency measures in industry and the thermal power segment, as well as residential clean energy access a consistent policy framework, thereby fostering clean energy transition. While air pollution measures enable short-term CO_2 emissions stabilization, climate policies prevent

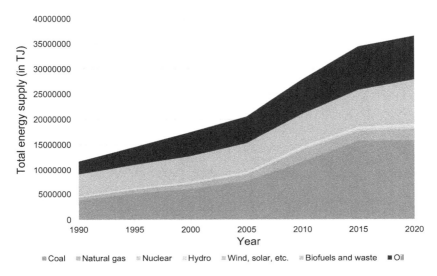

Fig. 2 Total Energy Supply (TES) by source, India 1990–2021 (*Source* IEA World Energy Balances)

long-term technology lock-in and deliver lasting air pollution reductions. A power sector transition from fossil to renewable energy, for example, addresses both concerns and delivers significant air pollution and CO_2 emissions reductions. To demonstrate co-benefit potential, this report provides a quantitative analysis of how flagship energy policies contribute to both air pollution reduction and climate change mitigation. Four key sectors are assessed: captive power plants, industrial energy efficiency, electrification of road transport, and expanded access to clean cooking (International Energy Agency 2022, 2023).

In the power sector, IEA analysis finds that timely and full implementation of the 2015 emissions standards notification for thermal power plants is crucial if India is to reduce air pollutants in the short term. The installation of emissions control technologies in thermal power plants would enable a 95% reduction in combustion-related emissions of SO_2 and an 80% reduction in PM2.5 emissions from the power sector by 2030 compared to 2019 levels. Strong renewables deployment could further abate air pollutants and mitigate CO_2 emissions in the long run (International Energy Agency 2022; PAGE 2023) (Table 1).

Table 1 Estimated direct and indirect jobs in renewable energy worldwide, by industry, 2021–2022 (in thousands)

Renewable energy Source	World	China	Brazil	India
Solar PV	4,902	2,760	241	282
Liquid biofuels	2,490	55	856	35
Hydropower	2,485	876	194	466
Wind power	1,400	681	68	40
Others	2,443	1,058	41	165
Total	13,720	5,548	1,400	988

Source International Renewable Energy Agency and International Energy Agency

The investment in renewable energy is estimated to create **988,000** jobs in India by **2022**. Hydropower, with around **466,000** jobs, holds the position of the largest renewable employer, followed by solar photovoltaic. However, it still lags behind other BASIC nations such as China and Brazil.

The recent evolution of India's domestic climate policy took a momentous turn on **3 August 2022**, when the Union Cabinet, under the guidance of the Prime Minister, endorsed the revised Nationally Determined Contribution (NDC). This updated commitment, slated for submission to the United Nations Framework Convention on Climate Change (UNFCCC) under the Paris Agreement, crystallizes India's resolute pledge to achieve net-zero emissions by **2070**. This redefined NDC encapsulates the essence of *"Panchamrit"* (five nectar elements), India's comprehensive climate action plan articulated during COP26 in Glasgow (Ministry of Environment Forest and Climate Change 2022a, 2022b). It signifies an evolution in India's domestic climate policy, showcasing a steadfast dedication to steering the nation towards a sustainable and resilient future, while playing a proactive role on the global climate stage. Climate change policies in India have primarily focused on supporting synergies between development and outcomes for the climate.

4 India, BRICS, and International Climate Negotiations

The sixth Assessment Report of IPCC in 2021 has consolidated and evaluated global research endeavours regarding climate change (Intergovernmental Panel on Climate Change [IPCC] 2023). With the advanced earth-monitoring systems that provide real-time geophysical data, enhancing comprehension of how global warming manifests across various regions, the question of the reality of climate change has settled. Today it is widely accepted that the world is warming due to human-caused greenhouse gas emissions (Intergovernmental Panel on Climate Change [IPCC] 2023).

From 1992, when the UNFCCC was signed, the global population who lived in extreme poverty has decreased from 35% to less than 10% in 2022 (World Bank 2020). An increasing number of people have improved living standards, health, and educational opportunities. Today, the climate crisis persists with evident effects, and it is marked by a 1 °C warming since preindustrial times that will lead to a 2–3 ft rise in sea levels by 2100 (Intergovernmental Panel on Climate Change [IPCC] 2023).

With the growing challenges to multilateralism, climate negotiations are increasingly regarded as a game to be played by major powers, thus making it challenging to compromise on responsibilities between historical and present emissions contributors. The geopolitical dynamics in the last few years with the Russia–Ukraine and Israel–Palestine conflicts complicate the feasibility of a binding global climate agreement. Notwithstanding the limitations, the international climate negotiations have been the base for extensive scientific collaboration, highlighting the ethical aspects of the climate crisis, inspiring youth action, and laying the groundwork for national climate action plans. However, the efficiency of these negotiations is limited by the absence of strong commitments and practical implementation.

As the emissions of developing countries increase rapidly, the participation of the developing nations in international climate policy decisions has become increasingly important, pushing countries such as India and China to be the dealmakers and dealbreakers of climate negotiations. This has led to the strengthening of linkages between climate change mitigation measures and development, so as to incentivize and motivate the developing nations to participate in the negotiations (Stahlke 2023).

In 2009, India allied with Brazil, China, and South Africa, forming a coalition at COP15 called BASIC to strengthen the collective voice of fast-growing, developing nations that are historically low emitters in climate negotiations. Through this collaboration, India aimed to enhance its influence in discussions with industrialized nations. These emerging economies together account for a significant portion of global emissions, underscoring their role in addressing climate change (Table 2).

Despite the efforts of the BRICS and BASIC alliance, the Copenhagen Accord fell short of achieving its goals (Stahlke 2023). The countries had to be satisfied with general statements about their climate goals instead of enforceable commitments. The BASIC alliance reiterated the principles of

Table 2 BRICS countries' 2020 targets under the Copenhagen Accord vs Actual Performance

Country	2020 targets	Emissions reduction performances
Brazil	In 2020, there are plans to reduce the predicted emissions by 36.1–38.9% by implementing changes in land use and land-use change	In 2010, the amount of greenhouse gas emissions totalled 2.27 gigatonnes, which were reduced to 1.58 gigatonnes in 2020. However, in order to meet the target, the emissions increased to 0.35 gigatonnes
India	By 2020, the aim is to reduce the emissions intensity of the GDP by 20–25% compared to the 2005 level	In 2005, the amount of greenhouse gas emissions per million dollars of GDP was 2.375 CO_2e. By 2019, this number had decreased to 1.172 CO_2e per million dollars of GDP
China	By 2020, we aim to decrease carbon dioxide emissions per unit of GDP by 40–45% compared to the levels recorded in 2005	The amount of carbon dioxide equivalent emissions decreased from 3.034 kilotonnes per million dollars of GDP to 844 kilotonnes per million dollars of GDP between 2005 and 2019
Russia	Reducing emissions to a range of 15–25% less than the levels recorded in 1990	In 2020, there was a reduction of 36.69% in greenhouse gas emissions
South Africa	In 2020, the aim is to decrease the rate of emission growth to 34% below the business-as-usual (BAU) scenario	The target range of 414–599 $MtCO_2$e has been met by limiting the total greenhouse gas emissions to 550 $MtCO_2$e, which falls within this range

Source https://climateactiontracker.org

"differentiated responsibilities" and equity considerations, underscoring that developing countries prioritize social and economic development and poverty eradication as the immediate goals and developmental goals over immediate climate actions.

The ongoing deadlock in climate negotiations offers a significant opening for BRICS nations to reshape the long-standing challenge that has persisted for over two decades, where divisions between developed and developing countries have remained a contentious issue. The crux of the dispute lies in questioning the validity of maintaining the differentiation between these two groups, a classification based on income per capita according to United Nations categorizations. This debate extends beyond climate policy, carrying implications for other realms such as trade regimes, making any potential changes a matter to be addressed within the broader framework of the United Nations.

Within this contentious environment, the text under negotiation at Lima introduces critical issues that could redefine the fundamental architecture of the climate regime. It proposes a separation between various aspects such as mitigation, adaptation, finance, technology, transparency, and capacity-building from what is termed the "means of implementation". This divergence from the established global consensus articulated in the convention's preamble, which emphasizes climate action based on scientific, technical, and economic considerations, is further underscored by recent reports from the Intergovernmental Panel on Climate Change (IPCC).

Moreover, specific proposed amendments introduce new commitments for developing nations, particularly regarding mitigation components. However, these additions seem to contradict the convention's core principles of differentiated responsibilities among countries. To navigate these complexities, there is a pressing need to reconfigure commitments in line with an evolved understanding of the intricate drivers behind climate change. Revisiting certain aspects of the convention's provisions, while integrating both environmental and sustainable development perspectives into global climate conferences, could pave the way for a more comprehensive and balanced approach to addressing the global climate challenge. This approach could potentially create a more adaptable and effective global climate framework that accommodates the diverse needs and aspirations of nations at different stages of development.

5   Critiques, Successes, and Future Directions

The BRICS nations have long encountered criticisms regarding their climate negotiations, as they set their sights on lofty climate targets and divergent interests among member nations. One major critique is that the BRICS nations need to prioritize economic growth over stringent climate actions, especially in matters regarding replacing fossil fuels with renewables. Critics argue that the group lacks the necessary ambition and motivation to address climate change effectively. There is also a prevalent perception that groups such as BRICS and BASIC are shields to developing nations from following stringent commitments and scrutiny by developed countries.

India, as part of the BRICS and BASIC grouping, responds to these critiques by emphasizing the need for equitable commitments that consider the member nation's developmental priorities. India as part of BRICS strongly advocates for the acknowledgement of the historical responsibility of developed nations while stressing the importance of financial support and technological transfer for developing countries as they transition towards cleaner technologies while skipping over the development trajectory of the developed nations. India clarifies that groupings such as BRICS platforms amplify the voices of developing nations in climate negotiations, ensuring that the needs of developing countries are adequately represented.

Despite criticisms, BRICS and BASIC have had significant successes in advancing climate policy that is favourable for developing nations. With initiatives such as the International Solar Alliance (ISA), spearheaded by India, these groupings have shown collective efforts that promote renewable energy. Initiatives such as BRICS and BASIC not only contribute to mitigating climate change at a pace that can be sustained by developing nations but also align with India's domestic objectives of energy security and economic growth. Knowledge-sharing and capacity-building initiatives within these groups have facilitated the exchange of best practices and technologies among member nations, thus accelerating the climate change adaptation mechanisms.

6 GOING FORWARD

India's initial climate policies faced scrutiny from scholars, pointing out limitations such as the exclusive focus on per capita emissions norms and the potential peril of aligning India's emissions with those of Western nations. The projections of escalating CO_2 emissions, soaring energy demands, and the substantial growth in urbanization and industrialization necessitate urgent attention.

Addressing the rising greenhouse gas emissions across various sectors—industries and urban and rural households—while amplifying renewable energy integration stands as a critical agenda for the nation's sustainable future. To avert the foreseen surge in carbon emissions, India's future climate policies must prioritize strategies that balance economic growth with environmental sustainability. Therefore, future endeavours should emphasize comprehensive policies geared towards mitigating emissions, fostering renewable energy uptake, and promoting sustainable practices across all sectors.

There is a pressing demand to develop a climate policy that garners global acceptance for India, and this imperative arises from the requirement for a sophisticated climate strategy, not just to navigate global politics and foreign relations but also to assert India's standing on the international stage (Barua 2017; Thaker and Leiserowitz 2014). India's active participation in global climate summits from its conception and its contributions to shaping international climate policies underscore its commitment to this endeavour. India should move forward by focusing on issues that can alleviate the country's greenhouse gas emissions while meeting its escalating energy demands and position itself as a significant player in global climate negotiations with strategies that address both the domestic and global demands.

India struggles with major socioeconomic challenges, including poverty, hunger, illiteracy, inequality, and displacement. Approximately 14.96% of the Indian population lives in multidimensionally poor households, with 19.28% of the rural population being multidimensionally poor with an intensity of poverty of 44.39% (NITI Aayog 2023). The poor are more vulnerable to the adverse effects of climate change (Sinha et al. 2022). Therefore, it is important that India's domestic climate policies prioritize reducing economic and social disparities to bolster resilience among these vulnerable segments of society.

India heavily relies on oil and natural gas imports due to the domestic demands, which is a major contributor to greenhouse gas emissions (Ministry of Petroleum and Natural Gas 2023). Energy transition to more renewable sources, particularly solar power and wind power, is a viable solution. India as a part of the five nectar elements (*Panchamrit*) of India's climate action in COP26 has declared that it will reach 500GW of non-fossil energy capacity by 2030 and 50% of its energy requirements from renewable energy by 2030 (Ministry of Environment Forest and Climate Change 2022a). This ambitious goal is both the biggest challenge and opportunity in India's hands. The shift towards greener and renewable energy can be the best opportunity to create more green jobs (approximately 988,000) for the youth, address the unemployment rates, and assist India in detaching growth from emissions (IRENA and ILO 2023; Ministry of Statistics & Programme Implementation 2023).

It is necessary that India recognizes the need to balance economic growth with emission reduction and embark on a long-term strategy to address its energy demands, economic aspirations, and climate challenges. By placing climate change policy at the core of its developmental policies, India will be capable of navigating the complex interplay between growth, energy requirements, and climate responsibilities.

Engrained with principles of equity, historical responsibility, and economic necessity, India's stance in international negotiations is intertwined with its pursuit of sustainable development goals. The nation has showcased resilience and commitment while facing challenges and criticisms through its proactive role in international climate forums. As India moves forward, it is of even greater importance that economic growth goes hand in hand with environmental stewardship. India's journey towards climate action not only offers insights for national policy frameworks but also underscores the interconnectedness of global efforts and emphasizes the need for collective, inclusive, and sustainable strategies to address the pressing challenges of climate change across the globe.

Bibliography

Atteridge, Aaron, Manish Kumar Shrivastava, Neha Pahuja, and Himani Upadhyay. 2012. "Climate Policy in India: What Shapes International, National and State Policy?" *Upadhyay Source: Ambio* 41.

Barua, Mintu. 2017. "India's Environmental Strategy in the Global Climate Negotiations." *International Studies* 51 (1–4): 195–211. https://doi.org/10.1177/0020881717719352

Blankespoor, Brian, Susmita Dasgupta, and Benoit Laplante. 2014. "Sea-Level Rise and Coastal Wetlands." *Ambio* 43 (8): 996–1005. https://doi.org/10.1007/s13280-014-0500-4

Chettri, Mona. 2017. Ethnicity and Democracy in the Eastern Himalayan Borderland Constructing Democracy.

Dasgupta, C. 2011. "Climate Change Negotiations: Guarding the "Overriding Priorities." *Indian Foreign Affairs Journal* 6 (2): 217–229.

Department of Science & Technology. 2020. Climate Change Programme. https://dst.gov.in/climate-change-programme

Dubash, Navroz K. 2013. The Politics of Climate Change in India: Narratives of Equity and Cobenefits. *Wiley Interdisciplinary Reviews: Climate Change* 4 (3): 191–201. https://doi.org/10.1002/wcc.210

Dubash, Navroz K. 2021. Varieties of Climate Governance: The Emergence and Functioning of climate institutions. *Environmental Politics* 30 (sup1): 1–25. https://doi.org/10.1080/09644016.2021.1979775

Dubash, Navroz K., Markus Hagemann, Niklas Höhne, and Prabhat Upadhyaya. 2013. "Developments in National Climate Change Mitigation Legislation and Strategy." *Climate Policy* 13 (6): 649–664. https://doi.org/10.1080/14693062.2013.845409

Gandhi, Indira. 1972. "Of Man and His Environment." United Nations Conference on Human Environment, Stockholm, Sweden.

Ghosh, M., and Ghosal, S. 2021. "India's Domestic Climate Policy: Past, Present and Future Strategies." *Annals of the National Association of Geographers India*, 41 (1): 156–175. https://doi.org/10.32381/ATNAGI.2021.41.01.10

Government of India. 2006. National Environment Policy. https://ibkp.dbtindia.gov.in/DBT_Content_Test/CMS/Guidelines/20190411103521431_National%20Environment%20Policy,%202006.pdf

Government of India. 2022. India's Updated First Nationally Determined Contribution Under Paris Agreement. https://unfccc.int/sites/default/files/NDC/2022-08/India%20Updated%20First%20Nationally%20Determined%20Contrib.pdf

Gupta, Himangana, Ravinder Kumar Kohli, and Amrik Singh Ahluwalia. 2015. "Mapping 'Consistency' in India's Climate Change Position: Dynamics and

Dilemmas of Science Diplomacy." *Ambio* 44 (6): 592–599. https://doi.org/10.1007/s13280-014-0609-5

Gupta, Rajat, Shirish Sankhe, Naveen Unni, and Divy Malik. 2022. Decarbonising India Charting a Pathway for Sustainable Growth.

Intergovernmental Panel on Climate Change (IPCC). 2023. Climate Change 2022—Impacts, Adaptation and Vulnerability. In *Climate Change 2022—Impacts, Adaptation and Vulnerability*. Cambridge University Press. https://doi.org/10.1017/9781009325844

International Energy Agency. 2022. Air Quality and Climate Policy Integration in India—Analysis. https://www.iea.org/reports/air-quality-and-climate-policy-integration-in-india

International Energy Agency. 2023. World Energy Outlook 2023. www.iea.org/terms

IRENA, and ILO. 2023. Renewable Energy and Jobs: Annual Review 2023. www.irena.org

Ministry of Environment Forest and Climate Change. 2022a. India's Stand at COP-26.

Ministry of Environment Forest and Climate Change. 2022b. India Stands Committed to Reduce Emissions Intensity of its GDP by 45 percent by 2030, from 2005 level. *PIB Delhi*.

Ministry of Petroleum and Natural Gas. 2023. Import and Export of Crude Oil and Petroleum Products. Petroleum Planning & Analysis Cell. https://ppac.gov.in/import-export

Ministry of Statistics & Programme Implementation. 2023. Periodic Labour Force Survey (PLFS)—Quarterly Bulletin for July–September 2023.

Mohan, Aniruddh. 2017. From Rio to Paris: India in Global Climate Politics.

Mohanty, Abinash, and Shreya Wadhawan. 2021. A District Level Assessment Mapping India's Climate Vulnerability.

Nirupama, A.K. 2020. "India's Climate Policy: Past, Present and Future Strategies." *Journal of Polity and Society*.

NITI Aayog. 2023. India a Progress Review 2023 National Multidimensional Poverty Index.

PAGE. 2023. Assessment of India's Green Jobs and Just Transition Policy Readiness.

Rattani, Vijeta. 2018. "Coping with Climate Change: An Analysis of India's National Action Plan on Climate Change." *Agriculture* 1.

Sengupta, Sandeep. 2019. "India's Engagement in Global Climate Negotiations from Rio to Paris." In *India in a Warming World*, ed. Navroz K. Dubash, 114–141. Delhi: Oxford University Press. https://doi.org/10.1093/oso/9780199498734.003.0007

Sinha, Manjisha, R. Sendhil, B.S. Chandel, Ravinder Malhotra, Ajmer Singh, Sujeet Kumar Jha, and Gopal Sankhala. 2022. "Are Multidimensional Poor

More Vulnerable to Climate Change? Evidence from Rural Bihar, India." *Social Indicators Research* 162 (1): 123–149. https://doi.org/10.1007/S11 205-021-02827-Z/TABLES/6

Stahlke, T. 2023. "Climate Policy and the Concept of Co-benefits in India." *Journal of Social and Economic Development* 25 (1): 86. https://doi.org/10. 1007/S40847-023-00235-2

Swami, Deepika, Prashant Dave, and Devanathan Parthasarathy. 2018. "Agricultural Susceptibility to Monsoon Variability: A District Level Analysis of Maharashtra, India." *Science of the Total Environment* 619–620: 559–577. https://doi.org/10.1016/J.SCITOTENV.2017.10.328

Thaker, Jagadish, and Anthony Leiserowitz. 2014. "Shifting Discourses of Climate Change in India." *Climatic Change* 123 (2): 107–119. https://doi. org/10.1007/S10584-014-1059-6

Vihma, Antto. 2011. "India and the Global Climate Governance: Between Principles and Pragmatism." *Journal of Environment and Development* 20 (1): 69–94. https://doi.org/10.1177/1070496510394325

Wang, Jun, Daniel G. Brown, and Arun Agrawa. 2013. "Climate Adaptation, Local Institutions, and Rural Livelihoods: A Comparative Study of Herder Communities in Mongolia and Inner Mongolia, China." *Global Environmental Change* 23 (6): 1673–1683. https://doi.org/10.1016/j.gloenvcha. 2013.08.014

World Bank. 2016. *India Sign Deal to Boost Solar Globally.* World Bank. https://www.worldbank.org/en/news/press-release/2016/06/30/world-bank-india-sign-deal-to-boost-solar-globally

World Bank. 2020. *Poverty and Shared Prosperity 2020: Reversals of Fortune.* https://doi.org/10.1596/978-1-4648-1602-4

World Commission on Environment and Development. 1992. Our Common Future.

China's Evolving Climate Change Strategy: a Dual Role in Mitigation and Adaptation

Jana de Kluiver

1 INTRODUCTION

Within the realm of global climate change efforts, China has emerged as a pivotal player whose strategy has transformed remarkably in the past decade. Notably, China's approach to climate change has evolved from being a mere facet of its energy consumption and economic development policy to a distinct, proactive endeavour encompassing mitigation and adaptation measures. China's approach to addressing climate change has experienced a noteworthy transformation in the past decade. This shift in its climate change strategy has been characterized by a move from a more defensive and cautious stance to one that emphasizes taking a global leadership role and actively participating in climate-related negotiations and initiatives (see Heggelund 2021: 10). This new era was ushered in by President Xi Jinping's landmark joint announcement with the United States promising to take steps to reduce its emissions alongside similar steps pledged by Washington (see The White House 2014).

China, the world's largest carbon-emitting economy since 2006, has seen its share of global carbon emissions rise significantly from 21% to

J. de Kluiver (✉)
University of the Free State, Bloemfontein, South Africa
e-mail: dekluiverjana@gmail.com

© The Author(s), under exclusive license to Springer Nature Singapore Pte Ltd. 2024
H. Solomon et al. (eds.), *BRICS and Climate Change*,
https://doi.org/10.1007/978-981-97-5532-5_6

27.4% by 2018. In contrast, the United States' contribution to global carbon emissions has steadily decreased from 19.93% to 14.9%, while the European Union's share has dropped from 12.4% to 8.4% during the same period. Consequently, by 2018, China's carbon emissions alone exceeded the combined total of the United States and the European Union, making it the largest carbon emitter globally (Lai 2021: 70). With China's share in global carbon emissions expected to continue growing, irrespective of its changing domestic demographic (see Man 2023), it has become crucial to comprehend the shifts in its climate policy and the underlying factors driving these changes, particularly in addressing the urgent issue of climate change. According to Cao et al. (2021), even if developed nations make significant strides in reducing emissions, global warming mitigation remains unattainable without China's active involvement. Consequently, China's climate policies hold global significance and are poised to play a decisive role in determining the attainment of worldwide climate objectives.

However, China's role in climate change mitigation presents a paradox that demands closer examination. On the one hand, Beijing is the source of significant greenhouse gas emissions (see Lai 2021), earning the nation the title of a major arsonist in the global climate landscape. On the other hand, China has also made significant strides in producing renewable energy sources, such as solar and wind power as well as electric cars (see Engels 2018: 2), establishing itself as a prominent fighter in the battle against climate change. The country already adds more green energy capacity annually than all other countries combined. China currently accounts for over three-quarters of new solar and wind capacity and 80% of the new hydropower capacity that is added annually (see Song-Pehamberger 2023). In 2021 alone, China added 17 gigawatts to its offshore wind energy grid—seven times that of the rest of the world combined. This resulted in 50% of the global offshore wind capacity now residing in China. China is also the world's largest electric vehicle market, with half of all electric vehicles sold there. The country's 500,000 electric vehicle bus fleet accounts for 98% of the global market share (Mordor Intelligence 2023).

This chapter examines China's comprehensive stance on climate change, scrutinizing its multifaceted role within the international environmental arena. First, the chapter will provide a historical overview of China's climate policy. Thereafter, it will explore China's alignment with the United Nations Sustainable Development Goals, particularly those addressing environmental and climate-related objectives. Furthermore, it will explore Beijing's approach to the Paris Agreement and its contributions to global climate action. Afterwards, China's bilateral attempts at climate change mitigation will be explored by examining the greening of the Belt and Road Initiative (BRI). To gain a more holistic perspective on China's position within the context of climate change, this research also examines the country's role as a member of BRICS (Brazil, Russia, India, China, and South Africa), a group of emerging economies with considerable influence on global politics and economics. By considering these facets, the chapter aims to elucidate China's evolving stance in the ever-important realm of climate change, offering valuable insights into its dynamic position as both a cause and a solution to the climate crisis.

2 Historical Perspective: From Energy Policy to Specific Climate Policies

China's export industry has been an engine for its economic growth since its opening up and economic reforms in the 1970s. China has become a prominent producer driven predominantly by affordable coal as its primary energy source. The nation has also expanded its presence in other energy-intensive industries, catering to global and domestic markets, including car manufacturing and shipbuilding (Conrad 2012: 435). The availability of dependable and economic energy was vital to sustain China's economic progress and, as a result, ensure its capacity to achieve overarching political objectives, such as poverty reduction and societal stability (Harris et al. 2013). According to Wu (2023: 1), China's climate actions can be traced back to global climate negotiations in the late 1980s. Climate change started gaining prominence as a public policy concern during this period, which was spurred by increasing scientific evidence and calls for action from influential states such as the United States and the United Kingdom. Meanwhile, the Chinese government was in the initial stages of introducing market-oriented reforms. In China, the early focus on climate change primarily revolved around scientific matters and was spearheaded by the State Science and Technology Commission (Sandalow et al. 2022).

122 J. DE KLUIVER

From the unsuccessful Copenhagen Climate Summit[1] in 2009 to the Paris Climate Agreement[2] in 2015, China's global climate governance efforts have made a definitive break from the ineffective Kyoto regime[3] (Keohane and Oppenheimer 2016). According to Lai (2021: 17), before 2009, particularly in the years leading up to 2006, China's climate policy leaned towards a defensive posture. From 1990 to 2005, China tended to minimize the urgency of climate-related concerns, emphasizing the paramount importance of economic development. This defensive posture could be explained by the country's domestic focus on achieving economic growth (see Cox 2022). However, Lai (2021) reasons that, from 2006 to 2008, China shifted its stance, acknowledging the adverse effects of climate change. Heggelund (2021: 12) attributed this shift to numerous core drivers such as air pollution, health issues, and energy security. The author added that this period saw the integration of climate change into China's economic development framework.

This transition continued from 2009 to 2011, when China, while avoiding internationally binding commitments, expressed its commitment to voluntary efforts to reduce carbon intensity. According to Yang (2022: 358), China's role in global climate governance has significantly shifted from the Copenhagen to the Paris Agreement. During the 2009 Copenhagen Summit, China refused to accept binding greenhouse gas emission targets. Having caused climate issues through their development, Beijing asserted that developed countries should lead climate change mitigation, with emission targets not binding developing nations (Harris et al. 2013). According to Dong (2017: 3), this period was characterized by

[1] The Copenhagen Accord emerged from the 2009 UNFCCC conference and marked a significant shift in international climate negotiations. While it was not a legally binding treaty, it introduced the concept of nationally determined contributions (NDCs) to emissions reductions. China pledged to reduce its carbon intensity under the Copenhagen Accord, signalling a willingness to engage more actively in climate action.

[2] The Paris Agreement, adopted in 2015 under the UNFCCC, represents a landmark international climate accord. China played a pivotal role in the negotiations and was a key signatory to the agreement. Under the Paris Agreement, China committed to peak its carbon emissions by 2030 and increase the share of non-fossil fuel energy in its total energy consumption.

[3] The Kyoto Protocol, established in 1997 as an extension of the UNFCCC, introduced legally binding emissions reduction targets for developed countries. While China was exempt from mandatory emissions reductions as a developing country, its participation in the Kyoto Protocol negotiations and discussions raised awareness of climate change issues within the Chinese government and the public.

a shift from a low-key approach to active engagement in global affairs. The author reasons that this transformation has profoundly impacted China's approach to climate negotiations, leading to more active summit-level climate diplomacy and a prominent role for Xi Jinping in shaping climate policies. Similarly, China's climate policy under Jinping has fluctuated. Initially, Jinping adopted an assertive and defensive stance from 2012 to 2014, but he subsequently pivoted towards positioning China as a morally grounded international climate leader from 2015 to 2019. However, from 2020 to 2021, the implementation of heavy industrial and carbon-intensive projects suggested a possible retreat from this proactive position on climate issues, despite public pronouncements of progressive goals (Lai 2021: 71). This shift in stance was a result of numerous external and internal pressures such as the economic impact of the COVID-19 pandemic (see Lui 2022), geopolitical developments, and domestic demand (see Li et al. 2023).

According to Schreurs (2016: 222), China's evolving stance on climate action is primarily shaped by domestic factors rather than international pressure. The author points out that China grapples with severe pollution issues, contributing to growing dissatisfaction among its citizens due to deteriorating air quality. This discontent has manifested through anti-incinerator protests throughout China.[4] In recent years, demonstrations opposing proposed incinerators have occurred in various Chinese provinces, including Hubei, Hunan, Guangdong, Shandong, Hainan, Jiangxi, and Zhejiang. Some of these protests have escalated into violence, revealing substantial public scepticism and distrust towards these facilities (see Ruwitch 2014; Standaert 2017; Bradsher 2019). The critical pollution levels can be attributed to the rapid proliferation of automobiles, persistent heavy reliance on coal, and an escalating demand for oil. Despite impressive growth in renewables since 2000, fossil fuels still accounted for 83% of China's primary energy mix in 2022, with coal accounting for 56% (Raj 2023). In contrast to this, Yang (2022: 358) reasons that China's adoption of international climate leadership is a component of a broader shift in its foreign policy and positioning within

---

[4] The anti-incinerator protests in China result from widespread public distrust and opposition to proposed projects in various provinces, driven by concerns about environmental and health risks as well as perceived transparency issues in decision-making processes. The affected communities fear adverse effects on air and water quality, public health, and the overall environment.

124   J. DE KLUIVER

global governance. Over the past decade, China's foreign policy strategy has evolved from a stance of Tao Guang Yang Hui (keeping a low profile) to Fen Fa You Wei (striving for achievement). These evolving trends underscore the interconnectedness of China's reform and globalization, highlighting the intricate interplay between China and the international community in global affairs. China's diplomacy has transitioned from traditional diplomatic practices to diplomacy for leadership, reflecting its growing aspiration to play a constructive and influential role on the world stage (Dong 2017: 3).

Nevertheless, as China's global influence has rapidly grown, there have been heightened domestic and international expectations for China to assume a more prominent role on the global stage. Simultaneously, doubts have arisen regarding China's status as a developing country, given its increasing material strength, reluctance to shoulder additional international responsibilities, and assertive behaviour in territorial disputes. These developments have generated uncertainties, concerns, and even apprehensions among China's Asian neighbours regarding its role in the regional and international order (Mearsheimer 2010). China's climate change policies are likely affected by an array of international and domestic factors such as energy security (see Conrad 2012), economic growth (see Ong 2012), severe air pollution and environmental problems (see Schreurs 2016), a need to position itself as a strong global power (see Rudd 2020), changes in China's economic development trajectory (see Dong 2017), technological innovation and development in renewable energy (see Heggelund 2021), and changing Chinese identity (Yang 2022).

3   CHINA AND THE UNITED NATIONS SUSTAINABLE DEVELOPMENT GOALS

The United Nations Sustainable Development Goals (SDGs), or Global Goals, are 17 interconnected objectives adopted by all United Nations member states in 2015 as part of the 2030 Agenda for Sustainable Development. They aim to eliminate poverty, protect the environment, and promote well-being worldwide by 2030, covering a range of critical issues. These goals serve as a comprehensive framework for global efforts to create a more equitable and sustainable world (UNDESA 2023). Bierman et al. (2017) assert that the 17 SDGs signify a ground-breaking approach to global governance, as they emphasize the significance of goal-setting within the international framework. This perspective aligns with a broader political discourse, as evidenced by Wood (2011), which has been ongoing concerning the United Nations' role in global governance and the potential for more effective outcomes through negotiations involving smaller groups of countries. Nevertheless, the success of the SDGs as a collective endeavour hinges on various institutional factors, as highlighted by Bierman et al. (2017). These factors encompass the formalization of state commitments, the reinforcement of global governance structures, the localization of global aspirations within national contexts, the integration of sectoral policies, and the maintenance of adaptable governance mechanisms.

Several SDGs are closely intertwined with climate change and environmental preservation. SDG 6 ensures clean water and sanitation, which are vital for environmental health; SDG 7 emphasizes affordable and clean energy, promoting renewables and energy efficiency to reduce emissions; SDG 11 seeks sustainable cities and communities, encouraging eco-friendly urban planning and waste management; SDG 12 underscores responsible consumption and production, advocating for resource efficiency and reduced environmental impact; SDG 13 addresses climate action, necessitating urgent measures to mitigate climate change effects; SDGs 14 and 15 address life below water and on land, preserving marine ecosystems and terrestrial biodiversity; SDG 16 highlights effective environmental governance through strong institutions; and SDG 17 underscores international partnerships for climate and environmental initiatives. Collectively, these SDGs provide a holistic framework for addressing climate change, environmental sustainability, and global development challenges (see UNDESA 2023).

Over several decades, China has employed five-year plans (FYPs) to steer its economic and social development efforts. Although it had already integrated sustainable development principles into its national planning, it did not explicitly synchronize its FYPs with the SDGs until their adoption of the goals. China's 13th FYP (2016–2020) marked the first instance of the SDGs being incorporated (see National Reform and Development Commission [NRDC] 2015). This plan acknowledged the significance of attaining sustainable development and included specific objectives related to various SDGs, such as poverty reduction, environmental conservation, and sustainable urban development. China subsequently continued to harmonize its successive FYPs with the SDGs. For instance, the 14th FYP (2021–2025) underscored the necessity of achieving higher-quality development in alignment with the SDGs, with a particular focus on environmental sustainability, innovation, and social equity (see CSET 2021). According to Sheng (2023), China has demonstrated remarkable progress, especially among developing nations, in advancing the SDGs ahead of schedule. Notably, China achieved the SDG poverty reduction target a decade earlier than anticipated, reflecting its effective strategies in addressing poverty. With a per capita GDP nearing $13,000, China is a testament to economic growth and development.

Furthermore, China has taken proactive steps on the global stage to promote the realization of SDGs. In 2021, the country introduced the Global Development Initiative (GDI), a comprehensive guideline and action plan to foster global consensus and expedite the worldwide implementation of SDGs in harmony with the United Nations' objectives. This initiative outlines eight key priority areas: poverty reduction, food security, pandemic response, development financing, climate change mitigation, digitalization, and green development, which are pivotal to achieving the SDGs (see the State Council Information Office of the PRC 2022). According to Siddharth Chatterjee, United Nations Resident Coordinator in China (2022), the GDI holds significant promise in supporting global recovery efforts and accelerating the attainment of SDGs worldwide.

The GDI has made specific progress regarding climate change and green development. It has focused on strengthening South–South cooperation and empowering developing countries to address climate change. As of May 2023, China has entered into 46 agreements for South–South cooperation on climate change with 39 developing nations. These agreements aim to enhance the climate resilience of these countries by collaborating on the establishment of low-carbon demonstration areas and the execution of assistance programmes in kind (CIKD 2023: 27). For example, the Declaration on China–Africa Cooperation On Combating Climate Change was launched as a three-year climate action plan (see Ministry of Foreign Affairs of the PRC 2021). Similarly, the China-Pacific Island Countries High-level Dialogue[5] on Climate Change was held, and the China-Pacific Island Countries Climate Action Cooperation Centre was established in April 2022 to support island countries in their response to climate change (see Ministry of Foreign Affairs of the PRC 2022a).

---

[5] Diplomatic envoys from Kiribati, Fiji, Tonga, Solomon Islands, the Federated States of Micronesia, Samoa, and Vanuatu were in attendance.

China has collaborated with international organizations and developing nations across Asia, Africa, and Latin America to engage in initiatives to prevent and manage desertification. An example of this is the work done under the BRI to combat desertification across the Silk Road region (see United Nations Convention to Combat Climate Desertification [UNCCD] 2018). Furthermore, China has promoted the application of its advanced expertise and technology in desertification control by encouraging its businesses to participate actively. Additionally, China has supported local reforestation efforts through modernized methods (CIKD 2023: 27). One notable instance of such efforts is establishing the China-Mongolia Cooperation Center for Desertification Control (see CIDCA 2023). Similarly, in November 2022, China, in partnership with the International Bamboo and Rattan Organization, initiated the Bamboo as an Alternative to Plastic Initiative. This initiative also involved launching the Project for the Innovative Development of Bamboo-based Alternatives to Plastics and a research and development project focused on key processing methods for bamboo products (see INBAR 2022). These efforts aimed to investigate eco-friendly and sustainable solutions to address the issue of plastic pollution using natural materials. These are merely singular examples among a much larger trend of initiatives under the GDI aimed at achieving the SDGs and Agenda 2060.

4 BEIJING'S STANCE TOWARDS THE PARIS SUMMIT

During the 21st Conference of Parties of the United Nations Framework Convention on Climate Change (UNFCCC), nearly all nations agreed on the adoption of the Paris Agreement on Climate Change in 2015 (Keohane and Oppenheimer 2016: 142). The Paris Agreement signifies a new era in global endeavours to advance climate mitigation and adaptation. This accord establishes the objective of limiting the global temperature increase to below 2 °C above preindustrial levels, with an even more ambitious aim of not exceeding 1.5 °C (UNFCCC 2016). Notably, the Paris Agreement holds a dual nature, being both legally binding and voluntary. It mandates all participating parties to undertake and communicate ambitious efforts and expects these endeavours to evolve progressively. Furthermore, each signatory must formulate, communicate, and uphold successive nationally determined contributions that they intend to fulfil. Additionally, the agreement stipulates that these contributions should be regularly communicated every five years, with

128   J. DE KLUIVER

the option to enhance their level of ambition (UNFCCC 2016: 2). It is worth acknowledging that the Paris Agreement's success was contingent on the proactive commitments of major greenhouse gas emitters, specifically China, the United States, and the European Union.

According to Jianfeng and Dauvergne (2022: 1), China's role in global climate discussions has shifted from an obstructive force to a proactive advocate for climate initiatives in developing nations. Together with India and Brazil, China was initially perceived as uncooperative and uninterested in leading global efforts to address climate change during the Copenhagen Climate Change Conference in 2009. However, within six years, China transformed by endorsing the 2015 Paris Agreement on climate change, which included a departure from its long-held negotiating positions. In the wake of the Paris Agreement, the primary policy shift has revolved around technological advancements within the power and transportation sectors. Notably, China has strongly emphasized implementing various measures, laws, and policies to foster the growth of renewable energy sources, particularly solar and wind energy. Additionally, China has embraced the concept of "green growth" as a strategic response to the challenges posed by climate change. These concerted efforts have borne fruit, positioning China as a global frontrunner in renewable energy (Heggelund 2021: 9).

According to Yang (2022: 358), China engaged in considerable international cooperation during the Paris Agreement, while concurrently increasing domestic climate action, effectively embracing international climate leadership (Yang 2022: 358). In the lead-up to the Paris Summit, China engaged proactively with major global players and issued three bilateral joint statements on climate change, in collaboration with the United States and the European Union. These statements, which outlined robust commitments and support for transparency measures, set the stage for the success of the Paris Agreement (European Council 2015). For example, China made substantial financial contributions to bolster climate action. At the 2015 China–US Summit and the Paris Summit, President Jinping announced the establishment of the China South–South Climate Cooperation Fund, pledging $3.1 billion to assist developing nations in their climate efforts. This commitment surpassed the US contribution of $3 billion to the United Nations' Green Climate Fund, marking a historic moment in China's role in international climate finance (Yang 2022).

China's ratification of the Paris Agreement in 2016 was notably swift, and it has since made strides to achieve its subsequent goals. China outlined specific, actionable commitments to achieve the goals set by the Paris Agreement. The 13th FYP for controlling greenhouse gas emissions was released after the Paris Summit. The plan references the need to set objectives for energy emissions and consumption and make provisions for the domestic implementation of the Paris Agreement (State Council of the PRC 2016). Reducing coal consumption and air pollution has been central to these efforts. The air pollution action plan of 2013–2017 set clear goals and was ultimately followed by the air pollution action plan to bring back blue skies from 2018 to 2020 (State Council of the PRC 2018). Beijing also advocated implementing a national Emissions Trading System (ETS) as one of several policy instruments to mitigate greenhouse gas emissions. In late 2017, the announcement of a national carbon market was made, initially focusing on the power sector, which is the largest contributor to emissions (Heggelund 2021: 11). The inclusion of greater use of natural gas as opposed to fossil fuels under these action plans significantly improved the air quality in many cities. Beijing is an example of this, given the role that natural gas has played in reducing urban air pollution in the city (see Webster 2023). Natural gas was primarily considered a bridge fuel until technological advances made more renewable sources available. Official updates indicated that, by 2018, China had reduced CO_2 emissions per unit of GDP (carbon intensity) by 45.8% in comparison to 2005 levels (Ministry of Ecology and Environment of the PRC 2019), consequently achieving the 40–45% reduction before 2020 as outlined by the Copenhagen Accord.

Moreover, in 2020, China announced ambitious commitments to cap carbon emissions by 2030 and attain carbon neutrality by 2060 (Jianfeng and Dauvergne 2022: 1). As outlined in its 2014 bilateral agreement with the United States and reflected in its Paris Agreement commitment, it entails reaching an emissions peak by 2030, despite the apparent decline in carbon dioxide emissions from fossil fuel combustion between 2014 and 2015. In 2016, policies were introduced to counter the proliferation of coal-powered plants, but overcapacity and substantial coal subsidies persisted as challenges. At the central level, there was a growing recognition of the imperative to reduce coal consumption post-Paris. Nevertheless, subnational implementation remained challenging, especially in large provinces (Hart et al. 2019). Local-level hurdles included limited understanding of policies and inadequate investment in education and scientific knowledge. Local governments and investors continued to pose challenges in constructing coal-fired power stations post-Paris (see Yuan 2020).

Despite the government's commitments, coal power expansion in China continues unabated. In 2021, China experienced significant power shortages, leading to a major shift in the government's energy priorities. The cost of electricity surged as factories resumed operations to meet the global demand after the COVID-19 pandemic. The war in Ukraine placed further pressure on China's energy security (Hawkins 2023). Russia's invasion of Ukraine in February 2022 caused oil and gas prices to rise and become increasingly volatile as the markets attempted to grapple with the prospect of reduced flows from Russia and the impact of sanctions (Meidan 2022). This heightened instability over energy supplies, in combination with the power shortages in 2021, resulted in a renewed Chinese focus on domestic energy security (Bland 2023). In the first half of 2023, construction began on 37 GW of new coal power capacity, with 52 GW permitted and 41 GW announced, while 8 GW of previously shelved projects were restarted. Of the permitted projects, 10 GW has already entered the construction phase. As a result of this permitting surge, China now has 243 GW of coal-fired capacity permitted and under construction. If the trend persists, including projects in the announcement or pre-permit stages, there could be a total of 392 GW of new coal-fired power capacity in the pipeline. Unless permitting is halted, achieving a reduction in coal-fired power capacity during the 15th FYP will require cancelling already-permitted projects or retiring existing plants prematurely (CREA 2023). However, according to Russel (2023), this development does not necessarily contradict the goal of achieving net-zero carbon emissions by 2060. The author reasons that China's large coal-fired construction programme should be viewed in the context of China's rapid shift to electric vehicles and away from internal combustion engine cars and trucks. The sale of new energy vehicles, encompassing fully electric vehicles and various hybrid models, has been experiencing a significant surge and constituted 36.9% of total vehicle sales in August 2023 (Li and Goh 2023).

5 The Belt and Road Initiative: A Catalyst for Global Economic and Environmental Shifts

China's expansion of the BRI has had far-reaching implications, not only in terms of economic cooperation but also with regard to environmental considerations. As introduced by President Jinping in 2013, the BRI refers to a strategy initiated by China that seeks to connect Asia with Europe and Africa by means of land and maritime networks to increase trade, improve regional integration, and stimulate economic growth. The "Belt" part of the initiative refers to developing a Silk Road Economic Belt. This land-based route stretches through Central Asia and links Europe with Western China. The "Road" refers to a sea-based route that links Africa and Southeast Asia with China's eastern ports relations (Bouey et al. 2020: 1). However, the BRI aims to go beyond simply building infrastructure. It also seeks to include policy alignment, trade streamlining, financial cooperation, and cultural and scientific interchange (Politi 2021). Furthermore, the initiative has inspired other major BRICS countries to formulate their own global initiatives. For instance, India's alternative involves establishing an economic corridor connecting Russia through Iran and Central Asia, while Russia is actively integrating the economies of Central Asia into the framework of the Eurasian Economic Union (see Teo et al. 2019). More recently, India has announced plans for the India–Middle East–Europe Economic Corridor (IMEC), an initiative that could rival the BRI's presence in the region (see Inamdar 2023).

The BRI has grown significantly in scale, and its investment patterns mirror the Chinese model, showcasing noticeable trends related to environmental concerns and a pronounced increase in green project investments. Since 2013, the cumulative involvement in the BRI has reached a substantial $962 billion, roughly $573 billion in construction contracts, and $389 billion in nonfinancial investments. In 2022, new coal-related projects were introduced, including establishing a captive coal-fired power plant and coal-mining operations in Indonesia. Surprisingly, energy-related engagement remained at its lowest levels, amounting to $24.1 billion, despite strong participation in technology manufacturing, such as a significant $7.6 billion investment in a Gigafactory (see Nedopil Wang 2023a). Alarmingly, fossil fuels accounted for approximately 63% of China's BRI energy involvement overseas, particularly through gas pipelines, potentially undermining global climate objectives. However, there is a glimmer of hope, as green energy engagement, encompassing solar, wind, and hydropower, increased by 50% in 2022. Investments surged by \$0.1–\$2.7 billion, and construction projects soared by \$1.9 billion to \$5.3 billion (see Nedopil Wang 2023b). This trend is expected to persist in 2023, as a significant 56% of China's total engagement of \$8.61 billion, encompassing construction and investment in the energy sector in BRI countries during the first half of the year, was allocated to renewable energy projects such as solar, wind, and hydropower (Hayley 2023).

Scholars and civil society organizations have expressed concerns about the BRI's potentially negative environmental impact (see Teo et al. 2019; Coenen et al. 2021). According to Chaudhury (2023), the initiatives carried out as part of the BRI have been detrimental to the environment and have exacerbated environmental challenges in fragile areas by increasing air and water pollution and contributing to water scarcity and soil erosion. The Bar-Boljare motorway in Montenegro that cuts through a UNESCO Biosphere Reserve is an example of this. The highway's construction has resulted in damaged ecosystems and deforestation, increasing the risk of flooding and landslides (see Kajosevic 2021). Hughes (2019) echoes these concerns and reasons that infrastructure projects related to the BRI will inevitably pass through and compromise environmentally sensitive regions and vital biodiversity zones across the globe. The construction of the Batung Toru Power Plant in Indonesia is an example of this, as the construction site is located within the habitat of the endangered Tapanuli orangutan (see Thomas 2023). Furthermore, the BRI's extensive global footprint means that it plays a significant role in achieving international CO_2 emission reduction targets. This implies that even if all non-BRI countries meet their emission reduction goals, failing to adhere to environmental standards within BRI-related projects could still lead to a 2.7 °C increase in global temperatures (see Jun and Zadek 2019).

Balancing environmental protection with economic development as part of the BRI presents a significant challenge due to its extensive reach through various delicate ecosystems. These ecosystems range from Russian forests and steppes to Malaysia's icy Tibetan Plateau and tropical rainforests (see World Wildlife Forum [WWF] 2017). In response to growing international criticism, multiple Chinese ministries jointly introduced policies promoting a "green Belt and Road" or "green Silk Road" to align with the global trend towards environmentally friendly, low-carbon, and sustainable development. This initiative aims to balance environmental protection with economic development along the BRI by implementing specific policies as part of the "green Belt and Road" approach. Examples of these policies include promoting the development of green economies, the incorporation of renewable energy sources in development plans, and the implementation of biodiversity conservation measures (see Nedopil Wang 2023b). Following domestic commitments to establish an ecological civilization,[6] China increasingly incorporates this environmental policy framework into its international endeavours (see Belt and Road Portal 2017).

According to Teo et al. (2019), the BRI should set a positive example in addressing environmental impacts to raise the bar for future global infrastructure projects, ensuring that high environmental standards are inherently part of such schemes. In 2016, President Jinping committed to establishing an environmentally sustainable BRI. This commitment was aligned with the introduction of the ecological civilization concept, which was incorporated into the Constitution of the Communist Party in 2012 (see State Council of the PRC 2017). In 2013, Jinping endorsed this concept and pledged to cooperate on climate change while overseeing China's shift towards renewable energy sources. As part of the greening of the BRI initiative, Chinese financial institutions that are involved in financing BRI projects, including the New Development Bank, Asian Infrastructure Investment Bank, and Silk Road Fund, have striven to incorporate this concept into their investments, thus establishing their environmental guidelines (Politi 2021). However, as opposed to domestic guidelines that must adhere to a stringent regulatory framework to ensure compliance with environmental targets, the BRI is governed by a more flexible approach. Instead of binding regulations, the BRI employs nonbinding, goal-oriented documents (Coenen et al. 2021). Although this does indicate a positive shift, it can be detrimental within the context of the BRI. State-Owned Enterprises (SOEs) remain profit-maximizing entities, and, given their centrality to the BRI, the lack of clear frameworks can be ineffective in incentivizing climate-friendly business practices.

---

[6] The goal of advancing towards an "ecological civilization" is to encourage enhanced preservation of natural resources, promote low-carbon development, increase resource recycling, and nurture an ecological mindset. This policy framework advocates for reductions in carbon emissions and water usage, enhancing water quality and biodiversity protection, responsible land use and development, and integrating environmental principles into industrial structures and urban planning. This concept was introduced into the CCP's constitution in 2012.

134   J. DE KLUIVER

6   CHINA'S CLIMATE CHANGE POSITION WITHIN BRICS

The BRICS alliance, comprising significant emerging economies such as Brazil, Russia, India, China, and South Africa, was established in 2009 as an informal consortium, with Iran, Saudi Arabia, United Arab Emirates, Egypt, and Ethiopia set to join in 2024. Its primary purpose was to serve as a forum for its member nations to counterbalance the global influence of the United States and its Western partners. However, it is important to note that the BRICS group does not possess the formal organizational structure of entities such as the United Nations, World Bank, or the Organization of the Petroleum Exporting Countries (Acharya 2023). Although this can limit the grouping's capacity to produce binding protocols that pertain to climate, it is also likely that the grouping would lack political will. However, given the group's rising international prominence and expanding scope (see Vanek 2023) as an influential partner in this grouping, China can significantly share best practices and encourage member states to seek greener alternatives.

BRICS' self-perception places climate issues prominently on its agenda, at least in theory. As it unfolds within the BRICS agenda, the discourse surrounding the "Common Future", intertwined with a vision that spans generations, fosters a sense of obligation towards advancing the sustainable development paradigm and combatting climate change. The self-perception of the BRICS collective shapes a shared identity often called emerging powers.[7] Within this context, BRICS portrays itself as a group of nations that acknowledges the detrimental consequences of antiquated environmentally insensitive industrialization pathways and aspires to formulate sustainable practices with a profound sense of responsibility (Kıprızlı 2022: 72). In 2009, sustainable development first emerged on the BRICS agenda, signifying a pivotal shift in the economic development paradigm (see BRICS Information Centre 2009). The leaders of BRICS countries also recognized the significance of sustainable and environmentally friendly practices in addressing climate change challenges (see Delhi Declaration 2012). The BRICS leadership outlined their dedication

---

[7] Emerging powers, also known as emerging economies or growing nations, represent countries undergoing a phase of rapid industrialization and substantial economic expansion. They are in the process of shifting from developing economies to becoming influential participants in global affairs, marked by growing political clout, economic prowess, and technological advancements.

to adopting fresh models and strategies to achieve fairer development and foster inclusive global growth by 2013 (see Ethekwini Declaration 2013).

China is a proponent of the need for developing countries to work together to address climate change, while acknowledging historical differences in emissions and responsibilities. BRICS' approach to climate change is heavily guided by the principle of "common but differentiated responsibilities and respective capabilities" (CBDR-RC) (see Johannesburg II Declaration 2023). The principle of CBDR-RC establishes a shared obligation among nations to safeguard the global environment. However, it also sets distinct behavioural standards for developed and developing countries (see United Nations 1992). The interpretation and implementation of the CBDR-RC principle continues to be a contested subject, encompassing its legal standing and capacity to shape the framework of a prospective climate agreement. Additionally, as certain developing nations such as India, China, and Brazil experience economic growth, there have been calls from industrialized nations to progressively harmonize the responsibilities of developed and developing country parties (Leclerc 2021: 78).

China has transitioned from being a relatively passive participant in global climate negotiations to actively assuming a leadership role within BRICS and in the broader international climate arena. This shift has been particularly pronounced since 2015. According to Jianfeng and Dauvergne (2022: 2), China's impact on worldwide climate governance has been more pronounced since 2015. The authors' reason is that China has transitioned from a passive participant to a proactive driver of agendas and a disseminator of climate-related knowledge. This shift is partly attributed to the United States' withdrawal from climate negotiations during Donald Trump's presidency (2017–2021). However, the authors contend that it is even more significant due to China's efforts to chart a climate course for the developing world. To gather greater insights into China's role in BRICS' climate change position and achievements, assessing its actions as BRICS chair in 2022 is useful.[8] The XIV BRICS Summit concept paper identified three critical aspects of global development: multilateralism and macroeconomic coordination, COVID-19

---

[8] The country in the role of chair is tasked with defining the agenda for the BRICS Summit and selecting the main subjects and matters to be deliberated upon during the sessions. This necessitates engaging in discussions with other member states to ensure that their concerns and interests are taken into account.

solidarity and health cooperation, and the development of green and low-carbon economies. The need to actively cultivate a green, low-carbon, and circular economy was emphasized in this document. This entails an unwavering commitment to the full implementation of the Paris Agreement, guided by the principle of CBDR-RC (see Ministry of Foreign Affairs of the PRC 2022b). China convened the BRICS High-level Meeting on Climate Change and the Environment Ministers Meeting to achieve this goal of enhancing communication and coordination among BRICS nations. The objective was to facilitate the exchange of knowledge and technology to promote green and low-carbon transitions (see Ministry of Ecology and Environment of the PRC 2022).

China has championed the concept of South–South cooperation within BRICS. South–South solidarity has been a cornerstone of BRICS (see Johannesburg II Declaration 2023), and China's approach to climate change has aligned with this view. Establishing the South–South cooperation on climate change mechanism in 2011 is an example of this. Since the mechanism's inception from 2011 to 2022, China has earmarked approximately ¥1.2 billion for climate cooperation with countries in the Global South and inked 41 collaboration agreements with 36 nations. Diverse modes of cooperation have been employed, including aiding countries in establishing low-carbon demonstration areas and furnishing them with climate-related resources such as meteorological satellites, solar power generation equipment, lighting systems, electric vehicles, environmental monitoring devices, and eco-friendly cookstoves (see National Development and Reform Commission of the PRC 2022).

According to Jianfeng and Dauvergne (2022: 4), China has been working to establish climate alliances within the Global South, even when faced with significant disagreements among developing nations. This effort serves multiple purposes, including safeguarding its core interests and the CBDR-RC principle and countering the increasing international pressure on China to accelerate and broaden its climate initiatives. While China's growing influence in climate governance does contribute to the Global South's capacity to mitigate and adapt to climate change, it is important to acknowledge that these developments often promote technocratic, incremental, and industry-focused approaches to climate action, which some experts and practitioners consider insufficient within the context of the ongoing climate crisis (Dauvergne 2021).

China's bilateral agreements with fellow BRICS nations in climate and energy cooperation have a cascading impact on the group's climate policies. These agreements often include commitments to renewable energy development, emissions reduction targets, and joint initiatives to combat climate change. The relationship between China and India is an example of this. China and India have cooperated on numerous climate issues such as renewable energy production (see Tagotra 2023) and deforestation (see Mizo 2016). As their economic significance grows, the concept of CBDR-RC is becoming increasingly outdated. In the lead-up to COP21 in Paris in 2015, China and India jointly announced a commitment to more comprehensive measures. For example, in addition to upholding the principles of the Kyoto Protocol, they pledged to collaborate on new technologies and set ambitious NDCs. This collaborative effort played a pivotal role in the subsequent signing of the Paris Agreement. Their potential for cooperation was further underscored at COP26 in Glasgow in 2021, whether it was viewed positively or not. Behind the scenes, both countries advocated for a shift from a commitment to coal phase-out to a coal phase-down, despite objections from civil society and some of the most vulnerable, least-developed countries (Prys-Hansen 2022). This cooperation represents just one example of their long-standing alignment on the issue of coal and extends to renewable energy projects as well. China has invested in and aided the advancement of solar energy initiatives in BRICS member states. For example, China's engagement in India's solar energy industry has established extensive solar farms and exchanged knowledge in solar technology (see Tagotra 2023).

China advocates for a multilateral approach to global climate governance, focusing on upholding the UNFCCC principles. It opposes unilateralism and promotes international cooperation to address climate-related challenges. According to Dong (2017: 1), China has embraced a leading role in the BASIC grouping. The BASIC coalition, comprising Brazil, South Africa, India, and China, has emerged as a significant and unified force in international climate negotiations, particularly within the framework of the COP meetings (Dong 2017: 1). Established in 2009, these BASIC nations have united to champion their shared interests in climate discussions, with a primary focus on principles such as equity and the CBDR-RC concept. Through their collective efforts, the BASIC group has achieved noteworthy milestones at COPs. One noteworthy accomplishment is their advocacy for integrating the CBDR-RC principle into climate agreements, underscoring the historical accountability of developed nations for climate change and the necessity for distinct obligations for developed and developing countries (Olsson et al. 2010). Furthermore, BASIC member nations have played a substantial role in deliberations concerning climate finance, technology transfer, and support for adaptation measures. By presenting a unified front, these countries have heightened their impact, promoting fairness in global climate governance and furthering their shared objectives in addressing the challenges of climate change (Sen 2021).

China's economic power is a formidable force that shapes BRICS' climate policies. Massive investments in renewable energy, clean technologies, and sustainable infrastructure projects reduce its emissions and serve as a model for other BRICS countries. China's investments in renewable energy projects across BRICS can facilitate technology transfer and promote climate-friendly development. China committed to constructing extensive wind and solar power facilities totalling 450 million KW of installed capacity. Furthermore, China plans to vigorously advance the establishment of a domestic carbon market, increase its assistance to fellow developing nations in fostering environmentally friendly and low-carbon energy solutions, and refrain from initiating any fresh coal-fired power ventures abroad (see Ministry of Ecology and Environment of the PRC 2022).

7 Concluding Remarks and Recommendations

China's role in the global fight against climate change is of dual significance, encapsulating the challenges posed by its substantial carbon emissions and the promise inherent in its contributions to renewable energy and sustainable technologies. The shift from a more passive position to one of active global leadership on climate-related issues underscores China's evolving strategy in the face of an increasingly urgent challenge (see Heggelund 2021). With China's carbon emissions surpassing those of the United States and the European Union combined, its climate policies are of global significance and will play a decisive role in determining the achievement of international climate objectives (Lai 2021; Cao et al. 2021). Therefore, a comprehensive examination of China's multifaceted role within the international environmental arena is crucial.

A historical overview of China's climate policy outlines the dynamic and multifaceted nature of China's climate policy development, influenced by a wide array of international and domestic factors. Prior to

2009, its climate policy prioritized economic development over climate concerns. From 2009 to 2011, China shifted towards more active global climate engagement and voluntary carbon intensity reduction. Leadership transitions, especially under Jinping, brought policy fluctuations. Domestic factors such as pollution and energy security played significant roles. China's climate stance is also influenced by broader foreign policy changes reflecting global aspirations, as its rising global influence generates growing international expectations and scrutiny. International and domestic factors such as energy security, economic growth, and pollution shape China's climate policies.

Key findings reveal that China has incorporated the United Nations' SDGs into its national planning, with a notable focus on sustainability and environmental conservation in its FYPs. China has achieved significant progress in SDG-related areas, outpacing many developing nations. On the global stage, it has proactively promoted the SDGs through the GDI, emphasizing climate change mitigation and green development. Additionally, China has actively addressed climate change and environmental issues by collaborating with international organizations and developing nations in Asia, Africa, and Latin America on climate resilience, desertification control, reforestation, and sustainable alternatives to plastics. These efforts underline China's commitment to SDG achievement and Agenda 2060.

Regarding Beijing's stance towards the Paris Summit, China has made a notable transformation from an obstructionist force to a proactive advocate for climate initiatives, particularly after endorsing the 2015 Paris Agreement. This shift has primarily focused on advancements in renewable energy and "green growth" to address climate change. Despite ambitious commitments to cap carbon emissions by 2030 and achieve carbon neutrality by 2060, China faces challenges in reducing coal power expansion, with coal-fired projects continuing in 2023, although this is partially attributed to a shift towards electric vehicles and decreased reliance on internal combustion engine cars and trucks.

Within the BRI, China's investments have grown substantially, with a notable increase in green project funding. However, concerns about the BRI's environmental impact persist, especially with a significant proportion of fossil fuels in the initiative. Nonetheless, investments in renewable energy projects such as solar, wind, and hydropower have increased in recent years, indicating a positive shift. The BRI's extensive reach through sensitive ecosystems poses a significant challenge, requiring a balance between environmental protection and economic development. Initiatives towards a "green Belt and Road" have been introduced, and China's financial institutions involved in BRI projects aim to incorporate environmental guidelines, although these remain nonbinding, goal-oriented documents.

China plays a pivotal role within the BRICS alliance. While the BRICS group lacks a formal organizational structure, China's influence as a member can shape best practices for its partners. The BRICS group places climate and sustainable development high on its agenda, adhering to the CBDR-RC principle in addressing climate change. China has transitioned from passive participation to proactive leadership in climate discussions within BRICS. As the BRICS chair in 2022, China emphasized the need for a green, low-carbon economy and convened meetings to enhance green and low-carbon transitions. China also champions South–South cooperation within BRICS, investing in climate cooperation with countries in the Global South. Bilateral agreements between China and other BRICS nations further influence collective climate policies. China's multilateral approach to global climate governance, its role in the BASIC coalition, and its economic power in renewable energy investments significantly impact BRICS' climate strategies, offering lessons in sustainable development and climate-friendly practices to the group.

Within this context, certain policy recommendations can be put forth to reconcile China's role as both an arsonist and a firefighter. First, China should set more ambitious targets for emissions reduction and significantly increase its investments in renewable energy sources, in line with its commitment to carbon neutrality by 2060. Additionally, China should take more aggressive measures to phase out existing coal-fired power plants and expedite the transition to cleaner energy sources, with a particular emphasis on natural gas and renewables. The transition to electric vehicles is a top priority as China shifts away from internal combustion engine vehicles. To achieve this, the government should implement policies and incentives to encourage the widespread adoption of electric vehicles and build the necessary charging infrastructure.

Furthermore, enhanced transparency in reporting emissions and climate actions is essential to build trust in global climate efforts. Open and accurate data should be a cornerstone of China's climate strategy, ensuring accountability for its commitments. The BRI presents a unique opportunity to address environmental concerns. China can mitigate the initiative's environmental impact by prioritizing green and sustainable projects within the BRI, including increased investments in renewable energy and adherence to strict environmental guidelines.

China should continue to align its climate policies with the SDGs, especially in areas related to environmental conservation and sustainable development. Another significant recommendation is to enhance South–South cooperation on climate change by increasing financial support and knowledge sharing with developing nations in Asia, Africa, and Latin America. In its role within the BRICS alliance, China should actively promote sustainable practices, renewable energy investments, and collective efforts to address climate challenges. Supporting a multilateral approach to global climate governance, particularly within the BASIC coalition, is vital for advancing equitable and effective climate agreements. Finally, China should invest in innovative technologies that drive sustainable and low-carbon economic growth, such as advancements in renewable energy, carbon capture and storage, and energy-efficient infrastructure.

REFERENCES

Acharya, Bhargav. 2023. What is BRICS, Which Countries Want to Join and Why? https://www.reuters.com/world/what-is-brics-who-are-its-mem bers-2023-08-21/.

Belt and Road Portal. 2017. Guidance on Promoting Green Belt and Road. https://eng.yidaiyilu.gov.cn/p/12479.html.

Bierman, Frank, Norich Kanie, and Rakhyun E. Kima. 2017. "Global Governance by Goal-Setting: The Novel Approach of the UN Sustainable Development Goals." *Current Opinion in Environmental Sustainability* 26 (27): 26–31.

Bland, Taylah. 2023. For China, One Overlooked Consequence of the Russia-Ukraine War. https://asiasociety.org/policy-institute/china-one-overlooked-consequence-russia-ukraine-war.

Bradsher, Keith. 2019. Protests Over Incinerator Rattle Officials in Chinese City. https://www.nytimes.com/2019/07/05/world/asia/wuhan-china-pro tests.html

BRICS Information Centre. 2009. Joint Statement of the BRIC Countries' Leaders. http://www.brics.utoronto.ca/docs/090616-leaders.html.

Cao, Jing, Mun S. Ho, Rong Ma, and Fei Teng. 2021. "When Carbon Emission Trading Meets a Regulated Industry: Evidence from the Electricity Sector of China." *Journal of Public Economics* 200: 104470.

Centre for International Knowledge on Development. 2023. Progress Report on the Global Development Initiative 2023. https://www.mfa.gov.cn/eng/top ics_665678/GDI/wj/202306/P020230620670430885509.pdf.

Chaudhury, Dipanjan. 2023. Environmental Damage from Belt and Road Initiative Projects on Rise. https://economictimes.indiatimes.com/news/int ernational/world-news/environmental-damage-from-belt-and-road-initiative-projects-on-rise/articleshow/101715401.cms.

CIDCA (China International Development Cooperation Agency). 2023. China, Mongolia to Jointly Combat Desertification. Accessed: http://en.cidca.gov.cn/2023-09/05/c_917585.htm.

Coenen, Johanna, Simon Bager, Patrick Meyfroidt, Jens Newig, and Edward Challies. 2021. "Environmental Governance of China's Belt and Road Initiative." *Environmental Policy and Governance* 31 (1): 3–17.

Conrad, Bjorn. 2012. "China in Copenhagen: Reconciling the 'Beijing Climate Revolution' and the 'Copenhagen Climate Obstinacy.'" *The China Quarterly* 210: 435–455.

Cox, Samantha. 2022. Poverty Eradication: A Chinese Success Story Ministry of Foreign Affairs of the PRC. http://za.china-embassy.gov.cn/eng/sgxw/202 210/t20221019_10785796.htm.

CREA. 2023. China's New Coal Power Spree Continues as More Provinces Jump on the Bandwagon. https://energyandcleanair.org/publication/chinas-new-coal-power-spree-continues-as-more-provinces-jump-on-the-bandwagon/.

CSET. 2021. Outline of the People's Republic of China 14th Five-Year Plan for National Economic and Social Development and Long-Range Objectives for 2035 https://cset.georgetown.edu/publication/china-14th-five-year-plan/.

Dauvergne, Peter. 2021. "Global Governance and the Anthropocene: Explaining the Escalating Global Crisis." In *Global Governance Futures*, edited by Thoman Weiss and Rorden Wilkinson, 26–39. London: Routledge.

Delhi Declaration. 2012. IV BRICS Summit Delhi Declaration. http://brics2 022.mfa.gov.cn/eng/hywj/ODS/202203/t20220308_10649515.html.

Dong, Liang. 2017. "Bound to Lead? Rethinking China's Role After Paris in UNFCCC Negotiations." *Chinese Journal of Population Resources and Environment* 15 (1): 32–38.

Engels, Anita. 2018. "Understanding How China Is Championing Climate Change Mitigation." *Palgrave Communications* 4 (1): 1–6.

Ethekwini Declaration. 2013. BRICS and Africa: Partnership for Development, Integration and Industrialisation. http://brics2022.mfa.gov.cn/eng/hywj/ODS/202203/t20220308_10649513.html.

European Council. 2015. EU-China Joint Statement on Climate Change. https://www.consilium.europa.eu/media/23733/150629-eu-china-climate-statement-doc.pdf.

Harris, Paul, Chow, Alice, and Karlsson, Rasmus. 2013. China and Climate Justice: Moving Beyond Statism. *International Environmental Agreements: Politics, Law and Economics* 13 (3): 291–305.

Hart, Craig, Zhu, Jiayan, and Ying, Jiahui. 2019. Mapping China's Climate and Energy Policies https://assets.publishing.service.gov.uk/media/5c8f06 c940f0b640da22ec7d/China_Climate_Map_Public_Secured_2019-3-1.pdf.

Hawkins, Amy. 2023. "China Ramps up Coal Power Despite Carbon Neutral Pledges." *The Guardian*, 24 April. https://www.theguardian.com/world/ 2023/apr/24/china-ramps-up-coal-power-despite-carbon-neutral-pledges.

Hayley, Andrew. 2023. "China's Belt and Road Energy Projects Set for Greenest Year, Research Shows." Reuters, 2 August. https://www.reuters.com/bus iness/energy/chinas-belt-road-energy-projects-set-greenest-year-research-2023-08-02/.

Heggelund, Gørild M. 2021. "China's Climate and Energy Policy: At a Turning Point?" *International Environmental Agreements: Politics, Law and Economics* 21 (1): 9–23.

Hughes, Alice C. 2019. "Understanding and Minimizing Environmental Impacts of the Belt and Road Initiative." *Conservation Biology* 33 (4): 883–894.

Inamdar, Nikhil. 2023. Can India-Europe Corridor Rival China's Belt and Road? https://www.bbc.com/news/world-asia-india-66957019.

INBAR (International Network for Bamboo and Rattan). 2022. Statement from the International Network for Bamboo and Rattan. https://apps1.unep.org/ resolutions/uploads/inbarstatementinc1.pdf.

Jianfeng, Jeffrey Q., and Dauvergne, Peter. 2022. China's Rising Influence on Climate Governance: Forging a Path for the Global South. *Global Environmental Change* 73 (1): 1–13.

Johannesburg II Declaration. 2023. BRICS and Africa: Partnership for Mutually Accelerated Growth, Sustainable Development and Inclusive Multilateralism. https://brics2023.gov.za/wp-content/uploads/2023/08/Jhb-II-Dec laration-24-August-2023-1.pdf.

Jun, Ma, and Zadek, Simon. 2019. Decarbonizing the Belt and Road: A Green Finance Roadmap. https://www.climateworks.org/wp-content/upl oads/2019/08/BRI_Exec_Summary_v10-screen_pages_lo-1.pdf.

Kajosevic, Samir. 2021. Montenegro Probes Chinese Highway Builder's Damage to Protected River. https://balkaninsight.com/2021/03/03/montenegro-probes-chinese-highway-builders-damage-to-protected-river/.

Keohane, Robert O., and Oppenheimer, Michael. 2016. "Paris: Beyond the Climate Dead End Through Pledge and Review?" *Politics and Governance* 4 (3): 142–151.

Kıprızlı, Göktuğ. 2022. "Through the Lenses of Morality and Responsibility: BRICS, Climate Change and Sustainable Development." *Uluslararası İlişkiler* 19 (75): 65–82.

144   J. DE KLUIVER

Lai, Hongyi. 2021. "The Evolution of China's Climate Change Policy: International and Domestic Political Economy and a Strategy for Working with China." *Journal of the British Academy* 9 (10): 69–98.

Leclerc, Thomas. 2021. "The Notion of Common but Differentiated Responsibilities and Respective Capabilities: A Commendable But Failed Effort to Enhance Equity in Climate Law." In *Debating Climate Law*, edited by Benoît Mayer and Alexander Zahar, 76–85. Cambridge: Cambridge University Press.

Li, Qiaoyi, and Goh, Benda. 2023. "China Car Sales Return to Growth in August, Tesla Nearly Doubles EV Share." Reuters, 8 September. https://www.reuters.com/business/autos-transportation/china-car-sales-return-growth-aug-tesla-nearly-doubles-ev-share-2023-09-08/.

Li, Xiaoran, Philipp Pattberg, and Oscar Widerberg. 2023. China's Climate Governance from 2009 to 2019: Motivations, Instruments, Actors, and Geopolitics. https://doi.org/10.1080/14693062.2023.2260352?needAccess=true.

Lui, Coco. 2022. China's Covid Zero Policy is Putting Its Climate Action on Ice, Bloomberg, https://www.bloomberg.com/news/features/2022-11-29/china-s-covid-zero-policy-is-putting-its-climate-action-on-ice#xj4y7vzkg.

Mearsheimer, John J. 2010. "The Gathering Storm: China's Challenge to US Power in Asia." *The Chinese Journal of International Politics* 3 (4): 381–396.

Meidan, Michal. 2022. The Russian Invasion of Ukraine and China's Energy Markets. Accessed: https://www.oxfordenergy.org/publications/the-russian-invasion-of-ukraine-and-chinas-energy-markets/#:~:text=The%20invasion%20and%20its%20aftermath,like%20other%20energy%20importing%20countries.

Ministry of Ecology and Environment of the PRC. 2019. UN Climate Action Summit: China's Position and Action. http://english.mee.gov.cn/News_service/news_release/201909/t20190917_734051.shtml/qhs.mee.gov.cn/qqqhzl/201909/t20190917_734045.shtml.

Ministry of Ecology and Environment of the PRC. 2022. Joint Statement issued at the BRICS High-level Meeting on Climate Change. http://brics2022.mfa.gov.cn/eng/hywj/ODMM/202205/t20220529_10694182.html.

Ministry of Foreign Affairs of the PRC. 2021. Declaration on China-Africa Cooperation on Combating Climate Change. https://www.fmprc.gov.cn/mfa_eng/wjdt_665385/2649_665393/202112/t20211203_10461772.html#:~:text=We%20stand%20ready%20to%20deepen,%2C%20ocean%2C%20low%2Dcarbon%20infrastructure.

Ministry of Foreign Affairs of the PRC. 2022a. Cooperation Between China and Pacific Island Countries. https://www.fmprc.gov.cn/eng/wjdt_665385/2649_665393/202205/t20220524_10691917.html#:~:text=In%20April%202022%2C%20the%20China,and%20Low%2Dcarbon%20Development%E2%80%9D.

Ministry of Foreign Affairs of the PRC. 2022b. XVI BRICS Summit Concept Paper on Thematic Issues. http://brics2022.mfa.gov.cn/eng/zg2 022/CPTI/.

Mizo, Robert. 2016. "India, China, and Climate Cooperation." *India Quarterly* 72 (4): 375–394.

Mordor Intelligence. 2023. Asia-Pacific Electric Bus Market Size & Share Analysis—Growth Trends & Forecasts (2023–2028). https://www.mordorintell igence.com/industry-reports/asia-pacific-electric-bus-market.

National Development and Reform Commission of the PRC. 2022. South-South Cooperation on Climate Change Yields Tangible Results. https://en.ndrc. gov.cn/netcoo/achievements/202201/t20220126_1313903.html.

National Reform and Development Commission (NRDC). 2015. The 13th Five-Year-Plan for Economic and Social Development of the People's Republic of China 2016–2020. Central Compilation & Translation Press: Beijing. https://en.ndrc.gov.cn/policies/202105/P020210527785800103339.pdf.

Nedopil Wang, Christoph. 2023a. China Belt and Road Initiative (BRI) Investment Report 2022. https://greenfdc.org/china-belt-and-road-initiative-bri-investment-report-2022/.

Nedopil Wang, Christoph. 2023b. Ten Years of China's Belt and Road Initiative (BRI): Evolution and the Road Ahead. https://greenfdc.org/ten-years-of-chi nas-belt-and-road-initiative-bri-evolution-and-the-road-ahead/.

Olsson, Marie, Aaron Atteridge, Karl Hallding, and Joakim Hellberg. 2010. *Together Alone?: Brazil, South Africa, India, China (BASIC) and the Climate Change Conundrum.* Stockholm Environment Institute.

Ong, Lynette H. 2012. "The Apparent Paradox in China's Climate Policies." *Asian Survey* 52 (6): 1138–1160.

Politi, Alice. 2021. How Green Is China's Belt and Road Initiative? https:// www.iai.it/en/pubblicazioni/how-green-chinas-belt-and-road-initiative.

Prys-Hansen, Miriam. 2022. Competition and Cooperation: India and China in the Global Climate Regime. https://www.giga-hamburg.de/en/publicati ons/giga-focus/competition-and-cooperation-india-and-china-in-the-global-climate-regime.

Raj, Pritish. 2023. China's Coal Phase-Out Plan Still Unclear Amid Ample Reserves: Oxford Institute. https://www.spglobal.com/commodityinsights/ en/market-insights/latest-news/coal/062623-chinas-coal-phase-out-plan-still-unclear-amid-ample-reserves-oxford-institute#:~:text=%22Despite%20i mpressive%20growth%20in%20renewables,coal%20accounting%20for%2056% 25.%22.

Rudd, Kevin. 2020. The New Geopolitics of China's Climate Leadership. https://chinadialogue.net/en/climate/the-new-geopolitics-of-chinas-cli mate-leadership/.

Russel, Clyde. 2023. "China's Huge Coal Plant Building Has Weird Climate Logic." Reuters, 19 September. https://www.reuters.com/world/china/chinas-huge-coal-plant-building-has-weird-climate-logic-russell-2023-09-19/.

Ruwitch, John. 2014. "China Police Detain 24 After Anti-Incinerator Protest." Reuters, 15 September. https://www.reuters.com/article/us-china-protests-idUSKBN0HA01320140915.

Sandalow, David, Michal Meidan, Philip Andrews-Speed, Anders Hove, Sally Qiu, Edmund Downie. 2022. Guide to Chinese Climate Policy 2022, Oxford Institute of Energy Studies. https://chineseclimatepolicy.oxfordenergy.org/.

Schreurs, Miranda A. 2016. "The Paris Climate Agreement and the Three Largest Emitters: China, the United States, and the European Union." *Politics and Governance* 4 (3): 219–223.

Sen, Amiti. 2021. COP26: India, Brazil, China, S. Africa Demand $100-B Climate Finance Support. https://www.thehindubusinessline.com/news/cop-26-india-brazil-south-africa-china-demand-roadmap-for-100-billion-climate-finance-support/article37279999.ece.

Sheng. 2023. China Leads Global Efforts to Realize UN Sustainable Development Goals for 2030. https://www.globaltimes.cn/page/202306/1293251.shtml.

Song-Pehamberger, David. 2023. Green Tech Geopolitics: China and the Global Energy Transition. https://www.foreignbrief.com/analysis/green-tech-geopolitics/.

Standaert, Michael. 2017. As China Pushes Waste-to-Energy Incinerators, Protests Are Mounting. https://e360.yale.edu/features/as-china-pushes-waste-to-energy-incinerators-protests-are-mounting.

State Council Information Office of the PRC. 2022. Global Development Initiative: A Path to Sustainable Development. https://english.scio.gov.cn/in-depth/2022-09/22/content_78433261.htm.

State Council of the PRC. 2016. State Council Notice on the Work Plan for Controlling GHG emissions in the 13th FYP. https://www.gov.cn/zhengce/content/2016-11/04/content_5128619.htm.

State Council of the PRC. 2017. Constitution of the Communist Party of China. http://english.www.gov.cn/news/top_news/2017/09/27/content_281475888488000.htm.

State Council of the PRC. 2018. State Council Notice on the Three-Year Action Plan to Win the Blue Skies Defence War. http://www.legaldaily.com.cn/index_article/content/2018-07/03/content_7585363.htm.

Tagotra, Niharika. 2023. How Renewables are Shaping Policy Brief the India-China Relationship, Planetary Security Initiative. https://www.planetarysecurityinitiative.org/sites/default/files/2023-03/PB_How_renewables_are_shaping_the_India-China_relationship_2eproef.pdf.

Teo, Hoong C., Alex Mark Lechner, Grant W. Walton, Faith Ka Shun Chan, Ali Cheshmehzangi, May Tan-Mullins, Hing Kai Chan, Troy Sternberg, and Ahimsa Campos-Arceiz. 2019. "Environmental Impacts of Infrastructure Development Under the Belt and Road Initiative." *Environment, Policy and Governance* 6 (6): 3–17.

The White House. 2014. Remarks by President Obama and President Xi Jinping in Joint Press Conference. https://obamawhitehouse.archives.gov/the-press-office/2014/11/12/remarks-president-obama-and-president-xi-jinping-joint-press-conference.

Thomas, Vincent Fabian. 2023. Batang Toru Power Plant Project Hits Snag as Orangutan Conflict Worsens. https://asianews.network/batang-toru-power-plant-project-hits-snag-as-orangutan-conflict-worsens/.

UN. 1992. United Nations Framework Convention on Climate Change https://unfccc.int/resource/docs/convkp/conveng.pdf.

UNCCD. 2018. China's Efforts to Halt the Gobi Provide a Blueprint for Tackling Desertification. https://www.unccd.int/news-stories/stories/chinas-efforts-halt-gobi-provide-blueprint-tackling-desertification.

UNDESA. 2023. The 17 Goals. https://sdgs.un.org/goals.

UNFCCC. 2016. Paris Agreement. https://unfccc.int/files/meetings/paris_nov_2015/application/pdf/paris_agreement_english_.pdf.

Vanek, Monique. 2023. Growing BRICS Alliance to Rival G-7-Led World Order. https://www.bloomberg.com/news/newsletters/2023-08-21/global-economy-latest-why-brics-nations-are-challenging-the-west.

Webster, Joseph. 2023. Natural Gas Reduced China's Urban Air Pollution. Can It Be a Global Climate Solution? https://www.atlanticcouncil.org/blogs/energysource/natural-gas-reduced-chinas-urban-pollution-can-it-be-a-global-climate-solution/.

Wood, Peter J. 2011. "Climate Change and Game Theory." *Ecological Economics Reviews* 1219: 153–170.

Wu, Shy. 2023. "A Systematic Review of Climate Policies in China: Evolution, Effectiveness, and Challenges." *Environmental Impact Assessment Review* 99 (4): 1–12.

WWF. 2017. WWF and Greening the Belt and Road Initiative. https://www.wwf.org.hk/en/?19680/Feature-Story-WWF-and-Greening-the-Belt-and-Road-Initiative.

Yang, Jilong. 2022. "Understanding China's Changing Engagement in Global Climate Governance: A Struggle for Identity." *Asia Europe Journal* 20: 357–376.

Yuan, Jiahui. 2020. 2023 Coal-Fired Power Plant Planning and Construction Early Warning Green All Over, Reproduce the Great Leap Forward? https://opinion.caixin.com/2020-03-06/101524628.html.

South Africa's Commitment Towards Climate Security and a Just Transition

Sanet Solomon

1   Introduction

The African continent has been experiencing an unprecedented rate of weather-related events over the past few years. These range from floods, heatwaves, and droughts to wildfires and cyclones that have left millions without water, food, and shelter (CLIMADE Consortium 2023: 3; Greenpeace 2024; BBC World Service Trust 2010: 4). Notable examples include Tropical Cyclone Freddy and the persisting drought on the Horn of Africa. The former lasted 34 days and resulted in 860 fatalities, the destruction of numerous homes and cropland, as well as the outbreak of cholera, whilst the latter impacted over 29 million people in a region reliant on rain-fed agriculture and pastoralism—consequently resulting in crop failure, mass population displacement, and increased malnutrition (Reliefweb 2023). Similar to many African countries, South Africa is no stranger to the adverse effects of the phenomenon, given its climate sensitivity and position as the fifth most water-scarce area in Sub-Saharan Africa. This is further exacerbated by the fact that the country's annual

S. Solomon (✉)
Department of Political Sciences, University of South Africa, Pretoria, South Africa
e-mail: soloms@unisa.ac.za

© The Author(s), under exclusive license to Springer Nature Singapore Pte Ltd. 2024
H. Solomon et al. (eds.), *BRICS and Climate Change*,
https://doi.org/10.1007/978-981-97-5532-5_7

temperature has been twice that of the global average (0.65 °C) over the past 15 years. This has translated into changes in seasonal rainfall patterns as well as an increase in the frequency and extension of dry spells that cause livestock losses and a decrease in crop yields. Thus, these changes not only threaten the country's water resources but also its food security, health, infrastructure, ecosystem, and biodiversity. Between 1990 and 2017, the country experienced over 100 natural disasters that affected 22 million people and resulted in a financial loss exceeding R113 billion (USAID 2023: 1; Scholes and Engelbrecht 2021: 1; Ziervogel et al. 2014: 1–2; Imgamba 2023).

Simultaneously, the country ranks amongst the top 15 global emitters of greenhouse gas and occupies the top position as Africa's largest emitter of greenhouse gas. In 2017, its net carbon emissions were estimated at 512 metric tonnes of CO_2. This is a result of the country's dependence on coal for energy generation as an affordable and consistent energy source (USAID 2023: 1; Imgamba 2023; Oxfam 2009: 14, 15; Tladi et al. 2024: 1). Between 2000 and 2020, the energy sector's emissions increased by 2.2% (Thambiran and Perumal 2023: 7). It is worth noting that the national power utility, Eskom, generates 95% of the country's electricity. Seventy-three percent of the electricity is generated using coal, whilst liquid fuels account for the remaining 27% (Nguyen 2023; South African Government 2014). Coal is not only essential for energy generation but also for other sectors such as iron and steel production, cement manufacturing, and the industrial sector. In 2020, it contributed R130.57 billion to the total mining revenue of R608.99 billion, making it the third-largest employer in the mining sector (Department of Mineral Resources and Energy 2022). This is particularly important, given the country's staggering unemployment rate of 41.1% in the fourth quarter of 2023 (Statistics South Africa 2024). In the same year, the country was listed as one of the most unequal societies globally, necessitating a need to prioritize development that may translate into poverty reduction but consequently increase greenhouse gas emissions. In unison, the country also has an obligation to the United Nation Framework Convention on Climate Change (UNFCCC), which focuses on mitigating global warming and climate change. These conflicting priorities place the country in a peculiar position as it requires a balancing of domestic interest with climate security and a just transition (Valodia 2023; Department of Energy, 2023: 21). All this warrants further analysis of the country's strategy and approach to balancing these competing interests.

2   Just Energy Transition

The notion of a just energy transition dates to the 1970s union movement in North America and stems from the concern of industrial transformation and workers' rights. Thereafter, it spread to other branches of trade unionism in the 1990s and eventually contributed towards the establishment of a Just Transition Coalition. The term was subsequently enriched in international meaning over a period of 30 years and adopted by the 2015 Paris Agreement and the 2030 Sustainable Development Goals. Over time, it was also linked to political power struggles and issues of development, which necessitate holistic assessments, as these transitions may have different effects on developed and developing countries (Sun et al. 2023: 1; Wang and Lo 2021: 1).

Conventionally, just transitions are associated with a gradual shift from fossil fuels towards renewable energy sources such as wind and solar. This process is often aimed at promoting sustainable human development, reducing pollution, and improving environmental quality. It also seeks to contribute towards the advancement of sustainable development goals (Wang and Lo 2021: 1).

During the process, developing countries may experience greater challenges than their developed counterparts, given their dependence on fossil fuels and traditional biomass. Thus, making them more susceptible to the poverty trap should they lack access to modern energy services. These transitions can also result in social and economic changes such as employment changes or possible reductions in income. Those employed in fossil fuel industries might encounter challenges such as finding alternative employment opportunities. Additionally, the loss of employment might also affect the local tax base and have an adverse impact on other industries such as transportation and waste management. The transition to ecological goods may also result in an increase in the price of goods (Sun et al., 2023: 1–2; Wang and Lo 2021: 1). Contrary to this, a just transition could usher in green jobs, minimize deforestation and wasteful production practices, and advance the attainment of the sustainable development goals (United Nations Development Programme 2022).

The importance of a just transition to climate change was initially stressed by the 2011 South African National Climate Change Response White Paper. In the same year, the country introduced its Renewable Energy Independent Power Producers Procurement Programme

(REIPPPP), which sought to undertake signed Power Purchasing Agreements (PPA) for a duration of 20 years. This programme encouraged the participation of small and medium enterprises (SMEs) with some capacity for solar, wind, and hybrid storage solutions. The need for a just transition was later reemphasized by the National Development Plan, which highlighted the country's contribution to the phenomenon and the need to shift towards a climate resilient economy (Presidential Climate Commission 2022: 6; National Development Plan 2011: 23, 38; Naidu 2023; Irena 2021: 1; McDaid et al. 2016: 5).

This was followed by the adoption of the 2018 National Strategy for the Electricity Sector, the establishment of the Presidential Climate Change Commission in 2019, and the Nationally Determined Contribution (NCD) under the Paris Agreement (Naidu 2023). The Climate Change Bill was introduced to the National Assembly in February 2022 and adopted by October 2023. The bill outlines the country's response to climate change and seeks to serve as a comprehensive legislative document encouraging an effective climate change response for the country. It seeks to serve as a catalyst for a transition to a green, low-carbon and climate resilient economy (Climate Change Bill 2022: 11; University of Cape Town and the African Climate and Development Initiative 2022: 4). Similarly, in 2022, Cabinet endorsed the Just Transition Framework, which is a nexus between climate change and development that seeks to support the country's broader goal of redesigning the economy to benefit more citizens. Thus, addressing the country's response to climate change, the reduction of greenhouse gas emissions, and the promotion of healthy communities. Whilst it does not explicitly work with climate migration and adoption policies, it focuses on the social and economic impacts of the policies (Naidu 2023; Presidential Climate Commission 2023 5). This signals commitment towards climate security. It is worth noting that the country's Just Transition Partnership with Germany, France, the United Kingdom, the United States, and the European Union is worth $8.5 billion. This amount comprises loans, grants, blended financing, and public–private partnerships (Institute for Economic Justice 2022: 1; Presidency of South Africa 2023: 19). One fifth of the ledge amount will be accessible in grant form. The purpose of the plan is to transition the country away from fossil fuels towards renewable energy options that would create employment opportunities for some previously employed in the coal sector (Guarascio 2022).

This JET also raises interesting questions for provinces such as Mpumalanga, where coal contributes 68% towards employment in an area plagued with high levels of poverty and unemployment. A survey conducted by the United Nations Development Programme in Sasol-burg found that 56.7% of the sample had not heard of JET, whilst 33.2% of participants indicated that they would move if the coal mines in their area were shut down. Members of the community feared job losses due to JET and have considered the likelihood that the transition would not offer sufficient alterative employment. Contrary to this, some believe that the transition would alleviate health challenges such as respiratory illnesses caused by ash. Amid all of this, it should be noted that mines contributed to infrastructure development such as schools and clinics amongst other facilities that benefit communities (Smit 2023a). Whilst some experts welcome these changes due to the continued coal power station breakdowns, others caution against these plans, given the country's high debt-to-GDP ratio of 74% for 2023–2024 (Reuters 2022; National Treasury 2024: 71). The former is rooted in the fact that the country experienced over 100 days of power outages in 2022, whilst the latter is rooted in the fact that the country's debt-to-GDP ratio increased from 49% in 2018 to 74% in 2024. Consequently, the International Monetary Fund has recommended implementing a legislative debt ceiling. It is recommended that countries maintain a debt-to-GDP ratio of 44% to ensure that governments avoid fiscal slippages (Winker 2022; Van Niekerk 2024; Mutizwa 2024).

3   South Africa's Alternative Energy Solutions

South Africa has long history of coal mining that dates back to 1875. To date, the country is globally ranked amongst the top 10 coal producers, with fields in the Free State, Witbank, the Waterberg, and the Highveld, amongst others. Coal has been the nation's preferred energy source, given its vast reserves and the affordability and dependability of this fossil fuel (Tladi et al. 2024: 2). However, over time, this form of energy generation has taken a toll on the country's water resources and biodiversity. This is particularly true in the Highveld grassland and bushveld where mining ash and waste is occasionally disposed of unsustainably. These practices subsequently result in rivers and water resources becoming acidic waste streams (Smit 2023b: 26).

Whilst the global utilization of renewable energy has increased by 60% since 2016, the adoption of alternative energy sources has been slower within the South African context, as the country's energy system is largely dependent on power generated from fossil fuels (Okunlola et al. 2019: 8). Over the past few years, the power utility, Eskom, has been struggling to meet the country's energy demands. This resulted in rolling power outages that cost the country between R59 and R118 billion in 2019 (*Mail & Guardian* 2021). This has also ushered in relevant conversations and the implementation of alternative energy solutions that are environmentally friendly. Hence, renewable energy now contributes 25% towards the country's energy generation capacity. The north-western part of the country has attracted several independent power producers who have ventured into solar farming. This is essentially done through the utilization of photovoltaic (PV) panels and concentrated solar power. In October 2023, South Africa had 51 active solar power stations adding renewable energy into the power grid. This form of energy generation is particularly attractive given the vast number of sunny days the country experiences (Ndlovu 2024; Labuschagne 2023a). Research conducted by the CSIR suggests that this industry could have conservatively created 33,000–35,000 jobs between 2022 and 2023 (Solar Power Systems 2021). Similarly, the utilization of wind energy has been favourable, as the country has 34 operational wind farms primarily located in the windy Cape provinces (Labuschagne 2023b). It is worth mentioning that both of these forms of renewable energy sources work well in South Africa given its climatic advantage. However, these need to be used in addition to traditional energy generation methods to ensure that power providers can meet domestic energy needs until a more sustainable option is available (Grobler 2023).

4   Balancing Domestic Interest with Climate Responsibility: The Exploration of Natural Gas Off the Coast of South Africa

In February 2019, French-owned company Total discovered gas 175 km off the coast of South Africa (Total 2019). The field is estimated to hold one billion barrels of gas, which could be converted into electricity or petrol at the gas-to-fuel refinery in Mossel Bay. This could translate into 28% corporate tax for the South African government and an additional 5% on the sale of oil and gas. Moreover, this would reduce the amount of oil the country would need to import (Wasserman 2019) and contribute towards job creation (Cliffe Dekker Hoffmeyer 2021). Nevertheless, local scientists have cautioned against seismic activity, labelling it "short-sighted, nationalistic and environmentally irresponsible" (Carnie 2022). They believe that it would increase the release of greenhouse gas into the atmosphere, threaten marine life, and cause marine noise and possible oil spills. Whilst environmental activists managed to halt this seismic blasting in 2021, the South African government granted Total permission to continue its oil and gas drilling in 2023 (Carnie 2022; Roelf 2023).

Despite the adoption of a climate change policy, there is a perception that the country would not be stopping the oil and gas operations. This directly contradicts its stance embracing a just transition. The Minister of Mineral and Energy Resources has been quoted stating that nongovernmental organizations were inhibiting economic development. He also stresses that climate change standards are set by developed countries and imposed on developing countries (Bradstock 2023; Burkhardt 2023). This stance aligns with the belief that an evaluation of carbon footprints reveals the power imbalances that exist between the developed and developing world. Research by Oxfam revealed that the top 1% of global economies had a carbon footprint 175 times higher than the poorest 10% of countries, thus corroborating the Minister's stance (Madonsela 2023: 53–54). Nevertheless, his stance reiterates the country's conflicting position on balancing domestic interests with climate security and a just transition.

5   Green Hydrogen as an Alternative Sustainable Energy Source

In 2021, the Department of Science and Innovation released the *Hydrogen Society Roadmap for South Africa 2021*. This document outlined the country's hydrogen ambition as aligned to its decarbonization goals and highlights the opportunity to remodel the country's industrial sector utilizing hydrogen to create a cohesive domestic value chain. The strategy outlines the government's desire to create a local demand for green hydrogen and hydrogen-related products (Salma and Tsafos 2022).

Hydrogen is a storage medium, whilst green hydrogen is a zero-emission fuel produced through electrolysis using renewable energy sources. It is labelled "green" due to its use of renewable energy such as wind and solar (BusinessTech, 2023). Its by-product is oxygen (Lawlor and Booth 2021). It can be used to produce low-carbon alternative fuels in the aviation sector; to produce ammonia, fertilizers, and synthetic acid; to convert trucks from diesel to fuel cell trucks; and in desalination plants, storage facilities, and the production of green ammonia (Salma and Tsafos 2022). It is believed that South Africa could become a leading green hydrogen producer given its climatic advantage. Should it actively pursue this route, the country could capture 4% of the global market share by 2050, add $4–9 billion to its GDP, create 380,000 jobs by 2050, cement itself as an investment destination, and take the lead in areas such as transportation and heavy industries. Moreover, it would enable the country to decarbonize its economy and achieve its goal of a just transition (BusinessTech 2023; Salgmann et al. 2023).

The CEOs of Sasol and Toyota South Africa have embarked on a joint venture in the development of a green hydrogen mobility corridor. This requires Sasol to create green hydrogen, which Toyota would use to develop zero-emission hydrogen fuel cell cars. The Toyota Mirai, which takes five minutes to refuel, is an example of their first hydrogen collaboration (Lawlor and Booth 2021).

However, as with other green alternatives, green hydrogen also has shortcomings. First, hydrogen is a highly volatile and flammable element, which would require manufactures to implement safety measures to prevent leaks and explosions. Second, it is challenging to store and transport, as it needs to be stored at -252.8 °C in liquid form, and approximately 10% of the energy is lost during this phase. In addition, 50% of the energy is lost when hydrogen is converted to electricity inside a fuel cell. Third, the production thereof requires high energy consumption. Green hydrogen in particular requires more energy than other fossil fuels. The World Economic Forum has stated that 30–35% of the energy used to produce green hydrogen is lost during the electrolysis process. More research needs to be conducted to make hydrogen energy more efficient. Despite this, countries such as Germany and the United Kingdom have embarked on the development of low-carbon hydrogen industries (Wu 2022). South Africa, Egypt, Kenya, Mauritania, Morocco, Namibia, Ethiopia, and Angola have also created a green hydrogen alliance aimed at providing each other with technical support, funding, and market access to partners. With time, this alliance could yield favourable results that translate into a just transition (Marwala 2023).

6 Resistance Towards Climate Adaptation and Mitigation

The International Energy Agency (IEA) has anticipated that coal consumption will remain largely unchanged until 2025 despite global investments in renewable energy infrastructure reaching $500 billion per annum. This is directly linked to countries' challenges with aligning their decarbonization goals with national interests. This hesitance is further exacerbated by scholarly research that documents the risks associated with current just transitions, as outlined in Sect. 2 of this chapter. These transitions can create economic risks and energy injustices for coal-producing countries such as South Africa, which is dependent on coal for its energy generation and 5% of its national GDP. Simultaneously, the country has embarked on a race against climate change (Mirzania et al. 2023: 2, 12). This places it in a distinctive position to balance its domestic interest with climate commitments. To understand this, one needs to examine the South African context.

South Africa has a difficult past marked by social and environmental injustices. Post-1994, the government inherited a fossil-based energy system and a lack of environmental governance that continued the cycle of poverty, inequality, and pollution in the country (Mirzania et al. 2023: 2). The government implemented two energy subsidy policies to redress these challenges. The Free Basic Electricity subsidy was introduced in 2003 followed by the Free Basic Alternative Electricity subsidy in 2007. These subsidies are dated and no longer provide an accurate reflection of the country's energy needs. Therefore, updated solutions are needed to resolve these energy needs as the continued power outages are negatively impacting productivity (Swilling et al. 2023: 24–25). Research suggests that building new wind and solar energy would be 40% more affordable than new coal-based energy plants, thus ensuring that the country aligns with its carbon emission plans (Centre for Sustainability Transitions and the Blended Finance Taskforce 2022: 8). Moreover, the country would need $250 billion in climate finance to successfully transition its energy system over the next three decades. This is an enormous undertaking, as the South African economy was worth $175 billion in 2022 (Centre for Sustainability Transitions and the Blended Finance Taskforce 2022: 15). This would translate to the creation of 50,000 jobs, 30% of which would be in the manufacturing of components and systems. The final plan needs to be people-centred for it to be labelled "just". It should translate into good health outcomes, quality education, and poverty alleviation (Centre for Sustainability Transitions and the Blended Finance Taskforce 2022: 10). Additionally, the country needs to work towards resolving its existing governance challenges, corruption, and its ailing fleet of power stations (Swilling et al. 2023: 10). It could also make positive strides towards social and economic progress, should it work towards achieving a capable state that is autonomous from ideological interest and focused on development challenges.

REFERENCES

Bradstock, Felicity. 2023. New Oil and Gas Discoveries Propel South Africa's Energy Renaissance. https://oilprice.com/Energy/Crude-Oil/New-Oil-And-Gas-Discoveries-Propel-South-Africas-Energy-Renaissance.html

Burkhardt, Paul. 2023. South African Minister Says US-Funded NGOs Stifling Development. https://www.bloomberg.com/news/articles/2023-10-10/south-african-minister-says-us-funded-ngos-stifling-development

Carnie, Tony. 2022. Stop Oil and Gas Exploration Madness, SA Scientists Urge Government. https://www.dailymaverick.co.za/article/2022-03-30-stop-oil-and-gas-exploration-madness-sa-scientists-urge-government/

Cliffe Dekker Hoffmeyer. 2021. The Brulpadda and Luiperd Gas Discoveries: A Game Changer for South Africa's Petroleum Offshore Exploration. https://www.cliffedekkerhofmeyr.com/en/news/publications/2021/Oil-Gas/oil-and-gas-alert-10-february-The-Brulpadda-and-Luiperd-gas-discoveries-A-game-changer-for-South-Africas-petroleum-offshore-exploration.html

CLIMADE Consortium. 2023. Summary for Policymakers: COP28. In *Climate Change and Epidemics 2023. CLIMADE Consortium Report*. Core writing team, ed. T. de Oliveira and C. Baxter, 1–23. Stellenbosch, South Africa: CLIMADE. https://doi.org/10.25413/sun.24599043].

Climate Change Bill. 2022. Republic of South Africa Climate Change Bill. https://www.gov.za/sites/default/files/gcis_document/202203/b9-2022.pdf

Cock, J. 2019. *Resistance to Coal and the Possibilities of a Just Transition in South Africa*. SWOP Working Paper 13. University of Witwatersrand.

Department of Energy. 2023. South African Coal Sector Report. https://www.energy.gov.za/files/media/explained/south-african-coal-sector-report.pdf

Grobler, Leenta. 2023. "Renewable Energy to Save South Africa from Energy Crisis." News24. https://www.news24.com/news24/partnercontent/renewable-energy-to-save-south-africa-from-energy-crisis-20230316-2

Imgamba, Joan. 2023. Climate Change in South Africa: 21 Stunning Facts About South Africa's Climate Breakdown. https://www.greenpeace.org/africa/en/blogs/54171/climate-change-in-south-africa-21-stunning-facts-about-south-africas-climate-breakdown/

Irena. 2021. Scaling Up Renewable Energy Investment in South Africa. Accessed 2 May 2024, from https://coalition.irena.org/-/media/Files/IRENA/Coalition-for-Action/Coalition-for-Action-BusinessInvestors-GroupScalingRenewableEnergyInvestmentSouth-AfricaDec2021.pdf

Labuschagne, Hanno. 2023a. All 51 Solar Farms Providing Power to South Africa. Accessed 3 May 2024, from https://mybroadband.co.za/news/energy/509176-all-51-solar-farms-providing-power-to-south-africa.html

Labuschagne, Hanno, 2023b. All 34 Wind Farms Providing Power to South Africa. Accessed 3 May 2024, from https://mybroadband.co.za/news/energy/508804-all-34-wind-farms-providing-power-to-south-africa.html

Lawlor, Patrick, and Ingrid Booth. 2021. Hydrogen Production in South Africa—The Fuel of a Green Future? Accessed 3 May 2024, from https://www.investec.com/en_za/focus/beyond-wealth/hydrogen-the-fuel-of-south-africas-green-future.html

Madonsela, Sanet. 2023. Climate-Security and the Anthropocene: The Case of Mali. In *African Security in the Anthropocene*, ed. Hussein Solomon and Jude Cocodia. Springer.

Marwala, Tshilidzi. 2023. "A Hydrogen Economy May Fuel a More Solid Development Drive in Southern Africa." *Daily Maverick*, 10 July. https://www.dailymaverick.co.za/opinionista/2023-07-10-a-hydrogen-economy-may-fuel-a-more-solid-development-drive-in-southern-africa/

McDaid, Liziwe, Jeeten Moran, and Sizwe Manqele. 2016. Renewable Energy Independent Power Producer Procurement Programme Review 2016: A Critique of Process of Implementation of Socio-Economic Benefits Including Job Creation.

Mirzania, Pegah, Joel A. Gordon, Nazmiye Balta-Ozkan, Ramazan Caner Sayan, and Lochner Marais. 2023. Barriers to Powering Past Coal: Implications for a Just Energy Transition in South Africa. *Energy Research & Social Science*. https://doi.org/10.1016/j.erss.2023.103122

Mutizwa, Godfrey. 2024. "IMF Says South Africa Needs a Debt Ceiling as Public Debt Spirals." CNBC Africa, 18 April. https://www.cnbcafrica.com/2024/imf-says-south-africa-needs-a-debt-ceiling-as-public-debt-spirals/

Naidu, Ronda. 2023. "South Africa Puts Labor Market at the Centre of a Just Energy Transition." Development Aid, 20 December. https://www.developmentaid.org/news-stream/post/172398/south-africa-just-energy-transition

National Development Plan. 2011. National Development Plan 2023: Our Future—Make It Work. https://www.gov.za/sites/default/files/Executive%20Summary-NDP%202030%20-%20Our%20future%20-%20make%20it%20work.pdf

National Treasury. 2024. 2024 Budget Review Government Debt and Contingent Liabilities. https://www.treasury.gov.za/documents/National%20Budget/2024/review/Chapter%207.pdf

Ndlovu, Nkosinathi. 2024. "Utility Scale: 10 Biggest Solar Projects in South Africa." Tech Central, 28 March. https://techcentral.co.za/10-biggest-solar-projects-in-south-africa/242137/

Nguyen, Lei. 2023. Understanding the Energy Crisis in South Africa. https://earth.org/energy-crisis-south-africa/

Okunlola, Ayodeji, David Jacobs, Ntombifuthi Ntuli, Ruan Fourie, Sylvia Borbonus, Laura Nagel, and Sebastian Helgenberger. 2019. Future Skills and Job Creation Through Renewable Energy in South Africa: Assessing the Co-benefits of Decarbonising the Power Sector. https://www.cobenefits.info/wp-content/uploads/2019/03/COBENEFITS-Study-South-Africa-Employment.pdf

Oxfam. 2009. Climate Change, Development and Energy Problems in South Africa: Another World Is Possible. https://www.preventionweb.net/files/11490_oiclimatechangesouthafrica1.pdf

Presidential Climate Commission. 2022. A Framework for a Juts Transition in South Africa. https://pccommissionflow.imgix.net/uploads/images/A-Just-Transition-Framework-for-South-Africa-2022.pdf

Presidential Climate Commission. 2023. Reflections Key Outcomes from COP28. https://pccommissionflo.imgix.net/uploads/images/Key-Outcomes-from-COP28-and-PCC-Participation-002Newsletter.pdf

Reliefweb. 2023. Rising Climate Death Toll in Africa Underscores Urgency for COP28 Action. https://reliefweb.int/report/world/rising-climate-death-toll-africa-underscores-urgency-cop28-action

Reuters. 2022. "World Bank Approves $1 bln Loan to Help South Africa Tackle Power Crisis." Reuters, 25 October. https://www.reuters.com/world/africa/world-bank-approves-1-bln-loan-help-south-africa-tackle-power-crisis-2023-10-25/

Roelf, Wendell. 2023. "South Africa Gives Go-Ahead for Total Energies to Drill Offshore." Reuters, 2 October. https://www.reuters.com/business/energy/south-african-minister-gives-green-light-totalenergies-drilling-off-cape-coast-2023-10-02/

Salgmann, Rico, Maximilian Weidenhammer, and Dominik Englert. 2023. "Green Shipping Fuels Made in South Africa." World Bank Blogs, 29

November. https://blogs.worldbank.org/en/transport/green-shipping-fuels-made-south-africa#:~:text=The%20Saldanha%20steel%20plant%20is,like%20transportation%20and%20heavy%20industries

Salma, Tani, and Nikos Tsafos. 2022. South Africa's Hydrogen Strategy. https://www.csis.org/analysis/south-africas-hydrogen-strategy

Scholes, Robert, and Francois Engelbrecht. 2021. Climate Impacts in Southern Africa During the 21st Century. Report for the Centre for Environmental Rights, September. https://cer.org.za/wp-content/uploads/2021/09/Climate-impacts-in-South-Africa_Final_September_2021.FINAL_.pdf?_ga=2.7071218.1741064849.1714073010-457181587.1714073010

Shields, Michelle. 2024. "What Climate Change Means for South Africa and Its People." UCT News, 11 March. https://www.news.uct.ac.za/article/-2024-03-11-what-climate-change-means-for-south-africa-and-its-people

Smit, Simone. 2023a. Including Diverse Insights to Increase the Justice of the Just Energy Transition—Collective Intelligence and Climate Change. https://www.undp.org/south-africa/blog/including-diverse-insights-increase-justice-just-energy-transition-collective-intelligence-and-climate-change

Smit, Danie. 2023b. Alternative Sources of Energy for South Africa in Various Shades of Green. Accessed 3 May 2024, from https://www.up.ac.za/media/shared/Legacy/sitefiles/file/44/1026/2163/8121/alternativesourcesofenergyforsouthafricainvariousshadesofgreen.pdf

Solar Power Systems. 2021. New Report Shows That Job Creation in the PV Sector Is Inevitable. https://solagroup.co.za/new-report-shows-that-job-creation-in-the-pv-sector-is-inevitable/

South African Government. 2014. National Climate Change Response White Paper. https://www.gov.za/sites/default/files/gcis_document/201409/nationalclimatechangeresponsewhitepaper0.pdf

Special Reports. 2021. "The Quest for Renewable and Sustainable Energy." *Main & Guardian*, 26 March. https://mg.co.za/special-reports/2021-03-26-the-quest-for-renewable-and-sustainable-energy/

Statistics South Africa. 2024. Media Release: Quarterly Labour Force Survey (QLFS)—Q4: 2023. https://www.statssa.gov.za/publications/P0211/Media%20release%20QLFS%20Q4%202023.pdf

Sun, Zhonggen, Furong Zhang, Yifei Wang, and Ziting Shao. 2023. "Literature Review and Analysis of the Social Impact of a Just Energy Transition." *Frontiers in Sustainable Food Systems* 7: 1119877.

Swilling, Mark Jacob, M. McCallum, Richards William, Nico D. Cloete, and Leon Jentel. 2023. Special Report 1 Geopolitical Energy Futures October 2023. Southern African Institute of International Affairs.

Thambiran, Tirusha, and Sarisha Perumal. 2023. National Greenhouse Gas Inventory Summary. In *South Africa's 5th Biennial Update Report (BUR-5) to the United Nations Framework Convention on Climate change (UNFCCC).*

https://unfccc.int/sites/default/files/resource/Fifth%20Biennial%20U
pdate%20Report%20%20of%20South%20Africa%20Submission%20to%20U
NFCCC.pdf

Tladi, Bonolo, Njabulo Kambule, and Lee-Ann Modley. 2024. Assessing the Social and Environmental Impacts of the Just Energy Transition in Komati, Mpumalanga Province, South Africa. *Energy Research & Social Science.* https://doi.org/10.1016/j.erss.2024.103489

Total. 2019. Total Makes Significant Discovery and Opens A New Petroleum Province Offshore South Africa. Accessed 3 May 2024, from https://totalenergies.com/media/news/press-releases/total-makes-sig nificant-discovery-and-opens-new-petroleum-province-offshore-south-africa

United Nations Development Programme. 2022. What Is Just Transition? And Why Is It Important? Accessed 3 May 2024 from https://climatepromise. undp.org/news-and-stories/what-just-transition-and-why-it-important

University of Cape Town and the African Climate and Development Initiative. 2022. Comments on the Climate Change Bill. Accessed 2 May 2024, from https://acdi.uct.ac.za/sites/default/files/content_migration/acdi_uct_ac_ za/1205/files/Climate%2520Change%2520Bill%2520Comments_Final.pdf

USAID. 2023. South Africa: Climate Change Country Profile. Accessed 25 April 2024, from https://www.usaid.gov/sites/default/files/2023-11/2023-USAID-South-Africa-Climate-Change-Profile.pdf

Valodia, Imraan. 2023. "South Africa Can't Crack the Inequality Curse. Why, and What Can Be Done." Wits News, 15 September. https://www.wits.ac. za/news/latest-news/opinion/2023/2023-09/south-africa-cant-crack-the-inequality-curse-why-and-what-can-be-done.html#:~:text=According%20to% 20the%20most%20recent,value%20between%200%20and%201

Van Niekerk, Ryk. 2024. "South Africa Urgently Needs a Debt Ceiling." Moneyweb, 26 February. https://www.moneyweb.co.za/news/economy/ south-africa-urgently-needs-a-debt-ceiling/

Wang, Xinxin, and Kevin Lo. 2021. "Just Transition: A Conceptual Review." *Energy Research & Social Science* 82 (102291). https://doi.org/10.1016/j. erss.2021.102291

Wasserman, Helena. 2019. "Everything You Need to Know About South Africa's Massive Gas Find." News24, 15 February. https://www.news24.com/new s24/bi-archive/impact-of-brulpadda-2019-2

Winker, Hartmut. 2022. "South Africa Could Produce a Lot More Renewable Energy: Here's What it Needs." *The Conversation*, 12 July. https://theconver sation.com/south-africa-could-produce-a-lot-more-renewable-energy-heres-what-it-needs-185897

Wu, Tin Lok. 2022. "Examining the Pros and Cons of Hydrogen Energy." Earth.org, 25 June. https://earth.org/pros-and-cons-of-hydrogen-energy/

Ziervogel, Gina, Mark New, Emma Archer van Garderen, Guy Midgley, Anna Taylor, Ralph Hamann, Sabine Stuart-Hill, Jonny Myers, and Michele Warburton. 2014. "Climate Change Impacts and Adaptation in South Africa." *WIREs Climate Change* 5: 605–620. https://doi.org/10.1002/wcc.295

BRICS Plus and Climate Change

Hussein Solomon⦿

1 Introduction

The twenty-first century will be characterized by two major developments. The first relates to the existential crisis confronting humanity as a consequence of climate change. The world is warming faster than at any other point in human history, with catastrophic implications for plant and animal life on the planet. According to the United Nations, the primary drivers of such global warming are the 90% carbon dioxide and 75% greenhouse gas emissions, which are produced by fossil fuels—coal, oil, and gas are the primary challenge here (UN Climate Action 2024).

The grave impact on human life is considered to be palpable. According to the World Health Organization (WHO), the deleterious impact of climate change is mostly felt by those living in areas highly vulnerable to climate change. These are generally the poor and marginalized and total 3.6 billion people. Moreover, a further 250,000 people per year will die between 2030 and 2050 as a result of diarrhoea, malaria, malnutrition, and heat stress as a direct result of climate change. The WHO estimates that, by 2030, an additional $4 billion per annum would

---

H. Solomon (✉)
University of the Free State, Bloemfontein, South Africa
e-mail: solomonh@ufs.ac.za

© The Author(s), under exclusive license to Springer Nature
Singapore Pte Ltd. 2024
H. Solomon et al. (eds.), *BRICS and Climate Change*,
https://doi.org/10.1007/978-981-97-5532-5_8

be needed in the health sector to respond to the health challenges arising from climate change (WHO 2023). With drought and desertification, food insecurity is also expected to further increase, thereby potentially exacerbating conflict between communities and states over arable land and water resources (Cocodia and Solomon 2023: 1–8).

There are further areas of concern. According to the US National Oceanic and Atmospheric Administration (NOAA), climate change could also collapse ocean currents. NOAA researchers have warned of the danger of the Atlantic Meridional Overturning Circulation (AMOC) current collapsing. AMOC plays an instrumental role in circulating warm and salt water around the world, thereby regulating global temperatures, transporting life-giving nutrients to sea life, and supporting worldwide water flows. In this sense, AMOC plays the role of a conveyor belt—controlling the climate (National Ocean Service 2024). However, NOAA scientists have now discovered that AMOC has been slowing down. This has been a direct result of the ice sheets off the coast of Greenland melting. Consequently, more freshwater is released into the North Atlantic, which decelerates AMOC. The simulation models developed by scientists at NOAA suggest the likelihood of an abrupt AMOC collapse in the future with catastrophic results for humanity (Lynn 2024).

The second major development relates to the tectonic shifts and disruptions occurring at the geostrategic level as the world moves away from a Euro-American Western order to a more multilateral order where power is diffused. One of the structures which has emerged to challenge Western hegemony is BRICS or, more accurately, BRICS Plus. The acronym was first popularized in 2001 by Goldman Sachs banker Jim O' Neill. BRIC began as a designation to suggest that the future of economic growth would no longer be in the United States and Europe but may well be situated in Brazil, Russia, India, and China (Library of Congress, n.d.). South Africa was soon added to this nascent bloc, and it came to be regarded as BRICS. Whilst BRICS has its challenges, it has grown more organizationally sophisticated with each summit. For instance, it possesses a BRICS Development Bank, which rivals that of the Bretton Woods system. In 2023, more than 40 countries wanted to become members of the BRICS group. This is a significant number and potentially reflects the strategic importance of the bloc.

After the conclusion of the 2023 BRICS Summit in Johannesburg, it was officially declared that Argentina, Egypt, Ethiopia, Iran, Saudi Arabia, and the United Arab Emirates would join what is now officially known as

BRICS Plus in 2024. The new BRICS Plus represents nearly 42% of the world's population and accounts for nearly 36% of global Gross Domestic Product (GDP) (Ashby et al. 2023). Under the new government of President Javier Mile, Argentina withdrew its application to BRICS on account of its scepticism of the bloc (Dsouza 2024). Despite Argentina's abrupt withdrawal, there is every indication that BRICS Plus will continue to grow apace. Indeed, BRICS Plus could herald the dawn of a significantly alternative world order.

The recent addition of Iran, Egypt, Ethiopia, Saudi Arabia, and the United Arab Emirates (UAE), from January 2024, represents a major achievement for BRICS, now BRICS Plus, as it includes a number of major energy and other geostrategic states within its fold. On the occasion of the announcement to expand BRICS, UN Secretary-General António Guterres acknowledged the bloc's expanding influence and strategic relevance. He also cited BRICS' lobbying for the reform of outdated structures such as the United Nations Security Council, International Monetary Fund, and World Bank. The United Nations Secretary General also noted that today's global governance structures reflect yesterday's power configurations. The Secretary General stressed that multilateral institutions needed to be more inclusive, and, to this end, they need to better represent current realities—shifting power dynamics to demographic shifts (Reuters 2023).

The BRICS expansion promises to further increase economic cooperation, geopolitical influence, and the emergence of a more diverse set of views and perspectives. The expansion is also likely to lead towards BRICS becoming a more dynamic organization (Bhowmick 2024). This renewed dynamism is critical in addressing climate change going forward.

The expansion of BRICS undeniably represents a significant geopolitical reordering.

As observed by the CFR:

> If not a new world order, the BRICS expansion is certainly an attempt at an alternative world order, one with a more sympathetic ear for the developing many versus the developed few. (CFR, 2023)

As preparations are underway for the 2024 BRICS Summit to be held in Kazan, Russia, no fewer than 30 countries have applied for BRICS membership, which is a significant number (Watcher Guru 2024).

168   H. SOLOMON

Given the enormity of the threat posed by climate change, it would make sense for BRICS Plus to champion the cause of climate change as one of its top priorities. This chapter seeks to briefly explore the evolution of BRICS and BRICS Plus positions in relation to climate change. It also seeks to provide an understanding of the challenges confronting BRICS Plus as it seeks to achieve a consensual approach on this pressing environmental challenge.

The following section will briefly examine BRICS' climate change position. Overall, the grouping has attempted to forge consensus on multiple issue areas, including that of climate change.

2   From BRICS to BRICS Plus: The Climate Change Agenda

Judging by their pronouncements and declarations, it is abundantly evident that issues of climate change are increasingly coming to occupy the minds of BRICS policymakers.

The BRICS grouping formally gathered at a High-level Meeting in May 2022 to address the challenge posed by climate change. This gathering came about as a result of a proposal by Chinese President Xi Jinping the previous year. Subsequently, member states gathered in Beijing for the first BRICS High-level Meeting on Climate Change in May 2022. This meeting was pivotal to revealing the official BRICS position on the climate change crisis as well as taking stock of BRICS efforts—nationally and as a bloc—to mitigate the impact of climate change. The BRICS High-level Meeting on Climate Change subsequently issued a critically important joint statement. This statement revealed BRICS' substantive views on the climate change challenge going forward. Here, they emphasized the need for both a low-carbon economy and one which emphasized inclusive and sustainable growth and development. The BRICS High-level Meeting on Climate Change set out to develop measures to jointly address climate change, including the exploration of approaches to accelerate low-carbon and climate resilient transition and achieving sustainable, balanced, and inclusive recovery and development (BRICS 2022).

There was further tacit recognition by the High-level Meeting that all parties needed to abide by multilateralism as a means of addressing climate change and focus on the development of concrete climate actions (BRICS 2022).

The High-level Meeting further called upon all Parties to:

Firmly adhere to the principles of the UN Convention and its Paris Agreement, including common but differentiated responsibilities and respective capabilities, in light of different national circumstances, and to increase mutual trust, strengthen cooperation, implement the Convention and its Paris Agreement in an accurate, balanced and comprehensive way, in accordance with the institutional arrangement of nationally determined contributions, and based on existing consensus. (BRICS 2022)

The High-level Meeting further noted that BRICS countries, through the utilization of multilateral means, had made significant contributions towards achieving low-carbon, climate resilient and sustainable development (BRICS 2022).

However, the High-level Meeting stressed that developing countries were facing a greater challenge in reaching the important goal of global carbon neutrality whilst reducing poverty in their respective countries. BRICS noted that this attempt at carbon neutrality was occurring amid a sluggish economic recovery following the COVID-19 pandemic. Importantly, the bloc attempted to frame its response to climate change within through the United Nations' Sustainable Development Goals (SDGs) (BRICS 2022).

According to the High-level Meeting statement, BRICS member countries had already set forth nationally determined contributions, which was deemed to be a reflection of their goal to secure a green economy whilst understanding their context—essentially their levels of development, resources, and overall capabilities (BRICS 2022). The High-level Meeting statement also acknowledged the successes that respective BRICS member countries achieved in attempts to address climate change in their respective countries.

Opposing unilateral actions in the climate change domain, the High-level Meeting also expressed the view that unilateral actions further threatened to gravely undermine multilateral cooperation, which in turn undermined global efforts to arrest climate change (BRICS 2022). This was perhaps the strongest statement reflecting the commitment of BRICS countries to consistently seek a consensus-driven approach in addressing climate change. This High-level Meeting and subsequent statement of 2022 reflected that BRICS was beginning to position itself as a leading actor in the fight to comprehensively address climate change.

The BRICS Summit held in Johannesburg, South Africa in August 2023 continued this trajectory. Here, BRICS member states reaffirmed their commitment to the fundamental founding principles of the organization, which includes respect for the sovereign equality of all member states, multilateralism, and consensus-seeking as opposed to unilateral measures and attempting to force solution on others. Without spelling it out, it was clear that the BRICS countries were contrasting their position with the manner in which those countries in the Global North approach international affairs—with a very top-down approach.

The XV BRICS Summit held under the theme, "BRICS and Africa: Partnership for Mutually Accelerated Growth, Sustainable Development and Inclusive Multilateralism", adopted the Johannesburg II Declaration in August 2023. The declaration reflected a sense of cohesion and consensus amongst BRICS member states that climate change has to be addressed more proactively. The tone here was certainly a positive departure from previous conservative and defensive BRICS positioning on climate change.

The Johannesburg II Declaration in particular reiterated the importance of implementing the United Nations Framework Convention on Climate Change (UNFCCC) and its Paris Agreement and the principle of "common but differentiated responsibilities and respective capabilities" (CBDR-RC) (BRICS 2023). This is an important principle, as developing countries who lack the technical expertise and financial resources cannot be expected to transition to a green economy at the same rates as their more developed counterparts. The declaration also aimed to transfer technology to countries which do not have the technical means to transition to green economies. Related to this was the securing of cheap financing to assist countries with their energy transitions (BRICS 2023). On the issue of finance, BRICS stressed two principles: First, that the developed world, who were historically the greatest greenhouse gas emitters, should make financing and the necessary technical expertise available to developing nations. This would be in keeping with the principle of climate justice. Second, the second principle of CDRC-RC not only reinforced the need for funding form those in the Global North but also that the timescale of the transition to carbon neutral economies will be according to the circumstances and capacity of member states (BRICS 2023).

These two principles are in keeping with UNFCC COP27, where it was agreed to operationalize the Fund on Loss and Damage incurred as a result of climate change as well as the loss of livelihoods as a result of the transition to low-carbon economies. Those in the developing world were specifically supposed to be the beneficiaries of this financial support.

What particularly irked BRICS nations was the fact that, whilst rhetorically committing to these undertakings at these conferences, those in the Global North either met their commitments minimally or not at all (BRICS 2023). These interventions on the part of BRICS could serve as a catalyst for development for those nations in the Global South (Naidoo 2023).

In keeping with their commitment to multilateralism, BRICS members stressed the importance of multilateralism and that this needs to be defended, promoted, and strengthened. Stressing the importance of multilateralism is imperative when one considers that the threat of climate change is a global one. Within this context, national or regional plans would be of little use unless these are all coordinated at an international level. Importantly, this multilateralism is not only for BRICS members. By referencing and appealing to the United Nations Conference of the Parties of the United Nations Framework Convention on Climate Change (UNFCCC), the Johannesburg II Declaration stressed the importance of multilateralism as the approach in international affairs regarding climate change (BRICS 2023).

3   BRICS Plus and Africa

BRICS Plus could also become a critically important champion of the African continent in multilateral fora, especially where the question of climate change is concerned. It potentially represents a critical counterweight to the West's climate change agenda and a viable new partner to Africa in addressing the devastating impact climate change continues to inflict on fragile African countries. As of January 2024, Ethiopia and Egypt joined South Africa as formal BRICS Plus member countries, which will likely ensure an even more amplified African voice in BRICS deliberations. This is especially critical vis-à-vis the climate change conundrum the continent is facing. Indeed, Africa remains the most vulnerable to climate change despite its miniscule contribution to greenhouse gas emissions.

The seriousness with which climate change is viewed in Africa was evident in September 2023 when Kenya hosted the Africa Climate Summit. In the run-up to the summit, more than 400 African civil society organizations penned a letter to African heads of state urging them to be cautious of the West. According to the authors of the letter, the West had hijacked the climate change agenda whilst pursuing a hidden agenda which was inimical to African interests (Chime 2023). This letter highlights the distrust with which the Global North is viewed by those in the Global South. Much of the science underpinning the discourse of climate change emanates in the West. It is for this very reason that BRICS Plus—a grouping of nations in the Global South—taking up the issue of climate change will have greater receptivity for those in the Global South who are cynical of a Western "hidden agenda".

The focus on BRICS countries is also important for other reasons. China and India are the second- and fifth-largest economies in the world (StatisticsTimes, 2023). Therefore, they have economic and strategic clout. Moreover, if one considers that, whilst the fertility rate across the West has plummeted, the demographic momentum resides in the Global South. It is also the Global South which is uniquely vulnerable to the impact of climate change. This is a direct result of varying levels of adaptive capacity, the diffusion of technologies does not always reach the poorest and most remote areas, and most people in the Global South are highly dependent on agriculture for their livelihoods. In Sub-Saharan Africa, for instance, subsistence agriculture dominates 80% of cultivated lands (Cocodia and Solomon 2023: 1–7). Consequently, these small-scale farmers have neither the resources nor the technology to adapt to climate change. From this perspective, it makes sense for an organization representing the Global South and taking the lead in promoting the interests of its own citizens with resources and technology from the wealthier countries coming to the aid of less-endowed states.

African states arguably represent some of the more vulnerable constituents of the Global South and could benefit far more significantly from a more activist BRICS Plus where climate change is concerned. In the spirit of the 2023 BRICS Summit theme, greater collaboration and cooperation between BRICS Plus and the African Union and its organs tasked with addressing climate change on the continent could prove beneficial in addressing climate change on several fronts simultaneously.

The African Climate Summit in September 2023 culminated in the adoption of The African Leaders Nairobi Declaration on Climate Change and Call to Action. The declaration initially struck a pessimistic note, soberingly pointing out that the promise of the Paris Summit will not be reached. The world will not be able to reduce greenhouse gas emissions by 43% by 2030. Consequently, the target limit of 1.5 °C increase in temperature agreed in Paris will be breached (African Union 2023).

Moving to the African context, then, the drafters of the Nairobi Declaration pointed that Africa was warming faster than other continents, as seen in the prolonged droughts, wildfires, and the like, which have undermined African lives and livelihoods. African leaders issued a clarion call for global action to reduce greenhouse gas emissions as we all transition to a low-carbon economy (African Union 2023).

Importantly, African leaders pointed out the injustice surrounding climate change. Over centuries, the developed world contributed to greenhouse gas emissions, not Africa. Even now, the continent's emissions are the lowest. Despite this, Africa experiences the worst effects of climate change (African Union 2023). This appeal to climate justice resonates very strongly with BRICS Plus nations' approach to climate change as well as their CBDR-RC principle.

In keeping with the call for climate justice, African leaders noted that the developed nations did not abide by their own pledges—specifically the $100 billion promised at the Copenhagen Summit in 2010. This was imperative to assist developing countries to transition from coal and oil towards a green economy. The Nairobi Declaration also called on the Global North to abolish their subsidies of fossil fuels, which was further impeding a global carbon neutral economy from developing (African Union 2023). In concurrence with the BRICS Plus position, the African Climate Summit also called for all countries to abide by their promise at COP27 to operationalize the Loss and Damage Fund. This was imperative to compensate those whose livelihoods are threatened by the transition to a green economy (African Union 2023).

Whilst realistic about the current challenges, the Nairobi Declaration was also progressive. There was recognition amongst the architects of the Nairobi Declaration that Africa could play a major role in mitigating climate change (African Union 2023). Home to the most youthful fastest-growing labour force, Africa also has massive untapped renewable energy potential and an abundance of natural assets. With investments into the education of this work force as well as the transfer of technologies, Africa could become a competitive industrial hub which can support its people as well as other regions in the world to achieve carbon neutrality (African Union 2023). In this way, too, economic development does not need to be in contradiction to the goal of sustaining the economy. This position, too, is in keeping with the BRICS Plus approach to the environment—to enable economic growth which is environmentally sustainable. It is imperative to emphasize that the African Climate Summit and its resultant Nairobi Declaration did not merely exist rhetorically but was part of a concerted strategy of the African Union—note here the African Union Climate Change and Resilient Development Strategy and Action Plan (2022–2032).

Judging by the African continent's Nairobi Declaration, there is abundant synergy and scope for greater BRICS Plus—Africa cooperation in addressing climate change going forward. African states and BRICS nations share similar aims and ambitions of effectively addressing all areas affected by climate change. Moreover, their approaches and resultant strategies towards climate change are mutually reinforcing, as is evident. The inclusion of more African states in BRICS Plus could be beneficial towards further amplifying the bloc's voice in the Global South as well as further reinforcing the existing synergy between BRICS Plus and Africa. Here, BRICS Plus could possibly consider a BRICS Plus Associate or Partner Status with non-BRIC African member states to further consolidate the fight against climate change. In this way, bilateral ties and multilateral ties will be mutually reinforcing towards a global carbon neutral regime.

4   BRICS Plus, Climate Change, and the Challenge of Consensus

Whilst BRICS Plus has great potential to play a leading role in the creation of a progressive climate change regime, it is not without its challenges. These are highly disparate countries that often pursue their own national interests and have come together in a loose grouping to advance those national interests whilst also pursuing other alliances which may conflict with those of BRICS Plus. A case in point is Iran, given sanctions imposed upon it by much of the Western world, ostensibly because of its nuclear programme, Tehran has sought to minimize the impact of the sanctions by consolidating its ties with BRICS countries (Dsouza 2024).

Meanwhile, India and China—the two most populous countries in the world and anchor members of BRICS Plus—also happen to be bitter geostrategic rivals. The territorial dispute and lingering distrust between India and China are clearly evinced along their common border along the Himalayas. On the Western part of the border, China has in its possession 38,000 km^2, which India claims to be part of its territory.

Meanwhile, to the east of the Himalayas, New Delhi's continued possession of 90,000 km^2 of territory is a bone of contention in Beijing (International Crisis Group 2023). The two countries went to war in 1962 over their competing territorial claims, and, more recently, in 2020, tensions flared up again. Currently, 100,000 Indian and Chinese troops are facing each other off along their common Himalayan border, even as they are members of BRIC, BRICS, and now BRICS Plus (International Crisis Group 2023). As a result of perceived Chinese assertiveness under President Jinping, India has become a member of the American-initiated Quad—an alliance seeking to contain China's influence. Member states of the so-called "Quad" include Australia, India, Japan, and the United States (Australian Department of Foreign Affairs and Trade 2024).

On the surface, tensions over the expansion of BRICS also became apparent. Russia and China arguably advocated for the group's expansion in an attempt to strengthen BRICS as a potential alternative to Western dominance in international affairs (Cheatham and Gallagher 2023). Brazil and India expressed fears and concerns that this expansion exercise could potentially weaken their influence within the bloc.

Some analysts believe that China and Russia would like to position BRICS Plus as an alternative global ally and potential geopolitical counterweight to the G7 and other Western-led alliances (Cheatham and Gallagher 2023). Russia in particular has been significantly isolated by the West following its invasion of Ukraine and has looked towards the Global South to help keep its economy afloat (Cheatham and Gallagher 2023). An enlarged BRICS could potentially help insulate Moscow from more crippling Western sanctions and further international condemnation and isolation.

South Africa also emerged as an advocate of BRICS expansion. On the eve of the Johannesburg Summit, President Cyril Ramaphosa expressed his wish to see more African countries join and partner with the bloc. The South African president invited over 30 African leaders to participate in the 2023 Johannesburg Summit. As noted earlier, expanding African membership could translate into strengthening the bloc's climate change responses, given the high premium African states place on swiftly addressing the multiplying threats posed by climate change.

As BRICS Plus prepares for its first fully fledged summit of 10 states, there are likely to be some significant differences between member states on several issues. Significant policy differences over climate change could possibly still emerge within an enlarged BRICS configuration. New member states' views on the issue will soon be heard at the forthcoming BRICS Plus Summit. Whether new member states' climate change policies will fully align with that of existing BRICS policy to date remains to be seen. It is, however, unrealistic to believe that member states will achieve unequivocal consensus on this particularly vexing issue. BRICS Plus leaders will, however, likely seek to achieve a modicum of consensus on the issue.

Overall, BRICS Plus expansion could prove to be beneficial if potential policy differences amongst member states are addressed in the spirit of securing some form of mutual consensus.

5   Overcoming the National Towards Greater Cooperation

Whilst the expansion of BRICS undoubtedly complicates achieving consensus on particular issues, it is also a positive development in that it dilutes China's power within the alliance. Seventy percent of the GDP of BRICS emanated from China (Plummer 2024). The dilution of Chinese dominance within BRICS Plus opens the way for an organizational culture which has its roots in multilateralism, compromise, and consensus-seeking.

Beyond BRICS Plus, it allows BRICS Plus to use that same organizational culture as it attempts to serve as interlocutor between the Global South and Global North and between BRICS Plus member states and those who are non-members in the Global South. What remains to be seen in policy and practice going forward is whether BRICS Plus can indeed construct a viable and lasting consensus on the issue of climate change as an expanded bloc.

6   BRICS Plus: Towards a New Climate Change Consensus?

Despite the challenges alluded to above, it is important to stress that both BRICS and the new BRICS Plus are in agreement of the statement made following the May 2022 BRICS Summit mentioned earlier. They are in favour of multilateralism, consensus-seeking, enhancing climate resilience, and hastening the transition to low-carbon economies.

2022 was also a significant year, as it marked the 30th anniversary of the United Nations Convention. Whilst BRICS Plus countries may have their national differences and internal dynamics, it is also true that they all subscribe to various international regimes such as the UNFCC and the SDGs. These all assist in creating a common ground on which to build cooperation and focus on what united them. Thus, despite their geostrategic rivalries and the like, climate change may prove to be an area where they can cooperate.

Coincidentally (and perhaps strategically for BRICS Plus), the UAE—one of the newest members of BRICS Plus—hosted COP28. More than 15 heads of state and 85,000 delegates attended this gathering, making it the largest UNFCC gathering to date. It was momentous for other reasons too. At their Dubai gathering, delegates from states and civil society undertook the world's first effort to conduct a "stocktake" of their collective efforts to arrest climate change. Whilst acknowledging their failures (missing the deadlines set by the Paris Summit), delegates undertook to strengthen their efforts at reducing greenhouse gas emissions, facilitating the transfer of funds and technical skills to less developed countries to facilitate their transition to a green economy, and strengthen resilience in local communities that are vulnerable to climate change (UNFCCC 2023). More specifically, countries agreed to reduce global emission by 43% by 2030, and the repeated demand from African and BRICS nations was finally met when the Loss and Damage Fund agreed to assist with transitions to carbon neutral economies in the Global South as well as with building resilience. In addition, more than $174 million were pledged for the Least Developed Countries Fund and the Special Climate Change Fund (UNFCCC 2023). This resonates both with the African Climate Summit and the goals of BRICS Plus, which reinforces collaboration between different countries.

Delegates at COP28 also stressed the importance of renewable energy sources such as wind and solar power. In an effort to move away from fossil fuels, states committed to deep emission cuts and the scaling up of finance for the provision for these transitions (UNFCCC 2023). What was remarkable about this Dubai COP was the fact that these commitments were also made by energy producers. One of the criticisms levelled at BRICS Plus was the inclusion of such major oil producers such as Iran and Saudi Arabia and their alleged vested interest in the status quo. Their agreement with the decisions emanating from COP28 suggests that this should not be a problem for the smooth running of

BRICS Plus, especially in the area of climate change. This position is reinforced when Russia, a major energy producer, expressed its desire to assist in building consensus within BRICS Plus on climate change. As the COP28 talks concluded in Dubai in December 2023, Russia expressed its desire to rally a united front amongst BRICS Plus nations when confronting global climate issues. Going further, Ilya Torosov, Russia's First Deputy Economy Minister, spoke of Moscow's willingness "to combine efforts and common approaches in the Eurasian space and in the BRICS space" on issues of climate change (Bloomberg News 2023). Torosov's announcement was in keeping with the 2022 BRICS Summit where it was agreed that multilateralism will be the norm in how BRICS nations will approach the issue of climate change (Liqiang 2023).

The next few months in the run-up to the first official BRICS Plus Summit to be held in Russia will be critical in assessing the extent to which this new association of 10 states will act in unison on multiple issue areas and the extent to which it will be able to reach renewed consensus on the question of climate change.

7   Conclusion

This chapter sought to briefly appraise the evolution of BRICS' climate change policy and the possible trajectory this policy could take under the stewardship of the newly created BRICS Plus constellation. The aspiration to form a multipolar international order appears to be gaining traction and making headway under the BRICS stewardship.

The expanded BRICS Plus grouping is already seen in many developing and emerging countries as a potential alternative to the current Global North-dominated nascent governance structure (KAS 2023). The BRICS Plus could emerge as a critical negotiating bloc championing the Global South's agenda on how best to address climate change, *providing* it achieves consensus on the issue at the forthcoming Russia Summit to be held later in 2024.

As noted earlier, no official BRICS Plus declarations have been issued overtly on the issue of climate change. What has been said in these pages emanates from individual BRICS Plus countries and have been extrapolated from their actions. All eyes will now be on Russia, which will likely form and host a contact group on climate change, or perhaps a second High-level Meeting on climate change which will likely reveal the bloc's climate change policy and strategy going forward after the COP28

Summit. The Russian 2024 BRICS chairmanship is convened under the motto "Strengthening Multilateralism for Just Global Development and Security". As Russia prepares to host the next BRICS Summit, Moscow's goal appears to be that of enhancing and bolstering BRICS as a critical conduit through which countries can pursue an independent foreign policy agenda (O'Conner 2024). This, again, is in keeping with BRICS' emphasis on multilateralism and respect for sovereignty when responding to climate change. In that sense, the Russian Summit will reflect more continuity than change in the transition from BRICS to BRICS Plus.

Russia (most notably, newly re-elected President Vladimir Putin) in particular would benefit from an emboldened and strengthened BRICS Plus on the international stage, given its increasing isolation following its war with Ukraine. President Putin should, however, refrain from using the opportunity to host this important summit to popularize the idea of BRICS as a counterweight to the West (Adler 2023). Rather than a counterweight to the West, and in keeping with its own principles of multilateralism and respect for sovereignty, BRICS Plus should celebrate multipolarity and, in keeping with its own principle of consensus-seeking, seek to find common cause with the West. Those countries that have strong ties with the West, such as India and Saudi Arabia, could potentially serve as interlocuter between BRICS Plus and the West. The climate is everyone's business; after all, humanity is confronted with an existential crisis. What is desperately needed is a new climate consensus where old divisions of West and East, North and South hold no traction.

References

African Union. 2023. The African Leaders Nairobi Declaration on Climate Change and Call to Action, Nairobi, Kenya, 6 September. https://africaclimatesummit.org.

Adler, Nils. 2023. "Can BRICS Create a New World Order?" Al Jazeera, 22 August. https://www.aljazeera.com/features/2023/8/22/can-brics-create-a-new-world-order

Ashby, Heather, Daniel Markey, Kirk Randolph, Kirtika Sharad, Henry Tugendhat and Aly Verjee. 2023. What BRICS Expansion Means for the Bloc's Founding Members. United States Institute for Peace. Washington, DC, 30 August. https://www.usip.org/publications/2023/08/what-brics-expansion-means-blocs-founding-members

Australian Department of Foreign Affairs and Trade. 2024. The Quad. DFAT. Canberra. https://dfat.gov/au/international-relations/regional-archit ecture/quad.

Bhowmick, Soumya. 2024. BRICS Plus: Navigating Global Challenges and Broadening Influence, 28 February. https://www.orfonline.org/expert-speak/brics-plus-navigating-global-challenges-and-broadening-influence

Bloomberg News. 2023. Russia Seeks to Unite BRICS on Climate Initiatives After COP28, 14 December. https://www.moneyweb.co.za/news/africa/rus-sia-seeks-to-unite-brics-on-climate-initiatives-after-cop28/

BRICS. 2022. Joint Statement Issued at the High-Level Meeting on Climate Change, 24 May. http://brics2022.mfa.gov.cn/eng/hywj/ODMM/202205/t20220529_10694182.html

BRICS. 2023. XV BRICS Summit, Johannesburg II Declaration: "BRICS and Africa: Partnership for Mutually Accelerated Growth, Sustainable Development and Inclusive Multilateralism", Sandton, Gauteng, South Africa, 23 August, Internet: https://brics2023.gov.za/wp-content/uploads/2023/08/Jhb-II-Declaration-24-August-2023-1.pdf

CFR. 2023. The BRICS Summit 2023: Seeking an Alternate World Order? Global Memo by ORF, SWP, SAIIA, SVOP, SIIS, RSIS, FGV, and CFR, 31 August. https://www.cfr.org/councilofcouncils/global-memos/brics-sum mit-2023-seeking-alternate-world-order

Cheatham, Andrew, and Adam Gallagher. 2023. Why the BRICS Summit Could be a Big Deal, USIP, 23 August. https://www.usip.org/publications/2023/08/why-brics-summit-could-be-big-deal

Chime, Vivian. 2023. "CSOs: Africa Climate Summit Hijacked by Western Nations Pushing Hidden Agenda." The Cable, 17 August. Internet: http://thecable.ng/csos-africa-climate-summit-hijacked-by-western-nations-pushing-hidden-agenda

"China vs India," StatisticsTimes. 8 December 2023. http://statisticstimes.com/economy/china-vs-india-economy.

Cocodia, Jude, and Hussein Solomon. 2023. "Introduction: African Security in the Anthropocene." In *African Security in the Anthropocene*, edited by Hussein Solomon and Jude Cocodia. Switzerland: Cham, Springer.

Dsouza, Vinodh. 2024. "BRICS: Iran Explains Why It Joined the Alliance," Watcher Guru, 24 February. https://watcher.guru/news/brics-iran-explains-why-it-joined-the-alliance.

International Crisis Group. 2023. Ice in the Himalayas: Handling the India-China Border Dispute. ICG Report. Brussels, 14 November. http://cri sisgroup.org/asia/south-asia/india-china/334-thin-ice-himalayas-handling-india-china-border-dispute. Date accessed: 10 March 2024.

KAS. 2023. BRICS Expansion: Geopolitical Power Shift or Transactional Alliance? https://www.kas.de/en/brics-plus

Library of Congress. n.d. BRICS: Sources of Information. Library of Congress. Washington, DC. https://guides.loc.gov/brics.

Liqiang, Hou. 2023. BRICS Plays Role in Global Climate Fight, 9 September. http://global.chinadaily.com.cn/a/202309/09/WS64fba0eda310d2dce4bb4c98.html

Lynn, Bryan. 2024. "Study: Collapse of Ocean Currents Could Cause Major Climate Problems," Voice of America, 18 February. https://learningenglish.voanews.com/a/study-collapse-of-ocean-currents-could-cause-major-climate-problems/748499.html.

Naidoo, Dhesigen. 2023. "Towards a BRICS Climate Club." ISS Today, 24 August. https://issafrica.org/iss-today/towards-a-brics-climate-club

National Ocean Service. 2024. "What Is the Atlantic Meridional Overturning Circulation (AMOC)?" https://oceanservice.noaa.gov/facts/amoc.html

O'Conner, Tom. 2024. "Russia Plans to Usher in 'A New World Order'—More Powers are Signing Up." Newsweek, 14 February. https://www.newsweek.com/russia-plans-new-world-order-brics-nations-1869722

Plummer, Robert. 2024. "Argentina Pulls Out of Plans to Join BRICS Bloc." BBC, 29 December. https://www.bbc.com/news/world-latin-america-67842992

Reuters. 2023. "BRICS Welcomes 6 New Members in Push to Reshuffle World Order." Reuters, 24 August. https://www.voanews.com/amp/brics-welcomes-6-new-members-in-push-to-reshuffle-world-order-/7240130.html

UNFCCC. 2023. UN Climate Change Conference. https://unfccc.int/cop28

United Nations Climate Action. 2024. Causes and Effects of Climate Change. United Nations. New York. https://www.un.org/en/climatechange/science/causes-effects-climate-change#:~:text=The%20world%20is%20now%20warming,forms%20of%20life%20on%20Earth.

Watcher Guru. 2024. "BRICS: 30 New Countries Prepare to Join Alliance in 2024."

World Health Organization. 2023. Climate Change. https://www.who.int/news-room/fact-sheets/detail/climate-change-and-health.

Saudi Arabia's Climate Change Policy: An Effort towards a Sustainable Future for the Kingdom and the Middle East

Md. Muddassir Quamar

1   Introduction

Climate change has emerged as a key global concern of the twenty-first century, with the international community increasingly paying attention to the issue. The United Nations Framework Convention on Climate Change (UNFCCC) was adopted in June 1992 during the Earth Summit in Rio de Janeiro, Brazil with the aim to mitigate the adverse impact of anthropogenic activities on the climate by stabilizing the greenhouse gas concentration in the atmosphere (Bodansky 1993). The UNFCCC came into effect in March 1994 and launched the Conference of the Parties (COP) as the primary decision-making body for devising an international action plan to address global warming and climate change. Accordingly, in December 1997, the Kyoto Protocol was adopted during the COP3 and came into effect in February 2005. As per the Kyoto Protocol, 37 industrialized countries agreed to reduce their greenhouse gas emissions by 5% compared to the levels in the 1990s during the first five-year commitment

---

Md. M. Quamar (✉)
School of International Studies, Jawaharlal Nehru University, New Delhi, India
e-mail: mmquamar@mail.jnu.ac.in

© The Author(s), under exclusive license to Springer Nature
Singapore Pte Ltd. 2024
H. Solomon et al. (eds.), *BRICS and Climate Change*,
https://doi.org/10.1007/978-981-97-5532-5_9

period from 2008 to 2012 (Böhringer 2003). Later, a more comprehensive agreement amongst 196 countries was adopted in December 2015 during the COP21 in Paris. The Paris Agreement came into effect in November 2016 to limit the global average temperature increase to well below 2 °C above preindustrial level (Savaresi 2016).

With increased attention to climate change and its adverse impacts on the environment and sustainability, the United Nations, through the COP, has worked tirelessly to develop a consensus amongst the world nations to chalk out a comprehensive way forward to address climate change (Ivanova 2018). Nonetheless, as with any other international matters, the differences amongst the global community on how to address the issue have come to the fore and taken a defining role in preventing a consensus (Dalby 2013). The most important question that has been debated is fixing the responsibility for greenhouse gas emissions and their impact in the form of global warming and climate change. The developing world, or the Global South, puts the responsibility squarely on the industrialized and developed economies for their historic contribution. Hence, countries such as China, India, and others have underlined that the developed countries should undertake greater responsibility in mitigating climate change and its adverse impacts (Bolin 2008). Alternatively, the industrialized nations have argued for fixing an equitable responsibility, especially as the fast-growing largest economies in Asia have gradually emerged as the primary contributors to greenhouse gas emissions since the late twentieth century (Reid and Goldemberg 1998).

A few points need to be stated here. First, from a scientific and scholarly perspective, the approach has to be collective and comprehensive given the nature of the challenge that affects all of humanity without differentiating on the basis of rich–poor, developed–developing, and north–south divides. Concurrently, it is important to note that some countries and regions are more vulnerable compared to others due to their geographic location and/or economic volatility (Nath and Behera 2011). Whilst the economically advanced countries are considered more responsible for the devastating impacts of anthropogenic activities, it is the poor nations in the Global South that are more vulnerable to its adverse effects. Second, the question of global warming, climate change, and greenhouse gas emissions cannot be viewed in isolation from the debates on sustainable development, and the global community has increasingly begun to recognize the need for an action plan that addresses the issue of climate change and sustainability in tandem (Soergel et al. 2021).

The third important dimension of the debate on climate change is its impact on economic growth. This is a more pressing concern for the developing economies with a clear divide amongst G7 and G20 countries, and the poorer nations in Asia, Africa, and South America. Hence, if for economically advanced countries the issue of climate change is primarily a matter of decreasing greenhouse gas emissions by reducing the consumption of fossil fuels and hydrocarbons, for developing and underdeveloped countries, the challenge primarily pertains to dealing with the immediate impacts of climate change whilst maintaining economic growth (Reddy and Assenza 2009; Ülgen 2021). However, the situation becomes more complex for countries that are major hydrocarbon producers and exporters, especially the members of the Organization of the Petroleum Exporting Countries (OPEC) and OPEC + . For these countries, such as Russia, Saudi Arabia, and others, the task of dealing with climate change is more complex because of their economic dependence on hydrocarbon production and exports (Krane 2020; Contu et al. 2021). Additionally, for some countries that are oil-dependent developing economies, the situation is even more intricate if they are located in an ecologically volatile region. These countries find themselves in multiple jeopardy, whereby they are not only major contributors to greenhouse gas emissions but also more vulnerable to environmental and ecological degradation and simultaneously dependent on petroleum for economic growth. The Gulf Cooperation Council (GCC) countries, namely Bahrain, Kuwait, Oman, Qatar, Saudi Arabia, and the United Arab Emirates (UAE), fall under this category.

Few countries are at the centre stage of the issue of global warming, greenhouse gas emissions, and sustainable development as the Kingdom of Saudi Arabia. The Kingdom finds itself in an extraordinary situation, as it is not only a major producer and exporter of the fossil fuels contributing to global CO_2 and greenhouse gas emissions but it is also economically entirely dependent on hydrocarbon exports, making it extremely vulnerable to the shifts in global energy consumption patterns (Al-Sarihi 2019; Al Shehri et al. 2023). The Kingdom also lies in one of the most arid and climate-volatile regions in the world, thus being extremely vulnerable to climate change (Al-Wabel et al. 2020; Tarawneh and Chowdhury 2018). And, unlike its smaller neighbours, such as Bahrain, UAE, and Qatar, Saudi Arabia has to deal with a larger population, a regional expectation of playing a leadership role, and being a late starter in economic diversification efforts. Consequently, the stakes for Saudi Arabia are much higher as far as the global climate change and sustainability debate is concerned. Therefore, Saudi Arabia has become proactive in the debates on climate change by participating in international multilateral forums such as COP and G20, and in devising a national and regional response.

As Saudi Arabia joins BRICS, which has emerged as one of the key international multilateral forums for countries of the Global South to discuss and debate matters of international politics and key challenges facing the world, it becomes important to examine the Saudi policy response to climate change. This needs to be analysed within the extraordinary context, wherein Saudi Arabia is both a major contributor to global warming and climate change as the world's largest oil producer and exporter, and it is extremely vulnerable to its adverse impacts on both its economy and ecology.

2 BRICS AND THE CLIMATE CHANGE DISCOURSE

Since its inception, the BRICS (Brazil, Russia, India, China, and South Africa), which has, as of 2024, been expanded to include Egypt, Ethiopia, Iran, Saudi Arabia, and UAE,[1] has remained committed to the need for addressing the adverse impacts of climate change. The joint statement issued at the BRICS High-level Meeting on Climate Change in May 2022 underlined the commitment of the BRICS nations "to the goals, principles and institutional framework" of the UNFCCC (1992) and the Paris Agreement (2015) (Ministry of Ecology and Environment of the People's Republic of China [MEE, PRC] 2022). The grouping has, over the years, underlined the need for the developed nations to take a proactive and leading role in "scaling up mitigation actions and ambition and provision of climate financing, and respect the right to development and policy space of developing countries as well as countries in transition" (MEE, PRC 2022). Nonetheless, the position of BRICS has evolved with the initial emphasis on the responsibility of the developed nations to undertake mitigating action, giving way to the need for adopting a global consensus-based cooperative mechanism through multilateralism and equitable distribution of responsibilities (Leal-Arcas 2013). However, there are differences amongst BRICS members in their approaches and commitments to climate change and sustainable development, as was

[1] Argentina was also set to join BRICS, but the decision was reversed by President Javier Milei after his election in December 2023.

noted during the COP26 in Glasgow in 2021, where India and Brazil adopted different positions (Kıprızlı 2022: 67).

The most important divergences within BRICS regarding the climate change debate pertain to diverse economic structures, varied energy profiles, and different developmental stages. Hence, for example, both China and India emphasize the need for continued and rapid industrialization in order to meet their developmental needs (Mizo 2016). Given the huge population in both of these countries, and the large demography that remains below poverty, China and India have underlined the need to protect their economic interests and have often adopted protectionist policies, whilst continuing to integrate into the globalized economy. Brazil, on the other hand, under Joel Bolsonaro, was breaking away from the BRICS consensus on various economic matters, especially on climate change and sustainable development (Ferris 2022). There also remains the question of how to go about reducing the dependence on fossil fuels given that most BRICS members have been slow in transitioning to renewable energy sources. The Russian situation, for example, is peculiar given its heavy reliance on hydrocarbon production and exports. Even South Africa and Brazil have struggled to increase renewables in their energy mix (Bodas Freitas et al. 2012). Furthermore, there are developmental challenges, especially for Brazil, India, and South Africa, and although there remains a degree of consensus on the need to expedite mitigating actions, the policy approaches adopted by individual BRICS members vary (Lachapelle and Paterson 2013).

As BRICS expands to include new members from Africa and the Middle East, notwithstanding the internal divergences, the grouping is likely to undertake a more assertive position in the COP in setting the future agenda and chalking the global action plans to address climate change and sustainable development. Notably, BRICS has emphasized the need for multilateralism and opposed unilateral actions that can undermine the collective efforts as agreed upon through the COP under the UNFCCC (MEE, PRC 2022). BRICS, for example, opposes "any measures to restrict trade and investment and setting up new green trade barriers with the pretext of addressing climate change, such as the imposition of Carbon Border Adjustment Mechanisms" (ibid.). Moreover, the issue of climate financing to mitigate greenhouse gas emissions remains contentious, with the advanced economies underlining the need for a collaborative approach whilst the BRICS and Global South nations emphasize the historical responsibilities of the industrialized economies given that they have been the major emitters and contributors to anthropogenic activities including in the Global South (Leal-Arcas 2013; Kıprızlı 2022). During the COP28 in Dubai in November–December 2023, the BRICS members focused on highlighting a balanced approach to developmental needs and environmental concerns (Asian News International [ANI] 2023).

Technology transfer is another important aspect of the global climate change discourse. This has been debated since the 1990s when the UNFCCC was adopted, and it has since become an important part of the United Nations conventions and COP meetings. Hence, in 2010, during the COP meeting, a technology mechanism was established to accelerate and enhance "climate technology development and transfer" (United Nations Climate Change [UNCC] 2023). Accordingly, two bodies—the Technology Executive Committee (TEC) and the Climate Technology Centre and Network (CTCN)—were formed to work under it. The Paris Agreement formed the Technology Framework to provide overarching guidance for the technology mechanism. Despite being critical to the effective implementation of climate action plans, the issue of technology transfer remains convoluted with divergent interests prevailing over collective and cooperative actions.

Any consensus on both financing and technology transfer remains elusive both at the global level and amongst BRICS members. China has some advantages on these issues, but the geopolitical challenges remain a hurdle to greater cooperation, including amongst BRICS members, especially as India and China diverge on the direction of the regional and global order. Furthermore, the expansion of BRICS, whilst strengthening the position of the grouping at the international climate change discourse, poses new challenges for evolving a consensus within.

3   SAUDI ARABIA AND CLIMATE CHANGE

Saudi Arabia is located in an arid region with the majority of its land area being non-arable (76%) including nearly 38% desert with harsh climatic conditions and an extremely sensitive ecosystem. The Kingdom receives a very low average annual rainfall, and, except for some sweet water sources in the valleys and oases, there are no other sweet water sources such as rivers or lakes. Thus, ecologically, it is an extremely sensitive country. In recent years, extreme weather events have underlined its vulnerability to climate change and its adverse impacts on living conditions and livelihoods due to the possibility of natural disasters with the floods in the south-western parts of the country and extreme climate conditions during summers happening more frequently (World Bank 2021). In addition, the economic structure contributes to Saudi sensitivity to the climate change debate, given that it is an oil-producing and exporting country with extreme dependence on oil being a rentier state economy. This places Saudi Arabia at a greater risk compared to other countries.

In addition to the physical and economic conditions, other factors contribute to Saudi Arabia's climate change calculus, including greenhouse gas and CO_2 emissions. Saudi Arabia's greenhouse gas emissions have witnessed a significant increase since the 1980s. In 1990, Saudi Arabia's CO_2 emission was 173.6 million metric tonnes (mmt), which increased to 607.91 mmt in 2023 (Statista 2024). According to the World Bank (2022), Saudi Arabia's per capita emissions are three times higher than the G20 average, even though it decreased by 10.7% during the 2014–2019 period. According to Climate Transparency (2022), Saudi Arabia's Nationally Determined Contribution (NDC) "target range would increase emissions 416–562% above 1990 levels, or to approximately 524–799 MtCO2e" as of 2030, whereas to keep below the 1.5 °C, it should be 347 MtCO2e. The most important contributor to Saudi greenhouse gas emissions is fossil fuels in its domestic consumption, which constitutes nearly 90% of the energy mix, and this has increased significantly since the 1990s due to fast economic growth. In addition to the domestic and industrial power consumption, the transport sector is a major contributor to greenhouse gas emissions. Demographic growth and fast-paced urbanization have been major factors in increasing Saudi greenhouse gas emissions.

The high level of greenhouse gas emissions has forced the Kingdom to undertake a series of measures to mitigate its contribution to global warming and climate change and roll out an ambitious climate change mitigation plan. In 2021, Saudi Arabia submitted the updated NDC to the UNFCCC secretariat, underlining its commitment to achieving sustainable development objectives and reducing emissions (Clean Development Mechanism [CDM], Saudi Arabia 2021). Accordingly, the Kingdom has committed to achieve net-zero greenhouse gas emissions by 2060 and reduce it to 278 million tonnes by 2030 (ibid. p. 3). The intended NDC stated that Saudi Arabia "has embarked on a comprehensive and highly ambitious set of measures to realize its climate ambitions using the Circular Carbon Economy" (CCE) framework (ibid.). The CCE is an innovative idea developed by Eric Williams (2019), who, based on William MacDonough's (2016) argument of carbon as a usable resource, proposed the idea of regarding atmospheric carbon as circular and using the 4R (reduce, reuse, recycle, and remove carbon) technologies (Kondo 2022). The CCE has emerged as a major concept in Saudi Arabia's plan of action for mitigating climate change and reducing its contribution to greenhouse gas emissions.

Saudi Arabia's climate change challenge is multifaceted because of the nature of its economy and geography. Its substantive economic dependence on fossil fuel production and exports, as well as its need for fast economic growth given the rising population and urbanization, meant that, in the past, Saudi Arabia had dragged its feet regarding the need for a comprehensive and swift climate change plan (Climate Analytics 2015). Whilst recognizing the complex problem facing the world due to global warming and climate change, for long, Saudi policymakers and experts felt that the Kingdom is at an extraordinarily disadvantaged position given the international discourse and consensus on dealing with the problem (Al-Sarihi 2019). They believed, and rightly so, that despite being located in one of the most ecologically vulnerable regions in the world, and being most affected in the scenario of a comprehensive energy transition, the Saudi interests and positions are ignored at the global multilateral forums, especially the COP meetings (Presidency of Meteorology and Environment, Kingdom of Saudi Arabia [PME, Saudi Arabia] 2011). The Saudi position was focused on the need to have a more considered view of energy transition, especially given its economic dependence on hydrocarbons and the need for economic growth.

However, a change in approach arose with the generational transition in the leadership, with the Kingdom recognizing the need to adopt a comprehensive and futuristic view, wherein climate change was placed as a central challenge. As Saudi economic growth was placed within the debate on sustainability, it led to the recognition of the urgent need to reduce greenhouse gas emissions and arrest global warming trends. Therefore, economic diversification emerged as a most pressing challenge for Saudi Arabia, which was reflected through the slew of measures undertaken to reduce dependence on hydrocarbons. The Kingdom also started on the path to reduce its domestic consumption of fossil fuels by increasing the proportion of renewables in its energy mix. The idea is to reduce dependence on fossil fuels both as a rentier state and a fast-developing large economy. This was reflected in the slew of initiatives taken by Saudi Arabia, including the ambitious Vision 2030 programme and multiple projects under its aegis. The Saudi presidency of the G20 in 2019–2020, the advent of COVID-19 and the plummeting oil prices in 2020, and the increased global concern over global warming, climate change, and extreme weather events in different parts of the world contributed to the change in the Saudi approach.

Hence, the 2021, NDC stated that

> the Kingdom is developing and implementing holistic and harmonized programs, policies, initiatives, and collaboration platforms to address climate change challenges at the national, regional and global scale. Examples include the Saudi Green Initiative, the Middle East Green Initiative, the Circular Carbon Economy National Program, the National Renewable Energy Program, and the Saudi Energy Efficiency Program. The Kingdom is also a member and active participant in major international initiatives such as the Global Methane Initiative, Mission Innovation, Clean Energy Ministerial, and Net-Zero Producers Forum. (CDM, Saudi Arabia, 2021, p. 3)

This underlined that Saudi leadership recognized not only the need for a fresh approach at the international multilateral negotiations on climate change but also the urgency for taking mitigating actions at three different levels. First, the need to reduce dependence on fossil fuels was recognized as imminent for a secure and sustainable future. This meant that plans are now in place to increase the share of renewables in the energy mix. Second, the recognition of fast-paced economic diversification within a sustainable development framework has become imminent. This is important, because only a diversified economy, away from dependence on hydrocarbons, is considered necessary for sustainable growth and economic, political, and social stability. Third, the need for the restoration of a green environment through forestation initiatives and steps for the conservation of natural resources has come to the fore in policymaking. Notwithstanding, Saudi Arabia along with other oil and gas economies continues to underline the need for a more holistic approach and not rushing into the energy transition given its potential debilitating and destabilizing impacts on the global economy, and the economy, politics, and society of countries such as Saudi Arabia.

4 POLICY INITIATIVES

Saudi Arabia has undertaken several policy initiatives to address the challenges it faces in terms of the debate on climate change, which, in its case, is intrinsically linked to the nature of its economy, its extraordinary dependence on fossil fuels, and the need for a sustainable future in terms of preventing continuous environmental degradation within the Kingdom and the wider Middle Eastern region. The most important of these initiatives is Vision 2030, which focuses on economic diversification and growth and meeting the aspirations of the Saudi youth. This is followed by the Circular Carbon Economy (CCE), which proposes an innovative framework for reducing carbon emissions and enhancing the Saudi commitment to mitigating global warming and climate change. Additionally, the Kingdom has unveiled an ambitious Green Initiative to radically increase Saudi and regional green cover through forestation by conserving ecology at the local level through micro-initiatives by conserving water and reducing environmental and other pollutants. Finally, Saudi Arabia has been working on meeting the targets of the Sustainable Development Goals (SDGs), building on its successes in achieving the Millennium Development Goals (MDGs).

4.1 Vision 2030

Amongst the most important policy initiatives in light of the need to mitigate global warming and climate change is the plan for economic diversification as part of its Vision 2030 initiatives. Vision 2030 is a comprehensive plan that takes a holistic view of integrating sociopolitical aspirations with economic and sustainable growth targets, keeping in view the pressing concerns for sustainability (Quamar 2022). One of the key aspects of Vision 2030 is to ensure fast economic growth and simultaneous reduction of oil dependence. This means that different sectors of the economy need to be strengthened or built from scratch. For example, the areas of service, transport, building and infrastructure, shipping, logistics, retail, religious and leisure tourism, film, music, entertainment, games, and sports are areas in which the Kingdom is investing to reduce its economic dependence on oil (Al Naimi 2022). In addition, Saudi Arabia has planned for major international investments through the Public Investment Fund (PIF) to compensate for the future loss in oil revenues. The vision plan also takes the society and demography into account and has incorporated the need for greater employment generation for young Saudis, both men and women, to reduce unemployment amongst educated youth (Quamar 2022; Al Naimi 2022).

The ambitious economic diversification plan focuses on a futuristic and sustainable vision, wherein scientific and technological solutions to the contemporary problems facing humanity take centre stage. For example, Saudi Arabia has unveiled the plan for a futuristic city—NEOM—that promotes the idea of combining ambition with technology for a sustainable solution to the most pressing of human challenges (NEOM 2004). There are 14 sectors that the NEOM project targets—including manufacturing, water, technology and digital, entertainment and culture, education, research and innovation, design and construction, food, energy, sport, tourism, mobility, health, well-being and biotech, financial services, and media—to create a profitable, sustainable, and innovation-driven economy. NEOM wishes to attract the best in business and innovation to Saudi Arabia with the promise of a transformative impact on the society, economy, and future. Amongst its most prominent projects is "The Line", which promises to revolutionize urban living by reducing emissions to net-zero and minimizing land use for sustainable living (ibid.).

Vision 2030 ultimately aims for socioeconomic transformation through innovation, use of science and technology, and building on the education, economic, and political reforms during the decades since the early 1990s (Quamar 2021). It aims to develop a sustainable economy that provides ample opportunities for educated Saudi youth without necessarily shutting the door on skilled and talented expatriates from across the world. Vision 2030 is based on three pillars—a vibrant society, a thriving economy, and an ambitious nation. In the seven years since its launch in 2016, Vision 2030 has had somewhat of a transformative impact on the society and economy by reducing restrictions, especially on women and cultural and social activities, and by decreasing the role of the ulema in determining public and private values (Quamar 2021, 2022).

4.2 Circular Carbon Economy

The CCE is an innovative idea that is based on the premise that carbon can be useful if technological innovation is made to reduce, reuse, recycle, and remove it (William 2019). Hence, reducing carbon emissions can be done through increasing renewables in the energy mix and judicious use of fossil fuels, whilst the emitted carbon can be reused through enhanced oil recovery methods (Kondo 2022; Al Shehri et al. 2023). Furthermore, through technological innovations, carbon can be recycled as a chemical product of secondary fuel and can be removed through direct air capture (DAC), carbon capture and storage (CCS), and afforestation. During its G20 presidency in 2019–2020, Saudi Arabia proposed CCE as a possible breakthrough in fighting climate change, defining it as "a voluntary, holistic, integrated, inclusive, pragmatic and complementary approach to promote economic growth while enhancing environmental stewardship through managing emissions in all sectors including, but not limited to, energy, industry, mobility and food" (G20 2020). Through policy and scholarly initiatives, the CCE was eventually endorsed in the G20 summit as a possible way forward in combatting climate change and mitigating global warming.

Saudi Arabia has taken several initiatives that fall within the concept of CCE and can help it reduce greenhouse gas emissions. Amongst the most important is reducing carbon emissions in domestic consumption mostly by transitioning to renewables for power generation for domestic use. This is complemented by the Saudi Energy Efficiency Program, which covers nearly 90% of the power consumption sector and aims to reduce carbon emissions by adopting more efficient energy consumption practices at all levels (CDM, Saudi Arabia 2021). Saudi Arabia also has the potential to recycle and reuse carbon both in its petrochemical industry and through policy initiatives and technological innovations in hydrogen energy (ibid.). There are, however, challenges to the concept of CCE, and many have also raised questions about its effectiveness and viability. Notably, the resistance to and criticism of the CCE is due to the questions regarding its universal usefulness. However, it can certainly prove to be an effective idea for major emitters who can use the concept to invest in research and development and scientific and technological innovations to reduce, reuse, recycle, and remove atmospheric carbon.

4.3   *Saudi Green Initiative*

In 2021, Saudi Arabia launched the Saudi Green Initiative (SGI) to integrate environmental protection, energy transition, and sustainability programmes with an overarching aim of reducing emissions and fighting climate change. The SGI is integrated into the Middle East Green Initiative (MGI), which is also an initiative launched by the Crown Prince and Prime Minister Mohammed Bin-Salman, who in November 2022 announced a $2.5 billion fund to support the MGI. The MGI intends to plant nearly 50 billion trees across the MENA, including 10 billion within Saudi Arabia, as a massive afforestation measure to restore degraded land to help improve air quality, reduce land and soil erosion, prevent adverse weather events, such as flooding and dust storms, and restore wildlife and green habitats (Saudi Green Initiative [SGI] 2023). Protecting marine biodiversity also falls within the mandate of the SGI. Accordingly, the idea is to reach the ambition of net-zero emissions by 2060 by implementing the concept of CCE and by accelerating the Kingdom's transition to a green economy. Notably, "three overarching targets guide SGI's work – emissions reduction, afforestation, and land and sea protection" (Vision 2030, 2023).

Saudi Arabia has launched more than 80 initiatives to meet the targets under the SGI through various existing and new programmes. Amongst the most important initiatives is enhancing Saudi Arabia's energy efficiency programme by 2025. Accordingly, the National Energy Services Company (Tarshid) has incentivized implementing new energy efficiency standards across sectors, including power generation, water desalination, and electricity production and transmission (CDM, Saudi Arabia 2021). Hydrogen production and export, transforming the energy mix to increase the share of renewables, waste and water management, and Mangrove plantation are other ambitious plans that are both integral to SGI and futuristic. The CCE and SGI are part of the Saudi Vision 2030, which aims to transform the Kingdom from an oil-reliant economy to a multifaceted diversified economy and a leading country in the world in terms of meeting the demands of climate change and sustainability.

4.4   Sustainable Development

Sustainable development is at the heart of the need to fight global warming and climate change, and Saudi Arabia has taken policy initiatives to integrate its climate change policy to achieve SDGs. The 17 SDGs include no poverty, zero hunger, good health and well-being, quality education, gender equality, clean water and sanitation, affordable and clean energy, decent work and economic growth, reduced inequalities, sustainable cities and communities, responsible consumption and production, climate action, life below water, life on land, peace, justice and strong institutions, and, finally, partnership for the goals. The Kingdom has been mindful of achieving SDGs as part of its growth targets. During

196   MD. M. QUAMAR

its voluntary national review of the 2018 high-level political forum on
sustainable development in the United Nations, Saudi Arabia underlined
its commitment to achieving SDGs by integrating it into the national
action plans as part of Vision 2030 and other initiatives for combatting
climate change in a sustainable environment. The report noted that.

> Saudi Arabia's commitment to the international development agenda is
> reflected not only in the actions it has undertaken domestically but also in
> the contributions it has generously provided to the development efforts of
> low-income countries through humanitarian and development assistance.
> As highlighted in the report, Saudi Arabia is one of the largest donors
> in the world, with a wide reach across geographical areas and develop-
> ment sectors. It has also become a significant provider of foreign direct
> investment in several developing countries in sectors of great significance
> in poverty alleviation such as agriculture and food processing. (United
> Nations, 2018)

The SDGs are an integral part of the global action plan led by the
United Nations to improve the living standards for the global population sustainably without damaging the ecology, whilst simultaneously
encouraging governments across the world to take a sustainable approach
to economic growth. This has helped countries such as Saudi Arabia to
integrate policy initiatives to combat climate change within the broader
framework of economic growth and sustainability. Amongst the most
important aspects of SDGs wherein Saudi Arabia faces adverse conditions
is in food and water security. Thus far, Saudi Arabia has been able to meet
its demands for clean water and adequate food due to its financial wealth,
but it remains vulnerable to challenges emanating from both natural disasters and human conflicts. Amongst the steps taken by the Kingdom to
ensure water and food security is using desalination technology, but its
adverse impact on local ecology remains a challenge. Furthermore, some
efforts in the direction of water management can be useful. This is also
linked to the question of food security, wherein the Kingdom largely
depends on imports or buying land in poor African countries to be able
to meet its requirements. Investments in technology and research and
development for land use for irrigation and agriculture have remained
far-fetched, given past failures, but can be explored with the help of
technological innovations and scientific advancements.

4.5   Renewable Energy

Saudi Arabia has huge potential for the use of renewable energy across the spectrum, including solar, wind, and hydrogen. Through its National Renewable Energy Program, the Kingdom plans to increase the share of renewables to 50% by 2030 through investments in technological innovation and streamlining the renewable energy value chain in the Saudi economy. An ambitious green hydrogen plan was unveiled to this effect, expecting to produce 650 tonnes per day of green hydrogen by electrolysis and 1.2 million tonnes of green ammonia annually by 2025 (CDM, Saudi Arabia 2021). In addition to green hydrogen, Saudi Arabia has the potential to become a leading producer of blue hydrogen, which can help enhance carbon capture potentials. In addition, Saudi Arabia has become part of the Global Methane Pledge Initiative and has committed itself to help and collaborate in reducing global methane emissions by 30% by 2030 (ibid.).

5   CHALLENGES AND LIMITATIONS

Saudi Arabia is at the centre of the global energy transition and climate change debate, being a leading oil producer and exporter, a rentier oil-based economy, and lying in an extremely ecologically vulnerable area. For long, the Kingdom adopted a defensive approach to the global climate change debate, as it was viewed as harmful to the interests of the global oil and gas producers. However, as the global consensus on the need to fight climate change became stronger, Saudi Arabia has adopted a more nuanced position. It has integrated its climate change strategy into its action plan to achieve the SDGs and economic diversification. Through Vision 2030, the commitment to CCE, its promotion during its G20 presidency and the subsequent announcement of SGI and MGI, as well as its commitment to increase domestic renewable use, Saudi Arabia has put itself in the leadership position in the global climate change debate. As it joins BRICS and claims a more prominent role in global geopolitics, it is important to analyse the challenges and limitations it faces at the domestic, regional, and international levels as far as its climate change policy and action plans are concerned.

One of the key challenges Saudi Arabia faces is the need for continuing economic growth in a sustainable and climate-sensitive manner. Whilst the Kingdom has made strides in launching mega initiatives, their efficacy is yet to be proven, especially in terms of combatting the physical impacts of climate change. The limitations of the new initiatives in terms of Saudi Arabia's and the Middle East's vulnerability to extreme weather conditions, water shortages, food insecurity, and degradation of land and marine biodiversity remain seriously unexplored and understudied. In terms of the protection of local ecologies, the possible adverse impact of mega developmental projects also remains unknown. Therefore, ecological studies and urban planning in a sustainable manner should be prioritized within the mega transformation initiatives.

The other challenge emanates from the cost-effectiveness perspective, wherein some of the domestic and regional initiatives can prove to be less effective in contributing significantly to addressing the impact of climate change for local communities, whilst cornering a mega share in the budgetary allocations. This would mean lesser financial availability for micro-programmes, especially as the financial capabilities of most of the regional countries remain limited. Moreover, given the fast transition in the global energy market and its impact on oil prices due to fluctuation both due to grey rhino and black swan events, such as COVID-19 and the Russia–Ukraine War, the need to increase the share of renewable sources in the energy mix is urgent and imminent, and this will also require huge financial allocation and commitments.

Furthermore, regional and global geopolitical tensions and conflicts can limit Saudi manoeuvrability as far as its plan for mega-economic transformation and ecological preservation is concerned. At the regional level, the growing tensions due to the ongoing Israel–Palestine conflict and its possible adverse impacts on regional stability can lead to serious challenges for Saudi Arabia. Moreover, the hedging strategy of the Kingdom vis-à-vis the United States and China can be challenging given that global economic and environmental governance are prone to geopolitical impacts. Finally, for the Kingdom, it remains challenging to develop broader regional cooperation on combatting climate change and evolving a regional action plan, especially as the Gulf and Middle East region remains prone to conflicts, and civil wars and suffers from proliferation of disruptive non-state actors.

6 Conclusion

Saudi Arabia has the second-largest oil reserves in the world, and it is amongst the leading global energy producers and exporters. The Saudi economy is largely dependent on revenues generated through hydrocarbon exports and it lies in an arid and climate-vulnerable region, making it a dual stakeholder in the contemporary global debate on climate change. As Saudi Arabia joins BRICS, it has the potential to play a leading role in the debate on climate change at the regional and international level and set the future action plan for the world in combatting this serious challenge. Whilst Saudi Arabia has implemented many policy initiatives to combat climate change, and some of them are in the direction of meeting the global climate change goals such as reducing emissions and achieving zero-emissions goals by 2060, the urgency of the problems remains a concern. This is especially true within the context of extreme weather conditions, ecological damage, degradation of marine and land biodiversity, and the challenges to water and food security. As noted, Saudi Arabia can leverage its advantages and transform the challenges to emerge as a leading global actor in taking policy initiatives to mitigate the adverse impacts of climate change within the country, in the Middle East region and the world. Given the centrality of fossil fuels, and greenhouse gas and CO_2 emissions, in the debate on climate change, Saudi Arabia will be in a disadvantageous position if it does not take a proactive stance in steering the debate and devising the future plan of action. As it becomes a member of BRICS, Saudi Arabia has the advantage of building partnership with countries, such as India, China, and Russia, to devise a global plan of action by finding innovative solutions to contentious issues such as climate financing, technology transfer, carbon emissions, and renewable sources that remain unresolved despite decades of debate and discussions amongst global stakeholders.

References

Al-Naimi, Sarah Muhanna. 2022. "Economic Diversification Trends in the Gulf: The Case of Saudi Arabia." *Circular Economy and Sustainability* 2: 221–230.

Al-Sarihi, Aisha. 2019. "Climate Change and Economic Diversification in Saudi Arabia: Integrity, Challenges, and Opportunities." *Policy Paper*, no. 1, The Arab Gulf States Institute in Washington, 20 March, https://agsiw.org/climate-change-and-economic-diversification-in-saudi-arabia-integrity-challenges-and-opportunities/.

Al-Shehri, Thamir, Jan Frederik Braun, Nicholas Howarth, Alessandro Lanza, and Mari Luomi. 2023. "Saudi Arabia's Climate Change Policy and the Circular Carbon Economy Approach." *Climate Policy* 23 (2): 151–167.

Al-Wabel, Mohammad I., Sallam, Abdelazeem, Ahmad, Munir, Elanazi, Khaled, and Usman, Adel R.A. 2020. "Extent of Climate Change in Saudi Arabia and its Impacts on Agriculture: A Case Study from Qassim Region." In *Environment, Climate, Plant and Vegetation Growth*, edited by Shah Fahad et al., 635–57, Cham, Switzerland: Springer Nature.

Savaresi, Annalisa. 2016. "The Paris Agreement: A New Beginning?" *Journal of Energy & Natural Resources Law* 34 (1): 16–26.

Asian News International (ANI). 2023. "BRICS Countries Collaborate to Mobilise Climate Finance at COP28 in UAE." *Business Standard*, 3 December. https://www.business-standard.com/world-news/brics-countries-collaborate-to-mobilise-climate-finance-at-cop28-in-uae-123120301190_1.html.

Bodansky, Daniel. 1993. "The United Nations Framework Convention on Climate Change: A Commentary." *Yale Journal of International Law* 18 (451): 451–558.

Freitas, Bodas, M. Isabel, Eva Dantas, and Michiko Iizuka. 2012. "The Kyoto Mechanism and the Diffusion of Renewable Energy Technologies in BRICS." *Energy Policy* 42: 118–128.

Böhringer, Christoph. 2003. "The Kyoto Protocol: A Review and Perspectives." *Oxford Review of Economic Policy* 19 (3): 451–466.

Bolin, Bert. 2008. *A History of the Science and Politics of Climate Change: The Role of the Intergovernmental Panel on Climate Change*. Cambridge, UK: Cambridge University Press.

Clean Development Mechanism, Kingdom of Saudi Arabia [CDM, Saudi Arabia]. 2021. "Kingdom Of Saudi Arabia/Updated Nationally Determined Contribution," 16 November. https://www.cdmdna.gov.sa/reports/44/ksa-ndc-national-determined-contribution-2021.

Climate Analytics. 2015. "The Paradox of Saudi Arabia's Climate Plans," 24 November. https://climateanalytics.org/press-releases/the-paradox-of-saudi-arabias-climate-plans.

Climate Transparency. 2022. "Saudi Arabia." *Climate Transparency Report: Comparing G20 Climate Action*. https://www.climate-transparency.org/wp-content/uploads/2022/10/CT2022-Saudi-Arabia-Web.pdf.

Contu, Davide, Ozgur Kaya, and Ilker Kaya. 2021. "Attitudes towards Climate Change and Energy Sources in Oil Exporters." *Energy Strategy Reviews* 38: 1–12.

Dalby, Simon. 2013. "The Geopolitics of Climate Change." *Political Geography* 37: 38–47.

Ferris, Nick. 2022. "What Four Years of Non-Existent Climate Action has Done to Brazil," *Energy Monitor*, 29 September. https://www.energymonitor.ai/policy/bolsonaro-what-four-years-of-non-existent-climate-action-has-done-to-brazil/.

G20. 2020. "Leaders' Declaration," Riyadh Summit, 21–22 November, https://www.ilo.org/wcmsp5/groups/public/---dgreports/---dcomm/documents/meetingdocument/wcms_761761.pdf.

Ivanova, Maria. 2018. "Climate Change." In *Oxford Handbook on the United Nations*, edited by Thomas G. Weiss and Sam Daws, 716–733. Oxford, UK: Oxford University Press.

Kıprızlı, Göktuğ. 2022. "Through the Lenses of Morality and Responsibility: BRICS, Climate Change and Sustainable Development." *Uluslararası İlişkiler*, 19 (75): 65–82. https://doi.org/10.33458/uidergisi.1164936

Kondo, Shigeto. 2022. "Evaluation of Saudi Arabia's Climate Change Policy: Circular Carbon Economy and Green Initiatives." The Institute of Energy Economics, Japan, 13 May. http://eneken.ieej.or.jp/data/10286.pdf.

Krane, Jim. 2020. "Climate Action versus Inaction: Balancing the Costs for Gulf Energy Exporters." *British Journal of Middle Eastern Studies* 47 (1): 117–135.

Lachapelle, Erick, and Matthew Paterson. 2013. "Drivers of National Climate Policy." *Climate Policy* 13 (5): 547–571.

Leal-Arcas, Rafael. 2013. "The BRICS and Climate Change." *International Affairs Forum* 4 (1): 22–26.

McDonough, William. 2016. "Carbon is Not the Enemy." *Nature* 539: 349–351.

Ministry of Ecology and Environment of the People's Republic of China [MEE, PRC]. 2022. "Joint Statement issued at the BRICS High-level Meeting on Climate Change." 24 May 2022. http://brics2022.mfa.gov.cn/eng/hywj/ODMM/202205/t20220529_10694182.html

Mizo, Robert. 2016. "India, China and Climate Cooperation." *India Quarterly* 72 (4): 375–394.

Nath, Pradosh K., and Bhagirath Behera. 2011. "A Critical Review of Impact of and Adaptation to Climate Change in Developed and Developing Economies." *Environment, Development and Sustainability* 13: 141–162.

NEOM (2024), "About US." https://www.neom.com/en-us/about.

Presidency of Meteorology and Environment, Kingdom of Saudi Arabia (PME, Saudi Arabia). 2011. *Second National Communication, Kingdom of Saudi Arabia*, Submitted to United Nations Framework Convention on Climate Change (UNFCCC). https://unfccc.int/sites/default/files/resource/saunc2.pdf.

Quamar, Md. Muddassir. 2021. *Education System in Saudi Arabia: Of Change and Reforms*. New Delhi: Palgrave Macmillan.

Quamar, Md. Muddassir. 2022. "Demography, Governance and Reforms in Saudi Arabia: An Assessment of the Vision 2030." In *Youth Bloom in GCC*, edited by Sameena Hameed, 34–49. New Delhi: KW Publishers.

Reddy, B. Sudhakara., and Gaudenz B. Assenza. 2009. "Climate Change—A Developing Country Perspective." *Current Science* 97 (1): 50–62.

Reid, Walter V., and José Goldemberg. 1998. "Developing Countries are Combating Climate Change: Actions in Developing Countries that Slow Growth in Carbon Emissions." *Energy Policy* 26 (3): 233–237.

Saudi Green Initiative (SGI) (2023), "Saudi Climate Vision." https://www.greeninitiatives.gov.sa/saudi-climate-vision/.

Soergel, Bjoern, Elmar Kriegler, Isabelle Weindl, Sebastian Rauner, Alois Dirnaichner, Constantin Ruhe, Matthias Hofmann, et al. 2021. "A Sustainable Development Pathway for Climate Action within the UN 2030 Agenda." *Nature Climate Change* 11: 656–664.

Statista (2024), "Carbon dioxide (CO_2) Emissions from Fossil Fuel and Industrial Purposes in Saudi Arabia from 1970 to 2022." https://www.statista.com/statistics/486065/co2-emissions-saudi-arabia-fossil-fuel-and-industrial-purposes/

Tarawneh, Qassem Y., and Shakhawat Chowdhury. 2018. "Trends of Climate Change in Saudi Arabia: Implications on Water Resources." *Climate* 6 (1): 1–19.

Ülgen, Sinan (2021), "How Deep Is the North-South Divide on Climate Negotiations?" Carnegie Europe, 6 October. https://carnegieeurope.eu/2021/10/06/how-deep-is-north-south-divide-on-climate-negotiations-pub-85493.

United Nations. 2018. "Sustainable Development Goals Knowledge Platform: Saudi Arabia." https://sustainabledevelopment.un.org/memberstates/saudiarabia.

United Nations Climate Change (UNCC). 2023. "What is Technology Development and Transfer?" https://unfccc.int/topics/what-is-technology-development-and-transfer.

Vision 2030, Kingdom of Saudi Arabia. 2023. "Saudi Green Initiative." https://www.vision2030.gov.sa/en/projects/saudi-green-initiative/.

Williams, Eric. 2019. "Achieving Climate Goals by Closing the Loop in a Circular Carbon Economy." 6 November, King Abdullah Petroleum Studies and Research Center, https://www.kapsarc.org/research/publications/achieving-climate-goals-by-closing-the-loop-in-a-circular-carbon-economy/.

World Bank. 2021. "Saudi Arabia: Extreme Precipitation Events." *Climate Change Knowledge Portal.* https://climateknowledgeportal.worldbank.org/country/saudi-arabia/extremes.

World Bank. 2022. "CO2 Emissions (Metric Tons Per Capita)—Saudi Arabia." https://data.worldbank.org/indicator/EN.ATM.CO2E.PC?locations=SA.

India–Africa Cooperation: Joint Engagement in Adaptation to Climate Change

Shilpi Ghosh

1 INTRODUCTION

At the 15th BRICS Summit (2023), New Delhi's commitment to the Global South was reiterated by Prime Minister Narendra Modi, who stated that India is a trusted and close partner of Africa in its road to become a global powerhouse under Agenda 2063. With this inclusion (Sabka Sath) in mind, India successfully advocated for the African Union to become a permanent member of the G20 (2022). African nations too have responded well to these efforts. Africa and India have significant historical and geographical ties. The two regions' inhabitants have always remained close together due to their proximity to one another and easy access to the Indian Ocean. India has consistently supported Africa during its anticolonial struggles, and Satyagraha, introduced by Gandhi, influenced many African independence fighters. With the establishment of formal ties after independence, India helped Africa achieve its developmental objectives and restructure its economy through South–South cooperation. The relationship since then has evolved in a much

---

S. Ghosh (✉)
School of International Studies, JNU, New Delhi, India
e-mail: shilpi30_isi@jnu.ac.in

© The Author(s), under exclusive license to Springer Nature Singapore Pte Ltd. 2024
H. Solomon et al. (eds.), *BRICS and Climate Change*,
https://doi.org/10.1007/978-981-97-5532-5_10

204   S. GHOSH

more positive direction. India now considers Africa to be an important partner. Both regions have continuously collaborated to achieve their shared objectives of economic growth, peace, stability, and security. Furthermore, both are significantly impacted globally by issues such as climate change.

2   CLIMATE CHANGE IN AFRICA

Over the past few decades, climate change has been one of the most debated subjects. The impact of global warming is already being felt across the globe, and it is expected that it will become even worse. Despite the United Nations' historic climate agreements, global emissions have increased significantly. New research indicates that global warming will surpass the crucial 1.5 °C increase over preindustrial levels by the end of the decade (Joeri Rogelj 2018). Governments from across the world have promised to cut emissions; however, there is no doubt that people living in the Global South are experiencing more negative effects from climate change than people living in the Global North (Suri S. 2023). These communities have historically been neglected and have fewer means to respond to or adapt to natural disasters. Africa emits 3.8% of the world's greenhouse gases, which is the least amount compared to the biggest emitters in the world (23% United States, 19% China, and 12% European Union). When contrasted with India, which accounts for 6% of global emissions, Africa makes a smaller contribution to global warming. According to the Africa Progress Panel (2015), which was headed by Kofi Annan, it would take the average Ethiopian 240 years to have the same carbon footprint as the average American. This makes Africa stand out disproportionately.

According to a recent report, climate change in Africa is weakening food security systems, affecting economies, promoting more internal migration and displacement (WMO 2023), and creating new conflicts or exacerbating existing ones (UN 2020). Using information from the Emergency Event Database (2023), 20 meteorological, hydrological, and climate-related hazards were reported in 80 African countries in 2022; approximately 5,000 people died as a result of these natural hazards. These tragic events directly impacted over 110 million individuals and resulted in economic losses of over $8.5 billion.

Agriculture being the backbone of the continent's economy and means of subsistence has also suffered the brunt of climate change (Trisos 2022).

Agricultural productivity has gone down considerably. The COVID-19 pandemic and the Ukraine war have caused a series of shocks that have increased food costs and decreased incomes. As a result, 123 million people, or 12% of the population of sub-Saharan Africa, will fear going hungry and suffer from severe malnutrition by the 2030s (IMF, Sept 2022). Conflicts over limited amounts of arable land, water, and pastures may intensify as a result of climate change and the depletion of natural resource bases (WMO, The Global Climate 2011–2020: A decade of acceleration 2023). As a result of mounting land pressure, farmer–herder violence has also escalated over the past 10 years.

African countries today acknowledge that climate change is already occurring, and, if left unchecked, it might exert severe strain on the continent's economy, way of life, and natural environment in the decades and years to come. North Africa witnessed a sharp increase in temperature, which resulted in wildfires in Algeria and Tunisia. Droughts have become a common occurrence in the Horn of Africa, especially in Ethiopia, Kenya, and Somalia due to a prolonged La Niña event (Johnson 2021), as a result of which, there has been an increase in internal migration in recent years. More than half of the newly reported displacements in 2022 were caused by climate-related disasters (Siegfried 2023). According to a report, 48 of the 49 African nations—mostly those in the Central African Republic, Chad, Nigeria, Guinea, Somalia, and Guinea-Bissau—are at a high or extremely high risk of being impacted by climate change (UNICEF 2023). The security landscape in Africa is fast changing due to changes in the climate, population, and urbanization.

Significant flooding occurred in many Sahelian regions during the monsoon season, especially in Nigeria, Niger, Chad, and the southern portion of Sudan. Many tropical storms and cyclones that hit Southern Africa in 2023 caused flooding and forced people to flee. According to a study, if climate adaptation is not done quickly, 16–27 million people are predicted to be suffering from coastal flooding, with damage costs ranging from $5 to $9 billion (Hinkel 2011). These cataclysmic disasters have caused enormous harm to African populations and have had significant economic effects. Furthermore, climate change and its effects are also detrimental to human health because they can alter the spread of zoonotic illnesses such as coronaviruses and Ebola, as well as diseases such as cholera, malaria, and meningitis.

The African Development Bank (AfDB) estimates that, by 2040, the effects of climate change might cost the continent $50 billion year, and

GDP could decline by an additional 30% by 2050 (Africa 2017). There will be significant hazards to human, social, and economic development if the effects of climate change are not taken into account. It may even reverse development efforts in the most afflicted countries by exacerbating the high susceptibility and inadequate adaptive capacity of most African nations, especially the poorest. Extreme weather events are also contributing to higher government spending. Furthermore, it has resulted in a decrease in the amount of taxes collected, which could eventually raise the amount of debt owed by the government.

Moreover, many of the women in the region are employed primarily in manual labour and small-scale farming, two occupations that are vulnerable to the effects of climate change. Because of this, women become more vulnerable to the effects of extreme weather events such as frequent droughts and floods, which harm crops and kill cattle that are essential to their livelihoods. For instance, the 2022 Africa Migration Report states that between 1990 and 2020, the proportion of female foreign migrants in Africa rose by 69%.

3 Climate Change in India

Indian Prime Minister Narendra Modi at the United Nations' COP26 climate summit in Glasgow, Scotland (2021) states that "climate change is looming large over the existence of many developing countries. Today, we have to take bold action to save the world. This is what is really required". India acknowledges the gravity of climate change, but there remain several unresolved developmental issues that require immediate attention.

According to preliminary estimates done by the United Nations Environmental Programme Report, India's greenhouse gas emissions increased by more than 5% in the past decade. India is among the top seven worldwide greenhouse gas emitters. Nine G20 members (low- and middle-income nations), including India, contributed 53% in 2000, which rose to 69% in 2021 (UNEP 2023a). In the past few decades, extreme weather events have been reported in India. For several months, there were record-breaking temperature rises, and exceptionally heavy rainfall caused deluges in several parts of the nation. Floods resulting from this killed thousands of people and cattle (WMO 2023). In 2022–2023 alone, climate-related disasters claimed 2,923 lives, damaged 1.84 million hectares (ha) of cropland, destroyed over 80,563 homes, and killed over 92,519 cattle (CSE 2023). Madhya Pradesh recorded the most days with extreme weather events, Bihar recorded the largest number of fatalities, followed by Himachal Pradesh and Uttar Pradesh (CSE 2023).

UNICEF in its first global climate risk index with an emphasis on children (titled "The Climate Crisis is a Child Rights Crisis: Introducing the Children's Climate Risk Index", 2021) ranked India 26th out of 163 countries in the report. This suggested that the health, education, and safety of Indian children are among the most "at-risk" due to the effects of climate change (Nicholas Rees 2021). Large-scale relocation as a result of climate changes occurs frequently in densely populated nations such as India. India's worst-ever monsoon season flooding incident happened in June 2013; strong rains, melting mountain snow, and ice-lake eruptions caused severe flooding and landslides in Uttarakhand in which over 5,800 people perished. Kerala has been severely impacted by annual floods. Cyclone Amphan, the region's most expensive tropical storm on record with estimated losses of over $14 billion, struck landfall in May 2020 and caused significant damage to Bangladesh and India. However, advances in emergency planning and early warning systems lessened the damage (WMO, The Global Climate 2011–2020: A decade of acceleration 2023).

India experiences significant droughts due to El Niño, resulting in acute food and water shortages in several parts of the country (WMO, The Global Climate 2011–2020: A decade of acceleration 2023). The situation has become worse due to disparities in access to and availability of water supplies as well as significant crop failures. As a result, India is on the verge of suffering food insecurity. After all, rain-fed agriculture accounts for around 65% of India's cropland. Food insecurity has economic forces that are amplified by climate change. Wetlands have dried up, and ecosystems have suffered greatly as a result of India's droughts and precipitation decrease (Cruz 2007). Agriculture and associated industries employ almost two-thirds of India's labour force and generate close to 20% of the country's Gross Domestic Product (GDP). The fact that Indian agriculture remains essentially dependent on weather patterns makes it vulnerable to the effects of climate change (Sahastrabuddhe et al. 2023). The area most adversely impacted by agriculture include the coastal regions of Gujarat, Maharashtra, and Karnataka (Panda 2009). These regions may also experience heightened flooding in low-lying areas. This will pose a serious threat to those who live in parts of India that are susceptible to the effects of rising sea levels, as the country has more than 7,500 km of coastline. If sea levels rise by 50 cm, coastal flooding might affect six Indian port cities: Chennai, Kochi, Kolkata, Mumbai, Surat, and Visakhapatnam (Prof. Piyush Tiwari 2022).

Extreme heat and droughts reduce farmer incomes by 14% for important crops, according to the 2017–2018 Economic Survey. The hardest hit are poorer farmers in areas with inadequate irrigation and infrastructure. High temperatures may make life difficult for workers and reduce productivity in industries such as construction. The International Labour Organization (ILO) estimates that, by 2030, the loss of productivity due to heat stress might be as great as India losing 34 million full-time jobs (up from 15 million in 1995). A further sign of climate change is the increase of extremely hot days (over 35 °C) in Indian cities. Similar rises have also been observed in Hyderabad, Bengaluru, Mumbai, and other large cities.

Owing to its lack of readiness and geographic vulnerability to climate change, India also experiences the spread of diseases that kill people and ruin people's livelihoods. These effects are further compounded by extreme poverty and inequality (Dubash 2012). The largest socioeconomic group in India impacted by the combination of increased variability and climate change may be women in general and impoverished women in particular (Adve 2019). India is home to 21 of the 30 most polluted cities in the world (Report 2020), putting millions of people at risk for respiratory and other ailments linked to pollution. According to a 2018 report, 1.24 million Indians died as a result of air pollution in 2017 (Lancet 2019).

According to German Watch, India ranks 14th in the world in terms of the impact of climate change. These occurrences thus amply demonstrate how susceptible India is growing to climate change.

4   Africa and India's Joint Initiative to Address Climate Change

Climate change is an immediate problem. According to an OECD report, Asia and Africa, being heavily dependent on natural resources, will find it difficult to adjust to climate change, and the current levels of poverty in these regions would quadruple due to climate change (OECD 2015). By 2050, it is predicted that terrestrial biodiversity would have declined by an additional 10% worldwide, with notable declines in Asia and Southern Africa (OECD, Environmental Outlook to 2050, 2012).

Even though the effects of climate change are becoming more apparent across Africa, some nations are leading the charge in combatting it and making use of the continent's natural resources. Many African nations are already leading the way in the development of low-carbon, eco-friendly substitutes for harmful land, water, and air chemicals. Indigenous people, along with their knowledge systems, have been protecting places that provide both local and critical global benefits, such as food, medicine, and cultural well-being as well as mitigation of climate change and biodiversity preservation (UNDP 2023). India is also contributing to the solution and going above and beyond what is required to combat climate change. In accordance with NAPCC, 34 states and union territories have created State Action Plans on Climate Change (SAPCCs), taking into consideration state-specific climate change-related challenges (Ministry of Environment 2023). To address the issues posed by climate change, India has started participating in international coalitions such as the International Solar Alliance (ISA) and the Coalition for Disaster Resilient Infrastructure (CDRI).

Moreover, in order to address climate change and its effects, Goal 13 of the United Nations' Sustainable Development Goals demands immediate action from both the regions. The moment has come for Africa and India to work together to address this ongoing calamity and shield the area from some of the worst effects of the climate catastrophe. If both regions adopt a more concentrated and cooperative strategy, they could have a good effect on the world economy. The two regions—which already have close cultural, economic, educational, and security ties—will become even closer by cooperating to address climate change adaptations. Using the UNFCCC climate action pathways as a guide, eight cross-sectoral collaborative opportunities that may be crucial to reaching the SDGs for Africa and India, as well as development pathways that are climate resilient (Nation, Africa, & Commission 2022), are noted below.

4.1   Transforming Food Systems

To fight against climate change, a "code red for humanity", there is an urgent call to transform our global food and agriculture systems in both Africa and India. The hidden environmental costs—which are primarily related to greenhouse gas and nitrogen emissions—appears to be a bigger burden in these nations (FAO, The state of food and agriculture 2023). Climate change affects livelihoods and incomes in rural areas, marine and coastal ecosystems, and terrestrial and inland ecosystems, increasing the risk of food insecurity in these regions and populations (Shobha Suri 2023). Efforts to adapt are vital, because climate change has already begun to negatively impact livelihoods in these nations by disrupting supply chains and reducing agricultural productivity. This could lead to a sharp rise in hunger and malnutrition by 2050 (FAO, The future of food and agriculture, Alternative pathways to 2050, 2018).

The transformation of food systems is increasingly acknowledged as a critical component of the response to the climate emergency and the decline of biodiversity. According to the most recent IPCC Report (AR6), adaptation and mitigation strategies centred around "land, water, and food" have the most potential to address the climate crisis.

Agriculture currently contributes between 19 and 29% of global greenhouse gas emissions, making it a major cause of climate change. Given its size, diversity, and high population, India will likely face significant obstacles in changing its food system, even though the country stands to gain greatly from the change. In the case of Africa, despite having 25% of the world's arable land, 10% of the world's agricultural output comes from it. It has not yet reached the full extent of its abilities. Industry reports state that, with the help of science and technology, Africa's agricultural sector could reach $1 trillion by 2030. To help African agriculture move from labour-intensive, low-productivity practices to skills-intensive methods and create a resilient food system, more funding is required (Ogega 2024).

India and Africa can jointly engage in "climate-smart agriculture" (CSA), which refers to a broad range of agricultural practices that modify agricultural systems to support food security in the face of climate change. A CSA strategy seeks to incorporate climate change into the development and application of sustainable farming methods. It also seeks to lessen agriculture's contribution to global warming and improve agriculture's resilience to climatic variability through improved climate change adaptation (Suri S. 2022). Important CSA initiatives from the Indian government include the National Innovations in Climate Resilient Agriculture (NICRA) projects, which develop and apply enhanced production and risk management technologies to make Indian agriculture—which includes crops, livestock, and fisheries—more resilient to climatic variability and climate change. Additionally, programmes focusing on traditional farming, organic products, Bamboo, millets, agroforestry etc. are part of the National Mission for Sustainable Agriculture (NMSA)

(Vandana Chauhan 2022). The "More Crop Per Drop" scheme is another significant initiative that offers comprehensive solutions for water supply chain creation and distribution (Vandana Chauhan 2022). Farmers receive soil health cards (SHC), which include comprehensive information on the test-based soil nutrient status of their own land as well as suggested fertilizer dosages for enhancing productivity through prudent input use and management.

Climate-smart agriculture practices are also being adopted by African nations. More countries are pledging their commitment to a food system that is more climate-smart and sustainable. Families in Nyando, West Kenya, benefitted from the construction of climate-smart villages by having access to more food and better nutrition options. In areas where coffee is grown, shade trees can reduce the temperature by two to five °C and minimize crop losses, which, in the absence of adaptation, could exceed $100 million annually. This is why farmers in Uganda are using shade trees to increase their coffee crops. More research in the future will help in the creation of climate-smart cultivars of staple crops such as rice (Mali), plantains and bananas (Cote d'Ivoire), and maize (Benin) in West Africa.

India and Africa can collaborate on developing green infrastructure and promoting agroforestry policies. Africa can revamp their land-use policies as was done by India. Africa's food system needs to become more efficient in areas such as food production, storage, processing, and packaging. The most advantageous policies for these regions will be to foster an environment that is welcoming and open to the transfer of knowledge and technology, supports legislation that helps to establish public–private partnerships (PPPs) for investment, and increases communication within and between countries to better understand the variety of issues that different regions face (FICCI 2016). As the Indian presidency of the G20 Summit in 2023 shone a bright light on millets, it is true that they are a great crop for long-term food security and sustainable agriculture. It will be helpful for Kenyan farmers, because they thrive in arid regions with little input and offer remarkable nutritional and health benefits. The two nations can work towards becoming a more food-secure country by embracing millets (PIB 2023).

4.2 Protecting Land-Based Ecosystems

Another optimal way to combat climate change is to restore and preserve nature. Between 20 and 30% of the net emissions reductions required by 2050 to limit the rise in global average temperature to 1.5 °C–2 °C could be met by land-based mitigations and significant cuts in emissions from fossil fuels (Society 2022). Protecting the current carbon-rich native ecosystems, restoring damaged ecosystems, and enhancing agroforestry management and involving local communities are the top priorities for land-based mitigation.

The Indian government has implemented a number of actions to conserve the environment and safeguard the ecosystem, which can either directly or indirectly contribute to the fight against climate change. It has introduced programmes that serve as corrective actions for environmental preservation and the sustainable growth of diverse ecosystems. Through the Conservation of Natural Resources and Eco-systems scheme and its various sub-schemes designed to protect coral reefs, mangrove forests, biosphere reserves, wetlands, and lakes, India has attempted to preserve the nation's natural resources and ecosystems. India's forest cover is to be protected, restored, and enhanced by the National Mission for a Green India (GIM). Programmes such as the Mangrove Initiative for Shoreline Habitats & Tangible Incomes (MISHTI) and Amrit Dharohar promote the best possible use of wetlands and improve carbon storage, biodiversity, ecotourism, and local community revenue generation.

Paradoxically, despite facing the most difficult obstacles, Africa has the best answers to help the world transition to a safe, climate-resilient future. The Great Green Wall Project (2007) was started by the African Union with the goal of improving millions of people's lives in the Sahel and restoring the continent's damaged landscapes. "Environmentally sustainable climate and resilient economies and communities" are at the core of Agenda 2063's aspiration to create a prosperous Africa (UNEP, Agenda 2063: The Africa We Want, first ten-year implementation plan, 2013–2023). A significant issue facing African nations is desertification and land degradation. Nonetheless, Africa is working hard to rebuild its ecosystems (UNEP, Supporting sound ecosystem management 2022). With the Pan-African Action Agenda on Ecosystem Restoration for Increased Resilience, Africa was the first continent to have an ecosystem restoration action plan in place. With the implementation of ambitious integrated ecosystem restoration projects throughout the region, the Pan-African

Action Agenda seeks to establish Africa as a global leader in ecosystem restoration. The government of the Eastern Cape, South Africa, started an extensive ecological experiment to plant the native plant spekboom to restore vast tracts of degraded land. Spekboom improves groundwater supplies and lessens flooding by increasing water infiltration in the ground (UNEP, How Africa is using nature to adapt to climate change 2021). The African Forest Landscape Restoration Initiative, or AFR100, is another national initiative aimed at restoring 100 million hectares of African land by 2030. It seeks to lessen the effects of climate change on the continent, fight poverty, and improve food security. The Mikoko Pamoja Community Based Organization was able to guarantee the preservation of 117 ha of mangroves in Gazi Bay (Kenya) since its founding in 2014. Additionally, the team has created new mangrove forests spanning 10 ha with technical assistance from WWF-Kenya and the Kenya Marine and Fisheries Research Institute (KMFRI) (Mangrove 2024). Furthermore, Somalia has partnered with three universities, Moud University, Puntland State University (PSU), and SIMAD University, to implement its National Adaptation Plan (NAP) and close the capacity gap. The creation of essential outreach and training programmes is being outsourced by the Somalian government, who is taking advantage of university expertise through this partnership. Somalia is ensuring that the knowledge and lessons learnt during the implementation of its NAP project will long be beneficial to the country (UNDP, Africa offers creative solutions to climate change 2023).

One potential joint initiative between the two regions could be to identify "nature-based solutions" to climate change. To truly make land-based mitigation a major player in the fight and decelerate climate change, implementation and funding hurdles must first be removed. A quarter of the world's wildlife populations are already found in these two regions, which also has the youngest population and the most arable land, which means they have the greatest potential for restoration (Kgomotso, 2022). India could also help developing nations in sub-Saharan Africa rewrite their environmental laws and choose the best approaches to environmental management. The contribution of law to environmental protection and poverty alleviation has not received sufficient attention (Mabogunje 1995). India's efforts to boost Africa's economic development will be extremely advantageous for both continents.

4.3   Transforming Energy Systems

In order to prevent climate change and keep global temperatures within 1.5 °C of preindustrial levels, the energy transition must be successful. By the second half of this century, the world's energy sector must transition from fossil fuel-based to zero-carbon sources in order to fulfil regional and national commitments and expedite the global energy transition (IRENA 2024). In keeping with its goal of promoting clean energy, India is increasingly working on solar and renewable energy. The International Solar Alliance (ISA) initiative was introduced by Prime Minister Narendra Modi and French President Francois Hollande on 30 November 2015, during the United Nations Climate Change Conference in Paris (Jha 2023). The ISA is an action-oriented, member-driven, collaborative platform for increased deployment of solar energy technologies. The basic motive behind it was to facilitate energy access, ensure energy security, and drive successful energy transition in its member countries (Oguntuase 2023). A number of African nations as well as the African Development Bank and Pan-African investment platforms such as Africa 50 have also joined the ISA. Moreover, India's announcement under the "Panchamrit action plan" that it plans to attain net-zero emissions by 2070 and source half of its electricity from renewable sources by 2030 is a significant step in its fight against climate change. India is setting the standard for a new paradigm in economic development that could spare other developing nations from adopting the carbon-intensive strategies that many have in the past (PIB, Ministry of Science & Technology 2023).

India wants to become a global exporter and producer of green hydrogen. In order to promote the production and consumption of green hydrogen, India established the National Green Hydrogen Mission in 2022 (Sachin Kotak 2024). It can become an exporter of green hydrogen derivatives and stop importing energy if the correct steps are taken, and it will be able to create a win–win solution for energy security, economic growth, and environmental sustainability if it can fully realize the potential of green hydrogen.

Africa has the potential to lead the world in renewable energy innovation and production. The continent is blessed with an abundance of renewable energy resources, including significant solar capacity, wind resources, geothermal areas, hydro energy, and green hydrogen prospects, despite its many challenges. Furthermore, Africa is home to more than

40% of the world's mineral reserves, which are crucial for the development of low-carbon and renewable technologies. Energy has a significant multiplier effect on Africa's development. It is the cornerstone of ensuring food security, because it boosts productivity in food production, storage, and transportation, while also generating jobs through value addition. Africa's industrial revolution and the full potential of the African Continental Free Trade Area depend on having access to reliable, affordable, and sufficient energy.

The Africa Energy Commission (AFREC), under the African Union, develops policies, programmes, and initiatives for the African Energy transition programme. It aims to fully utilize Africa's own energy resources and potential while avoiding the fossil fuel lock-in that currently befalls most industrialized and emerging economies, even India (Chukwuemeka 2023). However, several countries, such as Ethiopia, Kenya, and South Africa, are rising to the top of the world development league for low-carbon, climate-resilient projects. Ethiopia, for example, aims to achieve net-zero emissions by 2027. The geographical diversity of the continent offers tremendous potential for wind and solar energy, and many of the minerals and rare earth elements required for clean energy technologies are found in its soils (National Planning Commission 2016).

Nevertheless, Africa's energy production has tripled in the past few decades, but because of the continent's high population growth rate, the energy production rate has essentially remained constant. It could be argued that inadequate energy infrastructure has impeded the continent's economic growth and advancement of living standards (Gracelin Baskaran 2024). The International Renewable Energy Agency (IRENA) estimates that Africa has a combined theoretical energy potential of about 1,590 petawatt hours from wind, solar, and photovoltaic energy sources. Creating green energy technology will help to mitigate the effects of climate change and promote economic growth. Africa is appealing to all parties involved, including potential public and private investors, to accept and uphold the continent's shared stance on energy access and a just transition. Africa and India can collaborate to produce green hydrogen, which has the potential to increase GDP in six "important" countries—Egypt, Kenya, Mauritania, Morocco, Namibia, and South Africa—and help Africa meet its industrial needs in a sustainable way (Radford 2023).

India with the finance and technical know-how needs to assist African nations in building their renewable energy infrastructure. Capacity-building programmes and research partnerships can be supported by

216   S. GHOSH

means of cooperative projects that foster technology transfer and address specific energy challenges faced by African nations. It can investigate investment opportunities in African real estate projects, thereby promoting regional economic growth. Indian companies can export renewable energy (RE) technology and equipment to African markets. Both regions stand to benefit from leveraging India's manufacturing prowess. This may require building energy corridors and transmission infrastructure in order to efficiently transport RE across borders and ensure a consistent and sustainable energy supply. According to the IEA study "Electricity 2024", coal will continue to be the primary energy source in India through 2026 (PIB, Coal Demand Likely to Peak Between 2030–2035, 2022). Therefore, if India wishes to diversify its energy matrix and meet its goal of achieving net zero by 2070 in 2021, it will require Africa.

4.4   Transforming Mobility and Transport

The transportation sector is expected to grow at the fastest rate in the coming years, contributing more than 30% of greenhouse gas emissions. Over 90% of the expected global increase in vehicles on the road by 2050 is predicted to occur in low- and middle-income countries (UNEP, Supporting the global shift to electric mobility, 2023b). To effectively combat climate change, new and emerging technologies—such as electric vehicles and buses and zero-carbon producing energy sources—are required. While making the transition to electric vehicles will be important, real systemic change will be required to completely transform transportation, so that it is both affordable and accessible to all societal segments.

Sustainable transportation must be accessible to all, secure and safe, reliable and effective, and most importantly, ecological, hygienic, and strong. To achieve a cleaner transportation sector, several policies need to be implemented globally. These include improved urban planning, facilities for safe and comfortable walking and bicycling, more public transportation, and cleaner, more efficient on-road fleets, including electric vehicles. Governments must provide clear policy guidelines in order to bring about real change, and this global action plan should include a strong push for carbon pricing, urban sustainability action plans in medium- and large-sized cities, and climate finance reform. More public and private investment can be made by raising Official Development Assistance (ODA) funding for climate-friendly transport projects in developing countries (UNFCCC 2007).

The COVID-19 pandemic has presented the transportation industry worldwide with various challenges, including the movement of people from public to private and personal modes of transportation. The third-highest emitter of greenhouse gases in India is the transportation sector, which accounts for 14% of all energy-related CO_2 emissions (Megha Kumar 2022). The Faster Adoption and Manufacturing of (Hybrid &) Electric Vehicles in India (FAME) scheme is one of the numerous initiatives the government has already taken to promote clean mobility and accelerate the adoption of electric vehicles. The railways have pledged to cut emissions by almost 450 million tonnes and reach net-zero emissions by 2030. Both metro rails and high-speed regional mobility are rapidly gaining traction across the country. Ropeways for Overhead Mass Rapid Transit (OMRTS) are already being researched in the north-eastern states (Sinha 2021). The global EV30@30 campaign, which aims to have at least 30% of new car sales be electric by 2030 also has the support of India (Aayog 2023).

Even though there are many domestic renewable energy sources available, many African nations have been importing petroleum fuels from overseas markets, which is increasing their foreign debt. Nevertheless, rather than depending entirely on fossil fuels, some African countries are now beginning to use renewable energy sources. For example, approximately 85% of Kenya's electricity comes from renewable sources, including hydro, geothermal, and increasingly wind and solar energy (Mungai Kihara 2024). In the past two decades, solar energy production has emerged as a viable means of delivering electricity to remote regions of Africa. The revolution in electric mobility is also occurring in Africa. In sub-Saharan Africa, there is a mushroom-like proliferation of electric motorcycle and tuktuk start-ups providing app-based mobility services, while used electric vehicles, such as the Nissan Leaf, are becoming increasingly common in African cities (Cerulli 2024). The growth of "green jobs", which increase the number of jobs available for vehicle assembly and manufacturing in many sub-Saharan African countries, has also been aided by electric mobility. Lithium resources have been discovered in Zimbabwe, Namibia, Ghana, Mali, Ethiopia, and the Democratic Republic of the Congo (DRC). However, most lithium projects in Africa remain in the exploration or development stages (Robertson 2023).

India has received offers from several African nations to service a portion of their development loans by granting Indian companies access to their mining operations and permitting the export of highly valued lithium and cobalt, which would greatly assist India's efforts to secure critical mineral supplies. With China emerging as Africa's largest trading and investment partner in the electric vehicle sector, New Delhi is also attempting to fortify its long-standing ties to other African nations.

5   ENHANCING INCLUSIVE, LOW-EMISSION INDUSTRIALIZATION

The industrial sector is essential to economic growth, but industrial pollution poses problems for the environment and the economy. The ninth SDG seeks to build resilient infrastructure, promote sustainable industrialization, and generate innovative solutions. The National Policy on Biofuels, the National Missions for Enhanced Energy Efficiency and Sustainable Habitat, and the Promotion of Natural Gas are some of India's initiatives to promote "green industrialization" (Ighobor 2016). The Indian government has implemented regulations regarding the recycling of steel, plastic and e-waste, resource efficiency, and the development of green hydrogen technology.

During the 2023–2024 fiscal year, India launched several noteworthy efforts to meet clean energy targets and reduce carbon emissions. The Green Credit Programme was a notable initiative. It encourages voluntary environmental actions as part of the Lifestyle for Environment (LIFE) movement. Under the Gobardhan scheme, India is establishing 500 "waste-to-wealth" plants in an effort to address the issue of waste management (Siddharth Ghanshyam Singh 2023). Initiatives to address climate change were implemented while India presided over the G20. These included the establishment of a global coalition for land restoration, the Resource Efficiency Circular Economy Industry Coalition, and high-level directives for a robust and sustainable economy. However, the bulk of India's industrial activities still rely on coal, so a more significant shift towards industries based on renewable energy will be needed.

As part of a more all-encompassing industrial policy, African countries are pursuing clean and green industrialization strategies. The South Africa Industrial Energy Efficiency Project in Ethiopia is an example of how industrialization can improve livelihoods and create jobs without having a detrimental effect on the environment (UNIDO 2020). India is dedicated to supporting the development of a prosperous Africa founded on inclusive growth and sustainable development, in line with Africa's Agenda 2063 and the Sustainable Development Goals. Energy management systems, smart grids, and the smooth integration of renewable energy sources—such as solar and wind power—into industrial processes are just a few of the ways in which Africa and India can collaborate to develop Industry 4.0. Utilizing renewable energy reduces carbon emissions in industries and boosts energy security and independence. The Economic Report on Africa 2016: Greening Africa's Industrialization, published by the United Nations Economic Commission for Africa (ECA), highlights the fact that "green industrialization is the only way for Africa, it is a precondition for sustainable and inclusive growth" (UN 2023).

Nevertheless, Africa does have a chance to grow its value-added industries at this early stage of the energy transition. Numerous African countries have the potential to become major producers of green hydrogen through the use of electrolysis powered by renewable energy sources. Uganda currently receives 80% of its energy from renewable sources, but it could produce much more with better transmission and storage systems. Green industrial transitions are predicted to result in a 10-year reduction in carbon emissions. Africa needs economic growth that protects its natural resources, creates new opportunities for development, and improves the lives of both current and future generations of Africans. Both regions should create policies that strike a balance between environmental preservation and economic growth in order to minimize emissions and increase economic activity. There is a pertinent need to reevaluate the industrial sector of India and Africa as well as their place in the global economy.

6   Transforming Water Systems

Water security is more crucial than ever, but it is becoming harder to achieve due to climate change. In order to support global goals for food systems, biodiversity, and sustainable development as well as adaptation and resilience in the energy sector, cities, and agriculture, water systems must change in response to climate change. Water is a basic component of climate; it is found everywhere, and all social groups and industries—including manufacturing, commerce, agriculture, sanitation, and energy—are impacted by climate change. Climate-resilient water management must take into account the ripple effects of climate change at all scales and in all industries (IWMI 2022).

Governance is at the heart of climate-resilient water management, and it requires participation from all parties, including marginalized communities. Often, conventional water supply systems are ill-equipped to handle rising temperatures, sporadic dry spells, and irregular rainfall patterns. By fusing green and grey infrastructure, climate-change-resistant water supply systems, such as rainwater collection, water recycling, and intelligent storage solutions, offer a safeguard against the unpredictability of climate change. Floods, droughts, and other water-related events have been the cause of more than 90% of major weather-related disasters over the past 25 years; if climate change is not halted as soon as possible, these events will probably become more frequent and intense. Forecasts indicate that a rise in global temperature of more than 1.5 °C will have catastrophic consequences for the amount and quality of water that is available to meet basic human needs, such as the production of food and energy. This will jeopardize billions of people's right to vital ecosystems, clean water and sanitation, and life itself.

There are several important, mostly unexplored opportunities for lowering carbon emissions that can be obtained through efficient management of freshwater ecosystems and water resources. For example, water and wastewater combined are used, stored, distributed, and treated to the tune of about 10% of greenhouse gas emissions globally. Freshwater ecosystems, such as wetlands, have the largest carbon stocks of any terrestrial ecosystem (Brears 2023). By strengthening the resilience of our water resources, services, and systems, we can reduce the risks that climate change poses to people, ecosystems, and economies.

The Jal Jeevan Mission, Har Ghar jal, Jal Mission for Rejuvenation and Urban Transformation (AMRUT), and Jal Bhujal Yojana are the largest community-led groundwater management initiatives in India (PIB, Steps Taken By Union Government To Increase Water Availability and Promote Conservation Of Water 2023). The African Development Bank's book, *Stories of a Rising Africa: Water for a Better Life,* describes how the availability of clean drinking water, sanitation services, and better management practices has transformed nations such as Senegal, Tunisia, Morocco, and Rwanda. However, water scarcity and irrigation projects have a long history in Africa, particularly in North Africa. India and Africa can work together to provide affordable solutions in several areas, such as the logistics of drinking water. According to the World Health Organization (WHO), 387 million people in sub-Saharan Africa did not have access to basic drinking water services in 2020, and one in three Africans do not have access to clean water, and the situation is becoming worse due to urbanization, climate change, and population growth. Experts predict that 460 million people in Africa will reside in water-stressed areas by 2025. Finding workable solutions to Africa's water scarcity is essential to confront this rapidly developing crisis (Tech 2023).

An agreement for cooperation in agriculture and related fields, such as irrigation and water management, has been approved by the Indian government and Egypt. The Barefoot College / engineers (joint Africa–India initiative) supply sustainable energy, clean water, and means of subsistence to their communities. The Nyabarongo Hydropower Project, built by Bharat Heavy Electricals Limited (BHEL) with the help of an Indian Line of Credit, has allowed Rwanda to make tremendous strides. Policies have been implemented by the Indian government to encourage rainwater harvesting, which is the act of collecting, storing, and reusing rainwater for irrigation purposes in residential, commercial, and agricultural settings. In addition, the Indian government promotes the use of renewable energy sources for water management, such as solar energy for water pumping, seawater desalination, and wastewater treatment. This is being done in an effort to reduce greenhouse gas emissions and dependency on fossil fuels. The Namami Gange Programme (India) aims to preserve and rejuvenate the National River Ganga in addition to effectively reducing pollution and the National Groundwater Management Improvement Scheme sought to improve groundwater management and promote water efficiency.

7   Transforming the Blue Economy

Most urban residents in West Africa reside in coastal cities. For instance, about 20 million people (or 22.6% of the total population) in Nigeria live near the coast, and about 4.5 million Senegalese people (66.6% of the total population) reside near the coast of Dakar. However, with 211.93 million people living there, India makes up less than 0.25% of the world's coastline. People who live in these areas depend on the ecosystem goods and services that robust coastal and marine systems provide. They are members of the coastal socioecological systems (SES). Coastal marine environments support livelihoods as the Blue Economy and is a major source of sustainability for billions of people worldwide.

In comparison to 40 years ago, sea surface temperatures over the Arabian Sea have risen between 1.2°C and 1.4°C in recent decades, per a paper published in Elsevier's Earth Science Reviews in 2023 (Vineet Singh 2022). In addition, over the past 20 years, the Arabian Sea's total cyclone duration has increased by 80%. Very severe cyclone durations have increased by 260%. Rising sea levels, ocean acidification, deoxygenation, warming sea surface temperatures, and extreme weather events are all consequences of climate change that particularly affect the Indian Ocean Region and the people living along its coast. Even though these effects of climate change take time to manifest, they also pose an immediate threat. Observations reveal that the oceans absorb over 90% of the trapped excess heat resulting from human-induced greenhouse gas emissions into the atmosphere, thereby playing a significant role in mitigating global warming. There has been a strong desire to strengthen the economic ties between India and Africa, and the IORA provides the ideal forum for this. In order to effectively combat climate change, India and Africa will need to map its coastal regions scientifically and accurately. Afterwards, integrated coastal and marine spatial plans can be created thanks to this mapping. We must adopt and adapt the UNESCO-IOC guide.

To address the increasing threat of marine pollution, especially from plastics and microplastics, a comprehensive Plastic Elimination and National Marine Litter policy that involves state and local governments as well as coastal communities in a time-bound manner is needed (Peter Manyara 2022). The National Coastal Mission of India will be included in the Blue Economy initiatives. The Sustainable Development Goals (SDGs) will be implemented as part of the Blue Economy Policy. Despite its difficulties, regional, South–South, and international cooperation in environmental conservation is crucial to ensuring that investments in the blue economy are sustainable over time. To "improve Integrated Coastal Zone/Area Management in Africa" and "minimize environmental damage and expedite recovery from catastrophic event", the African Union has proposed creating the Combined Exclusive Maritime Zone of Africa (CEMZA) (Bolaky 2023). Regional cooperation is also required for environmental conservation, joint exploration to find new sources of marine-based resources, and to conduct research and development (R&D) on marine-based products, cooperative maritime security and surveillance and environmental conservation.

The United Nations is pushing a concept called a "sustainable blue economy" to encourage the use of green methods in ocean management and the blue economy (UNDP, an ocean of oppurtunities 2023). The text emphasizes the importance of integrating sustainability into the utilization of blue resources, such as lowering carbon emissions during the process of developing the blue economy in order to prevent harm to the oceans and marine resources. It places a strong emphasis on minimizing harm to the seas and marine resources by incorporating sustainability into the utilization of blue resources, which includes cutting carbon emissions while fostering the blue economy. Africa and India can work together on projects such as cooperative marine security and surveillance, environmental preservation, cooperative marine area exploration, and cooperative research and development of marine-based products.

8   Digital Transformation

Though not without risks, digital technologies can accelerate the achievement of Agenda 2030's environmental goals. Digitalization presents risks to the environment, including pollution and excessive use of natural resources, but it also offers opportunities by making environmental data more accessible and facilitating creative solutions. Power and transportation are two infrastructure sectors that emit significant greenhouse gases, and they are being impacted by the rapid digital transformation. As a result, policymakers in developing nations are attempting to determine how digital technology fits into the green agenda. Though it increases the ICT sector's carbon footprint, digital innovation opens up new avenues for adaptation and mitigation of climate change (Zaki Khoury 2022). Digital technology has the potential to reduce greenhouse gas emissions by 15% according to the World Economic Forum.

Africa and India must adopt a systemic strategy that supports digital infrastructures, norms, and incentives that are sustainability-focused and encourage the development of innovative technological solutions to difficult environmental problems. To protect our environment, they must work together to advance environmental data and digital infrastructures, support sustainable practices and technology transformation, and advance global digital literacy. India has been a leader in the field of digital public infrastructure, advocating for a digital ecosystem that is both interoperable and secure. The goal of India's efforts to restructure multilateral financial institutions is to raise money for SDGs and green development

(Laskar 2023). Since India is not a large producer of fossil fuels, its efforts in the field of green energy are intended to both promote growth and decarbonize the energy system.

Critical obstacles to digital development in sub-Saharan Africa include inadequate policy and regulatory frameworks, a persistent gender gap in digitalization, underdeveloped digital infrastructure, and a lack of accessible and affordable connectivity. Though hundreds of millions of people now have internet access and are effectively using a wide range of digital services, including online learning platforms and mobile payments, due to a people-centred technological transformation and its focus on increasing affordable, inclusive connectivity, the region has made significant progress towards digital transformation in the past 10 years.

India can assist in the digitalization of meteorological services in Africa that will accelerate the speed at which data is transmitted and enhance the capacity to develop real-time information exchange products and services, which are essential for forecasting and warnings of hydro-meteorological hazards (AICCRA 2023). The goal of the African Union's 2020–2030 digital transformation strategy is to create an inclusive, integrated digital economy and society throughout the continent. In order to guarantee that climate services can boost resilience in Africa, digital solutions are essential. Mobile phone connectivity is necessary to improve last-mile communication. Data from the International Telecommunication Union (ITU) indicates that Africa lags behind many other regions in terms of 3G and 4G broadband coverage. An Indian telecom company called Bharati Airtel is currently operating successfully in several African countries. Because of its affordable data plans in Nigeria, Airtel Nigeria is the most profitable division of Airtel Africa. In 2019, Airtel stated of over 99 million subscribers across the continent (ET 2023).

9   Role as BRICS Members

Both India, the founding member of BRICS, and South Africa, who joined in 2010, are supporters of global cooperation in the area of energy efficiency. They are ready for a productive discussion on how to address climate change based on the idea of shared but differentiated responsibility, given the necessity of combining measures to protect the climate with steps to fulfil our socioeconomic development tasks. In order to improve the application of the Kyoto Protocol and the United Nations Framework Convention on Climate Change (UNFCCC), they pledge to work towards a comprehensive, equitable, and legally binding solution. In order to better adapt their economy and society to climate change, they decide to increase their practical cooperation (BRICS 2022).

They are dedicated to advancing agricultural cooperation and information sharing about methods for guaranteeing that the most vulnerable populations have access to food. Along with exploring and extracting natural resources, as well as processing, transforming, and using them, they are also working together to develop technology and innovation in the potential BRICS economies' sectors, such as mining and metals, pharmaceuticals, information technology, chemicals, and petrochemicals (ILO 2022). This cooperation includes creating an environment that is favourable to investment, climate-friendly, and will benefit both parties. In order to encourage sustainable development and lower greenhouse gas emissions in compliance with the Paris Agreement, they are in favour of utilizing natural gas more widely as a clean, cost-effective fuel (Dsouza 2022).

10   CONCLUSION

India places its top priority on Africa. Indian leaders have repeatedly reiterated this on various international platforms. India has made substantial investments in Africa to support its talk of helping the Global South, rather than just paying lip service to it. India and Africa want to address the problems caused by climate change. It is prepared to cooperate with Africa to protect biodiversity, establish a fair global climate order, and implement clean and efficient energy sources. Africa has also expressed gratitude to India for its steadfast support of the 55-nation continent's G20 membership. They have even dubbed India the fifth global superpower. However, India needs to take more proactive measures given China's increasing influence on the continent over the past decade.

Both regions stand to gain from collaborative research and innovation that produces long-term answers to shared problems such as climate change. Moreover, the alignment of cooperation between India and Africa with the BRICS platform amplifies the effect of these synergies. Africa's attempts to close the digital gap can be strengthened by India's technological prowess, which will make financial, healthcare, and educational services more accessible. There have been new networks and methods for starting a global dialogue about the effects of and remedies for climate change in recent years. The International Solar Alliance (ISA) and the

Coalition for Disaster Resilient Infrastructure (CDRI), of which Africa is a member, are two examples of the multistakeholder global partnerships that India founded. Together, India and Africa can turn around their respective fortunes and strengthen their respective positions as future global leaders in the fight against climate change through mutually beneficial development cooperation.

REFERENCES

Aayog, N. 2023. "NITI Aayog Convenes India's Electric Mobility Enablers under G20 Presidency." *PIB.*

Adve, Nagraj. 2019. "Impacts of Global Warming in India: Narratives from BelowNarratives from Below." In *India in a Warming World,* edited by Navroz K. Dubash, 64–78. Oxford University Press.

Africa, U. N. 2017. *Climate Change Impacts on Africa's Economic Growth.* Addis Ababa: UN. ECA.

Agarwal, Kabir. 2022. "Want to Fight Climate Change? Transform Our Food System." *First Post,* 9 November.

AICCRA. 2023. "New Digital Innovation Harnesses Power of Real-Time Weather Data." *AICCRA.*

Benton, P.T. 2023. *At COP28 Governments must Agree How to Transform Food Systems.* Chatham House.

Bolaky, B. 2023. "Operationalising Blue Economy in Africa: The Case of South West Indian Ocean." *OEF Issue Briefs,* 11 May.

Brears, R. 2023. "Climate Resilience and Water Supply: Innovative Strategies for Urban Water Management." *Our Future Water Newsletter.*

BRICS. 2022. "Joint Statement Issued at the BRICS High-level Meeting on Climate Change." *BRICS CHINA 2022.*

Carter, R. 2021. "How to Transform Food Systems in the Face of Climate Change." *World Resource Institute.* 23 June.

Cerulli, N. 2024. "E-Mobility in Sub-Saharan Africa: Electric Two Wheelers Gaining Momentum." *Cleantech group.*

Champions, C. 2023. "Transforming Food Systems for People, Nature and Climate: A shared call to action." *UNFCCC.*

Chukwuemeka, N.S. 2023. "The Challenges and Opportunities of Energy Transition across Africa." *African Union, 2023—Volume 13 [Issue 10],* 4312–4339.

Cooper, S. 2023. "10 Ways Forward to Transform Food Systems for Climate and Nature." *UNDP.*

Cruz, R. 2007. *Asia. Climate change 2007: Impacts, Adaptation and Vulnerability*. Contribution of Working Group II to the Fourth Assessment Report of the Intergovernmental Panel on Climate Change.

CSE, C.F. 2023. *Climate India 2023: An Assessment of Extreme Weather Events*. New Delhi: Down To Earth (DTE).

Doane, M. 2023, Sept. "Transforming Food Systems for a Healthy Planet and Healthy People." *FAO and GEF*.

Dsouza, R. 2022. "A Stocktaking of BRICS Performance in Climate Action." *ORF-Special Reports*.

Dubash, N.K. 2012. *Handbook of Climate Change and India*. New York: Earthscan.

Dubash, N.K. 2019. "Introduction." In *India in a Warming World: Integrating Climate Change and Development*, edited by N. K. Dubash, 1–30. Delhi: Oxford Academic.

ET. 2023. "Airtel's Perilous Safari: How Sunil Bharti Mittal conquered Africa." *The Economics Times*.

FAO. 2018. *The Future of Food and Agriculture, Alternative pathways to 2050*. Rome: Food and Agriculture Organization of the United Nations.

FAO. 2021. "The Nature of Food Security in the world." *Food and Agriculture Organization of the United Nations*, pp. ISSN 2663–8061.

FAO. 2023. *The State of Food and Agriculture*. publications@fao.org.

FICCI. 2016. *India-Africa Partnership in Agriculture*. FICCI.

Gracelin Baskaran, S.C. 2024, Jan 31. "Achieving Universal Energy Access in Africa amid Global Decarbonization." *Centre for Strategic and International Studies*.

Gupta, P.D. 2014. "Pricing Climate Change." *Sage Journals—Politics, Philosophy and Economics* 13 (4).

Hinkel, J. 2011. "Sea-Level Rise Impacts on Africa and the Effects of Mitigation and Adaptation: An Application of DIVA." *Regional Environmental Change*, 207–224.

Ighobor, K. 2016. "A Green Path to Industrialization." *Africa Renewal*.

ILO. 2022, March. "Employment and Just Transition to Sustainability in the BRICS Countries." *BRICS CHINA*.

IMF, I.M. Sept,. 2022. *Climate Change and Chronic Food Insecurity in Sub-Saharan Africa*. Washington, DC: International Monetary Fund, Publication Services.

IRENA. 2024. *Energy Transition Outlook*. International Renewable Energy Agency. https://www.irena.org/Energy-Transition/OutlookIWMI. 2022. Transformation of Water Systems for Climate Change Adaptation and Resilience. *International Water Management Institute, Water Issue Brief–18*.

Jha, V. 2023. "International Solar Alliance: Bridging the Gap." *Centre for Social and Economic Progress*.

Joeri Rogelj, e. a. 2018. *SPECIAL REPORT Global Warming of 1.5 °C*. Incheon, South Korea: Intergovernmental Panel on Climate Change (IPCC).

Johan Swinnen, C.A. 2022. "IFPRI Global Food Policy Report 2022: Accelerating Food Systems Transformation to Combat Climate Change." *IFPRI Blog: Issue Post*.

Johnson, K. 2021. "La Niña and Climate Change Cause Exceptional Drought in East Africa." *Climatelinks*. Feed the Future.

K. Niranjan Kumar, M.R. 2013. "On the Observed Variability of Monsoon Droughts Over India." *Weather and Climate Extremes*, 42–50.

Kgomotso, P. 2022. "Africa's Role in Saving the World's Damaged Lands and Ecosystems." *Africa Renewal*.

Lancet. 2019. *Indian Air Pollution: Loaded Dice* 3 (12): E500–E501.

Laskar, R.H. 2023, July. "India Pushing for Digital Transformation and Climate Justice in G20." *Hindustan Times*.

M. Crippa, E. S.-F. 2021. "Food Systems are Responsible for a Third of Global Anthropogenic GHG emissions." *Nature Food*, pp. 198–209.

Mabogunje, A.L. 1995. "The Environmental Challenges In Sub Saharan Africa." *African Technology Forum* 37 (4): 4.

Mangrove, G. 2024. "MIKOKO PAMOJA." *KNOWLEDGE HUB*.

Megha Kumar, Z.S. 2022. "Decarbonizing India's Road." *International Council on Clean Transportation*.

Ministry of Environment, F. a. 2023. *PIB*. PIB Delhi. https://pib.gov.in/PressR eleaseIframePage.aspx?PRID=1895857.

Monika Zurek, A.H. 2022. "Climate Change and the Urgency to Transform Food Systems." *Oxford University Research Archive*.

Mungai Kihara, P.L. 2024. "Mid- to Long-Term Capacity Planning for a Reliable Power System in Kenya." *Energy Strategy Reviews* 52.

Nation, U., Africa, E.C., and Commission, A.U. 2022. *African Union climate Change and Resilient Development Strategy and Action Plan*. Addis Ababa: UN. ECA. https://au.int/sites/default/files/documents/41959-doc-CC_ Strategy_and_Action_Plan_2022-2032_08_02_23_Single_Print_Ready.pdf.

National Planning Commission, A.A. 2016. "The Growth and Transformation Plan (GTP)." *Climate change laws of the world*.

Neugarten, R.A. 2024. *Mapping the Planet's Critical Areas for Biodiversity and Nature's Contributions to People*. Nature Communications.

Nicholas Rees, M.B. 2021. *The Climate Crisis is a Child Rights Crisis: Introducing the Children's Climate Risk Index*. New York: UNICEF.

OECD. 2012. *Environmental Outlook to 2050*.

OECD. 2015. *Poverty and Climate Change*.

Ogega, O. K.-B. 2024. How to Transform Africa's Food System. *Communications Earth & Environment*, 12 (3).

Oguntuase, O.J. 2023. "India and the Global Commons: A Case Study of the International Solar Alliance." *Observer Research Foundation*.

Panda, A. 2009. "Assessing Vulnerability to Climate Change in India." *Economic and Political Weekly* 44 (16): 105–107.

Patil, S. 2023. "A Recipe for Change: Reshaping Our Food Systems Amid Rising Costs and Climate Change." *The Wire*.

Peter Manyara, K.R. 2022. "Legal and Policy Frameworks to Address Marine Litter Through Improved Livelihoods." *The African Marine Litter Outlook*, 137–197.

PIB. 2022. *Coal Demand Likely to Peak Between 2030–2035*. Ministry of Coal: Press Information Bureau.

PIB. 2023. "Millets Strengthen Relations Between India and African Nations." *Ministry of Agriculture & Farmers Welfare*.

PIB. 2023. *Ministry of Science & Technology*. PIB Delhi. https://pib.gov.in/Pre ssReleaseIframePage.aspx?PRID=1961797#:~:text=Dr%20Jitendra%20Singh% 20said%2C%20India,1%20billion%20tons%20by%202030%3B.

PIB. 2023. "Steps Taken By Union Government to Increase Water Availability and Promote Conservation of Water." *Ministry of Jal Shakti, PIB*.

Prof. Piyush Tiwari, D.M. (2022). "Impact of Future Sea Level Rise on Coastal Real Estate and Infrastructure in India." *SHELTER* 23 (2).

Radford, C. 2023. "Green Hydrogen in Africa: A Continent of Possibilities?" *White & Case*.

Rampal, P. 2021. "A Roadmap for Sustainable Food Security." *India Matters, ORF*.

Report, I.A. 2020. World Air Quality Report.

Robertson, C. 2023. "A Rush for Lithium in Africa Risks Fuelling Corruption and Failing Citizens." *Global Witness*.

Sachin Kotak, J.S. 2024. "5 Ways to Power Up India's Green Hydrogen Ecosystem." *World Economic Forum*.

Sahastrabuddhe, R., S.A. Ghausi, J. Joseph, and S. Ghosh. 2023. "Indian Summer Monsoon Rainfall in a Changing Climate: A Review." *Journal of Water and Climate Change* 14 (4): 1061–1088.

Shobha Suri, S.R. 2023. "Building Climate-Resilient Food Systems." *Observer Research Foundation (ORF)*. Issue brief no. 566.

Siddharth Ghanshyam Singh, K.J. 2023. "GOBAR-Dhan: Scheme Announced in Budget a Welcome Step, but Challenges Ahead." *Down to Earth*.

Siegfried, K. 2023. "Climate Change and Displacement: The Myths and the Facts." *Stories*. United Nations High Commissioner for Refugees (UNHCR).

Sinha, S. 2021. "Decarbonising Transport: Redefining Mobility Policies in India." *National Portal of India*.

Society, T.R. 2022. "Climate Change and Land: The Science of Working with Nature Towards Net Zero." *The Royal Society*.

Sonja Leitner, D. E.-B. 2020. "Closing Maize Yield Gaps in sub-Saharan Africa Will Boost Soil N2O Emissions." *Current Opinion in Environmental Sustainability*, 95–105. ISSN 1877–3435.

Suri, S. 2022, Nov. "Climate Smart Agriculture for Sustainability and Food Security." *Observer Research Foundation (ORF).*

Suri, S. 2023. "It's Time for Climate Justice—A Global South Perspective on the Fight Against the Climate Crisis." *Internationale Politik.*

Tech, G.W. 2023. "Top Solutions to Water Scarcity in Africa." *Genesis Water Tech.*

Trisos, C.I. 2022. *2022: Africa.* In *Climate Change 2022: Impacts, Adaptation and Vulnerability, 1285–1455.* Cambridge, UK and New York, NY, USA: Cambridge University Press.

UN. 2023. "Economic Report on Africa, ISSN (online): 24118354." *UN iLibrary.* https://doi.org/10.18356/7ece2581-en.

UN. 2020. *Climate Change Exacerbates Existing Conflict Risks, Likely to Create New Ones, Assistant Secretary-General Warns Security Council [Press Release].* https://press.un.org/en/2020/sc14260.doc.htm

UNDP. 2023. "Africa Offers Creative Solutions to Climate Change." *Climate Promise.*

UNDP. 2023. *Africa Offers Creative Solutions to Climate Change—Here are 3 of Them.* New York: UNDP.

UNDP. 2023, Jan. "An Ocean of Opportunities." *UNDP Blue Economy Action Brief.*

UNEP. 2021, Sept 29. "How Africa is Using Nature to Adapt to Climate Change." *Climate Action.*

UNEP. 2022. "Supporting Sound Ecosystem Management." *In Nature Action.*

UNEP. 2023a. *Emissions Gap Report 2023.* Kenya: UN.

UNEP. 2023b. "Supporting the Global Shift to Electric Mobility." *UNEP.*

UNEP. n.d. *Agenda 2063: The Africa We Want, First Ten-Year Implementation Plan, 2013–2023.* UNEP: https://wedocs.unep.org/20.500.11822/20823.

UNFCCC. 2007. "Investment and Financial Flows." *United Nations Framework Convention on Climate Change.*

UNICEF. 2023, September 1. *Children in 98 per cent of African Countries at High or Extremely High Risk of the Impacts of Climate Change: UNICEF.* Retrieved from Unicef: https://www.unicef.org/press-releases/children-98-cent-african-countries-high-or-extremely-high-risk-impacts-climate.

UNIDO. 2020, Oct. "SA Industrial Energy Efficiency Project." *United Nations Industrial Development Organisation.*

Vandana Chauhan, E. 2022. *Climate Smart Agriculture: A Key to Sustainability.* New Delhi: Parliament Library and Reference, Research, Documentation and Information Service.

Varma, G. 2015, July 15. "Studies show Increasing Monsoon Variability, Intensity." *Nature India*.

Vineet Singh, R.M. 2022. "A Review of Ocean-Atmosphere Interactions during Tropical Cyclones in the North Indian Ocean." *Earth-Science Reviews* 226 (3): 103967. https://doi.org/10.1016/j.earscirev.2022.103967.

WMO. 2023. *Provisional State of the Global Climate in 2023.* Geneva: UN.

WMO. 2023. *The Global Climate 2011–2020: A Decade of Acceleration.*

WMO, W. M. 2023. *Africa Suffers Disproportionately from Climate Change.*

Zaki Khoury, J. L. 2022, April. "The Nexus of Green and Digital: An Opportunity or a Challenge?" *World Bank Brief*.

Zhen-Qiang Zhou, S.-P. X. 2019. "Variability and Predictability of Indian Rainfall During the Monsoon Onset Month of June." *Geophysical Research Letters, Advancing Earth and Space Sciences*.

BRICS Plus and Climate Change: Balancing National Interests, National Development Goals and Environmental Sustainability

Hussein Solomon and *Sanet Solomon*

1 INTRODUCTION

Climate change is real. This is a fact which **3.6** billion people can attest to as they suffer heatwaves, intense flooding, drought, desertification, food insecurity, and disease. Tragically, and unlike other natural disasters, this one was all too avoidable as its origins are entirely man-made, as Solomon attests too in this volume. The anthropogenic origins of climate change prompted the Nobel Prize winning chemist Paul Croetzen and Eugene Stoermer to label this epoch the Anthropocene (Madonsela 2023: 53). While contested by some geologists, one cannot deny that human activities have had a significant impact on the planet.

What is also undeniable is that existing initiatives—largely led by the Global North—from the Kyoto Protocol to the Paris Summit, have

H. Solomon (✉)
Centre for Gender and Africa Studies, University of the Free State,
Bloemfontein, South Africa
e-mail: solomonh@ufs.ac.za

S. Solomon
Department of Political Sciences, University of South Africa, Pretoria, South Africa

© The Author(s), under exclusive license to Springer Nature
Singapore Pte Ltd. 2024
H. Solomon et al. (eds.), *BRICS and Climate Change*,
https://doi.org/10.1007/978-981-97-5532-5_11

233

mostly failed to reverse the trend of harmful greenhouse gas emissions being released into the atmosphere. As Matthew Brown (2024) rather depressingly reminds us, heat-trapping carbon dioxide and methane levels spiked to an all-time high in 2023. Within this context, an initiative from those who identify as being part of the Global South—the BRICS nations—is a welcome initiative. Despite initial misgivings given their being latecomers to the climate change narrative, despite tensions within their respective states on issues of climate change, and despite differing national interests, BRICS, and now BRICS Plus, countries are individually and collectively taking great strides toward carbon neutrality and a green economy. This holds great promise not only for BRICS nations themselves but for humanity as a whole.

The strategic importance of BRICS nations taking up the mantle of climate change cannot be overstated given the geostrategic shift in power eastward with the likes of China and India looking likely to become the dominant powers of the twenty-first century. Russia, meanwhile, is a major global player whose influence is felt globally. Moreover, according to the International Energy Agency, Russia has the world's largest reserves of natural gas (International Energy Agency 2024). On the other hand, Brazil, in addition to being the dominant power in its region, has the Amazon rainforest, which Marina da Silva notes has been termed the "lungs of the earth" on account of its carbon absorption capacity. The inclusion of major global energy players such as Saudi Arabia and Iran as well as the addition of major regional actors such as Egypt and Ethiopia into BRICS Plus can only further solidify the strategic importance of BRICS Plus on the international stage.

2 BRICS Plus: Overcoming Initial Reluctance to Engage on Issues of Climate Change

The embracing of climate change by BRICS Plus nations is somewhat surprising, since their initial focus was on economic development, geostrategic concerns, and articulating a more robust voice for the Global South in international affairs. Some critics, Bianca Naudé reminds us, were rather dismissive of BRICS taking proactive measures on climate change given their dependence on fossil fuels, their own deforestation efforts, as well as their unsustainable land use. China, Jana de Kluiver notes, produces more greenhouse gas emissions than the rest of the world combined. India, Bashabi Gupta reminds us, is the world's third-largest emitter of greenhouse gases. Saudi Arabia, meanwhile, according to Mudassir Quamar, is a major emitter of greenhouse gases and a global exporter of petroleum, with fossil fuels constituting 90% of its energy mix. Despite Brazil hosting the Rio Earth Summit, Marina da Silva notes that it never responded to global warming with the seriousness it deserves. Naudé opines that compounding this dismissive attitude was the fact that BRICS countries had little in common. Their vast differences in size, capabilities, cultures, and values, critics argued, meant that BRICS countries could not act with one voice on the international stage. To put it differently, critics argued that BRICS states acted merely in their national interests and not in the collective interests of the bloc on the global stage.

There is, of course, some truth to this. For far too long, BRICS nations emphasized sovereign rights as opposed to their collective responsibility to our global commons. Moreover, as Bianca Naudé argues, BRICS nations initially viewed the climate change agenda as antithetic to their development goals. India, initially, was the chief proponent of this position, but as Gupta notes in her chapter, concerns about poverty and economic development in India are what drove these positions. India, Gupta soberly observes, scores the lowest on the Human Development Index.

The BRICS position has, however, shifted, as we have seen in the chapters in this volume, to reverse environmental degradation and carbon neutrality through promoting a green economy. Individual BRICS nations have also changed their stance. Initially sceptical of climate change, Moscow has changed its stance, and in its latest climate doctrine, which appeared in 2023, it speaks of the "significant, predominantly adverse effects" of climate change on Russian society—a sentiment with which Sergey Kostelyanets concurs. In recent years, Russia has experienced an increase in the frequency and scale of natural disasters. What motivated President Putin to declare in 2021 that carbon neutrality was Russia's goal, however, was the consensus reached by the United States and the European Union about the imposition of carbon-based tariffs on steel, aluminum, and other items that constituted a major portion of Russian exports. China, meanwhile, is the world leader in the production of electric cars and solar and wind power (see Jana de Kluiver's chapter in this volume). India's Prime Minister Modi, meanwhile, has pledged that India will achieve net-zero emission by 2070 and that renewable energy will constitute half of the country's energy mix by 2030 (see the chapter by Bashabi Gupta). Saudi Arabia has undertaken to reduce greenhouse gases to 278 million tonnes by 2030 through the circular carbon economy with its emphasis on new technologies.

The question, however, remains as to why BRICS nations have changed their stance. Four interconnected reasons explain this. First, according to Bianca Naudé, the collective identity of BRICS is that of emerging powers. As they all seek a leadership role—whether at regional or international levels, they are compelled to act as "responsive and constructive stakeholders concerning climate change". This is particularly evident in China's stance on the environment, according to De Kluiver, as it attempts to reposition its foreign policy on a more constructive and influential trajectory. This is in line with its aspirations of global leadership. Saudi Arabia, meanwhile, Mudassir Quamar emphasizes, sees itself as the leader in the Gulf and Middle East region.

Second, the environmental degradation as a result of climate change has had such a malevolent impact on ordinary citizens' lives, the myth that caring for the environment was an obstacle to development has been proven false. Simply put, one can embrace environmentally sustainable development paths which can produce employment opportunities. As Bashabi Gupta observes, 988,000 jobs were created in India's renewable energy sector by 2022. However, in addition to job creation, a green economy is what is needed to take the economy to the next level. This was very ably captured by First Deputy Minister of Economic Development, Ilya Torosov, who made the connection between low-carbon technologies and long-term competitiveness in June 2022 (see the chapter by Sergey Kostelyanets).

Third, popular anger with existing policies has also motivated BRICS countries to change their position on the environment. In the case of both Beijing and Pretoria, Naudé argues that environmental degradation has fuelled popular anger, which threatens the respective ruling parties' authority and legitimacy. De Kluiver, for instance, stresses how environmental protests have wreaked havoc in several Chinese provinces in recent years.

Then, there is the issue of political change. In Brazil, it was particularly stark with the election of right-wing populist Jair Bolsonaro in 2018. He rolled back many environmental policies during his years in office. According to Marina da Silva, these included the unrestricted exploitation of the Amazon, attacks on the scientific community and environmental institutions, reneging on international agreements on climate change and withdrawing Brazil as host nation for COP25. With the election of Luiz Inacio da Silva, however, there has been an attempt on the part of the Brasília to reengage the international community on climate change, to stop the deforestation of the Amazon, and strengthen institutions engaging in environmental oversight. Sergey Kostelyanets notes how the ebb and flow of climate change debates were intimately related to political shifts. While the Soviet Union was a leading voice in the world on climate change, climate skepticism has engulfed Russia largely as a result of the oil and gas lobby, which has grown long tentacles into the apparatus of state. The shift in generational leadership in Saudi Arabia, meanwhile, has witnessed a younger leadership sharing the global concerns about climate change and wanting their country to be less dependent on fossil fuels (see chapter by Mudassir Quamar).

3   BRICS Plus and Climate Change: The Search for Consensus and Multilateralism

Whatever the motivations, the BRICS Plus nations' new commitment is a welcome departure from their former defensive and reactive positions. The benefit of the more proactive stance on the part of BRICS Plus for the planet cannot be overstated. Four reasons account for this. First, most of the world's population live in the Global South, and as BRICS Plus membership expands, these countries will have more claim to represent the majority opinion. Second, while the Global North are largely post-industrial economies, the same cannot be said of those in the Global South who are intensifying industrial activity. Thus, from a climate change perspective, the future of greenhouse gas emissions, and by extension humanity as a whole, will be more impacted by developments in the Global South than those in the Global North.

Third, Western initiatives have largely failed on account of their top-down approach when pushing climate change. As such, their attitude toward those in the South was regarded as condescending and arrogant. In his chapter, Sergey Kostelyanets also raises the issue of the weaponization of climate change in how the West relates to Russia through the Carbon Border Adjustment Mechanism. While ostensibly imposing a tariff on embedded emissions of products entering the European Union, it really is another form of economic sanction against Moscow. Meanwhile, BRICS, and now BRICS Plus, emphasize cooperation and multilateralism while respecting national sovereignty, which is perceived as less threatening to the newly independent countries of the Global South. Moreover, BRICS Plus's common but differentiated responsibility principle is more attuned to the existing realities when engaging in the policy realms. Individual states are at different levels of development, have differing capabilities and different needs, and cannot be treated the same, as the West has been wont to do. Perhaps, more importantly, the lack of traction that Western initiatives have received among the global population is that the fundamental narrative was too Eurocentric, which the majority of the world's population could not relate to. As Naudé outlines in her chapter, Chinese approaches to the environment rooted in Confucianism with its emphasis on harmony with the cosmos, Indian approaches with its emphasis on *Advaita* monism, which is based on the single hidden connectedness of Brahma, and *Ubuntu* in the African context which emphasizes our collective humanity make for a more receptive audience to almost half of the world's population. While Sunni Saudi Arabia and Shia Iran have only just joined BRICS Plus, there are Islamic approaches to the environment which both governments can use to "sell" more environmentally friendly policies. The Qur'an emphasizes that God created the earth and humanity has been entrusted with the stewardship of it. Moreover, various Qur'anic verses (7:31, 6:141, 17–26–27 and 40:34) all warn against excessive consumption of the earth's resources. Cold Western rationalism, which is the basis of much of the current climate change policies, therefore held scant appeal to the majority of the world's population, since it was alien to their culture, traditions, and value systems.

Fourth, while some have been highly critical of the inclusion of fossil-producing states such as Iran and Saudi Arabia within the BRICS Plus fold, it is better to treat them as partners rather than pariahs and seek to moderate their stance on hydrocarbons. In his chapter, Mudassir Quamar notes that Riyadh understands full well that they exist in an ecologically stressed country that is extremely vulnerable to climate change. Moreover, their dependence on fossil fuels and their not diversifying their economy hold them hostage to market prices and geostrategic shifts that are out of their control. In similar fashion, others have been critical of the huge discrepancies between BRICS Plus countries. These discrepancies, however, may be a boon rather than a curse for the planet. The BRICS High-level Meeting on Climate Change, for instance, has not only enhanced communication and cooperation among BRICS members but has also sought to facilitate the exchange of knowledge and technology between member states to promote a green and low-carbon economy (see the chapters by De Kluiver and Solomon in this volume). This was a promise often made by those in the Global North but never implemented—something for which the BRICS nations have legitimately berated the Global North. The disparities between BRICS Plus states then, far from undermining cooperation, could well be a book for all humanity, as these countries are given the means to level up.

None of the preceding should suggest that national interests do not exist and that it would be easy to achieve consensus within BRICS Plus around climate change. However, between national interests and collective interests, there is also an enlightened national interest from preventive short-term national interests from detracting from the concerns of the global commons we all inhabit. The BRICS leadership has also demonstrated remarkable pragmatism when faced with issues they do not find agreement. As Bashabi Gupta notes in her chapter, Brazil, India, and China formed the BASIC alliance in 2009 to act as a platform for developing nations in the COP talks—specifically those who were fast growing but were historically low emitters. Thus, a precedent has been set for those BRICS Plus member states who may not be on the same page—another structure is then created within the larger BRICS Plus bloc among those who do agree on certain issues.

It is important to stress here that the BRICS Plus partnership is not merely an anti-West alliance and does not preclude partnership with the Global North. After all, climate change is a cross-cutting issue affecting all animal, human, and plant life on the planet. Despite the polarizing nature of politics, such partnership is not impossible to achieve, as there are historical precedents. Jana de Kluiver reminds us of the joint announcement by the US and Chinese presidents to reduce greenhouse gas emissions. Sergey Kostelyanets, meanwhile, reminds us of the 1972 Agreement on Cooperation in the Field of Environmental Protection between the United States and the Union of Soviet Socialist Republics during a heated Cold War. Marina da Silva also stresses that, while Brazil's new administration has prioritized South–South cooperation, Lula da Silva has also sought to engage with both the United States and Europe on climate change.

Perhaps more importantly, there have been more recent developments which could set the basis for further collaboration between BRICS Plus and non-BRICS Plus member states. Consider here the holistic approach to development set by the United Nations Sustainable Development

Goals (SDGs) which most states subscribe to or, for that matter, the United Nations Framework Convention on Climate Change (UNFCC). As countries globally integrate the SDGs into their national planning, it will increase synergy for cooperation and therefore multilateralism.

It is also important to note here that members of BRICS Plus are already playing a hugely positive role both in their respective regions and internationally. Mudassir Quamar observes that the Saudi initiative to build 50 billion trees includes the entire Middle East and North Africa (MENA) region. De Kluiver reminds us that Beijing has 46 agreements for South–South cooperation on climate change with 39 developing countries. Moreover, Beijing has launched a three-year climate action plan with African states to combat climate change. These could bolster the goals of the African Climate Summit (see the chapter by Hussein Solomon in this volume) and other Chinese efforts such as the China Pacific Island Countries High-level dialogue on Climate Change as well as the China-Mongolia Cooperation Center for Desertification Control. India, too, is playing a key role in the development of less developed countries through the creation of the International Solar Alliance and the Coalition for Disaster Resilient Infrastructure, according to Shilpi Ghosh. India has much in common with Africa, from anticolonial struggles to development and demographic challenges. Consequently, New Delhi's strategy to arrest climate change will have more resonance in the African context than those strategies emanating from the Global North. The inclusion of Egypt and Ethiopia into the fold of BRICS Plus in addition to South Africa could well bring Africa as a continent closer to BRICS Plus. However, there is a need for these BRICS Plus countries' bilateral relations to be better coordinated within the multilateral context of the BRICS bloc.

In conclusion, the positive evolution of BRICS and BRICS Plus positions on climate change is a boon to the planet and a triumph of multilateral and pragmatism. BRICS Plus is integral to our planet's survival and the future of succeeding generations.

REFERENCES

Brown, Michael. 2024. "Heat-Trapping Carbon Dioxide and Methane Levels in the Air Last Year Spiked to Record Highs Again." *NBC News*, 6 April. https://www.nbcnews.com/world/carbon-dioxide-emissions-reached-record-high-rcna166704.

International Energy Agency. 2024. "Russia." iea.org/countries/russia.

Madonsela, Sanet. 2023. "Climate-Security and the Anthropocene: The Case of Mali." In *African Security in the Anthropocene,* edited by Hussein Solomon and Jude Cocodia. Cham, Switzerland: Springer Nature.

The Holy Qur'an.

Index

A

Action Plan for the Prevention and Control of Deforestation in the Legal Amazon (PPCDAm), 41

Adaptation, 38, 42, 55, 58, 60, 81, 99, 100, 102, 105, 111, 112, 119, 127, 138, 205, 209–211, 219

Adaptation Fund, 81

Advaita, 23, 28–30, 238

African Climate Summit, 172–174, 177, 240

African Development Bank (AfDB), 205, 214, 220

African Union, 9, 172–174, 212, 222, 224

Amazon, 38, 39, 41, 43, 45–47, 49, 59, 69, 234, 237

anthropogenic, 5, 67, 70, 71, 79, 83, 88, 183, 188, 233

anti-colonial, 203, 240

B

Bali, 101

Belt and Road Initiative (BRI), 5, 121, 127, 131–133, 140

Bolsonaro, Jair Messias, 7, 38, 43, 44, 56, 61, 236

Brazil, 2, 6, 12, 13, 28, 38, 39, 41–43, 45, 49, 54, 55, 58–61, 135, 175, 187, 235, 237

Brazilian Institute of the Environment and Renewable Natural Resources (IBAMA), 45, 57

Brazil, Russia, India, China, and South Africa (BRICS), 1–5, 7, 9–11, 13, 14, 20, 21, 24, 31, 55, 58, 89, 98, 112, 121, 134, 135, 137, 140, 166–171, 175, 176, 178, 179, 186, 187, 197, 225, 234–236, 238–240

Brazil, South Africa, India, and China (BASIC), 6, 55, 108, 110, 112, 137, 138, 141, 239

BRICS High-level meeting on Climate Change, 89, 136, 168, 186, 238

© The Editor(s) (if applicable) and The Author(s), under exclusive license to Springer Nature Singapore Pte Ltd. 2024
H. Solomon et al. (eds.), *BRICS and Climate Change*,
https://doi.org/10.1007/978-981-97-5532-5

244 INDEX

BRICS Plus, 8, 9, 166–168, 171–179, 234, 237–240
BRICS Summit, 13, 30, 57, 60, 135, 166, 167, 169, 170, 172, 178, 203
Budyko, Mikhail I., 69, 70
Bush, George W., 72, 84

C
Carbon Border Adjustment Mechanism (CBAM), 85, 87, 187, 237
carbon emissions, 5, 14, 21, 40, 82, 84, 85, 98, 103, 119, 120, 130, 139, 150, 192, 194, 218, 220, 223
carbon neutrality, 5, 85–88, 91, 129, 140, 169, 234, 235
carbon sequestration, 51, 69
carbon sink, 38, 42, 45, 86
China, 2, 12, 73, 97, 109, 120–126, 128, 130, 133, 135–141, 166, 174, 175, 187, 188, 218, 239
China-Africa Cooperation on Combating Climate Change, 126
China-Mongolia Cooperation Center for Desertification Control, 127, 240
China Pacific Island Countries High-Level Dialogue on Climate Change, 240
Circular carbon economy (CCE), 7, 190–195, 236
Clean Development Mechanism (CDM), 54, 189, 191, 194, 195, 197
climate action, 3, 8, 11–14, 18, 22, 30, 31, 54, 55, 59, 89, 101, 108, 111, 112, 114, 121, 123, 126, 136, 168, 188, 209, 240
Climate Action Cooperation Centre, 126

climate change, 1, 5–9, 11, 13, 14, 20, 37, 39, 42–45, 54, 58–61, 70, 77, 81, 84, 91, 99, 103, 104, 107, 109, 112, 114, 119, 120, 122, 125, 126, 128, 136, 141, 152, 165, 168–174, 176, 178, 184–186, 189, 190, 195, 197, 198, 204, 205, 207, 209, 210, 218, 226, 234, 235, 237, 240
climate diplomacy, 6, 123
climate doctrine, 13, 77, 88, 235
climate finance, 4, 128, 138, 157, 216
climate justice, 9, 98, 100, 101, 170, 173
climate security, 4, 150, 152, 155
climate skepticism, 237
Coalition for Disaster Resilient Infrastructure (CDRI), 209, 226, 240
Common but Differentiated Responsibility (CBDR), 2, 13, 54, 56, 58, 60, 103, 169, 238
Conference of Parties (COP), 127, 137, 177, 186–188, 239
Confucian, 24, 25, 27, 28
Copenhagen Climate Summit, 98, 122

D
da Silva, Luiz Inácio Lula, 7, 58, 237, 239
decarbonization, 5, 79, 83, 85, 86, 88, 89, 91, 155, 157
deforestation, 6, 12, 37, 40, 41, 43, 45–49, 51, 52, 55, 58, 59, 61, 132, 137, 234, 237
Democratic Republic of the Congo (DRC), 217
desertification, 51, 127, 139, 212, 233
development, 3, 5, 7, 13, 14, 17, 30, 41, 44, 46, 54, 56, 59, 71, 74,

77, 81, 82, 85, 89, 97, 98,
102–105, 111, 114, 122, 125,
126, 132–134, 136, 140, 150,
151, 153, 156, 168, 171, 185,
188, 191, 195, 196, 206, 210,
215, 218, 219, 223, 224, 235,
236, 240
Dubai, 88, 89, 177, 178, 188

E

Earth Summit, 41, 54, 70–72, 98,
100, 183, 235
Economic Commission for Africa
(ECA), 219
ecosystems, 8, 21, 37, 49, 59, 102,
105, 132, 150, 188, 207, 210,
212, 220, 221
Egypt, 8, 87–89, 156, 166, 171, 215,
234, 240
electric cars, 120, 235
emerging powers, 2, 3, 12, 134, 236
Energy Conservation Act, 106
environmental degradation, 1, 9, 11,
12, 14, 17, 18, 20, 235, 236
Environment Ministers Meeting, 136
Ethiopia, 8, 89, 134, 156, 167, 186,
205, 215, 218, 240

F

fossil fuels, 7, 12, 13, 21, 37, 59, 68,
85, 102, 112, 129, 139, 151,
153, 156, 173, 185, 187, 190,
192, 199, 212, 215, 224, 235,
238

G

G20, 85, 185, 186, 189, 194, 197,
203, 206, 211, 225
Gandhi, Indira, 98, 99, 203
geothermal energy, 69

Ghana, 217
Global North, 14, 24, 170–173, 178,
233, 237, 239, 240
Global South, 6, 14, 58, 60, 72, 89,
91, 136, 140, 171, 172, 174,
176, 177, 184, 186, 188, 225,
234, 237, 238
Governance, 2, 3, 7, 10, 19, 21, 43,
56, 98, 122, 124, 125, 137, 141,
157, 158, 167, 198, 220
Green Climate Fund, 81, 128
green development, 126, 139, 223
green economy, 11–13, 169, 170,
173, 195, 234, 236
greenhouse gases (GHG), 5, 61, 68,
69, 72, 97, 204, 223, 235, 236
Greenland, 166
Guterres, Antonio, 167

H

heatwaves, 37, 149, 233
holism, 14, 23, 28
holist ontology, 14, 23, 25
hydrocarbon, 74, 76, 185, 187, 190,
191, 238

I

India, 2, 8, 73, 97, 98, 100, 101,
104, 105, 107, 108, 110, 113,
114, 131, 137, 174, 179, 187,
203, 206–209, 213, 214, 216,
218, 219, 222–226, 235
Intergovernmental Panel on Climate
Change (IPCC), 41, 71, 72, 81,
82, 109, 111, 210
International Bamboo and Rattan
Organization, 127
International Energy Forum
Ministerial Meet, 101
International Labour Organization
(ILO), 102, 114, 208

246 INDEX

International Monetary Fund (IMF), 153, 167
International Solar Alliance (ISA), 101, 112, 209, 214, 225, 240
Iran, 89, 131, 134, 166, 167, 174, 177, 186, 234, 238

J

Jinping, Xi, 30, 31, 119, 123, 128, 133, 139, 168, 175
Johannesburg II Declaration, 13, 135, 136, 170, 171
Just transition, 4, 150–152, 155, 157, 215

K

Kazan, 167
Kenya, 156, 171, 205, 211, 213, 215, 217
Kremlin, 79, 84, 91
Kyoto Protocol, 5, 54, 55, 73–76, 79, 80, 84, 90, 100, 137, 183, 224, 233

L

Least Developed Countries Fund, 177
Lifestyle for Environment (LIFE), 102, 218
Lithium, 217, 218
low carbon, 13
low-emission economy, 13

M

Mali, 211, 217
Mangrove Initiative for Shoreline Habitat and Tangible Incomes (MISHTI), 212
Medvedev, Dmitry, 77–79, 82, 84, 91
Metaphysics, 14, 21, 24, 27, 29, 31

mitigation, 5, 6, 38, 39, 42, 44, 57–61, 71, 81, 90, 91, 99–101, 104, 105, 107, 111, 119–121, 126, 139, 186, 209, 212, 213, 223
Modi, Narendra, 98, 203, 206, 214, 235
monism, 14, 23, 25, 28, 29, 238
multilateralism, 55, 109, 135, 168, 170, 171, 176, 178, 179, 186, 187, 237, 240

N

Nairobi, 172–174
Nairobi Declaration, 172–174
Namibia, 156, 215, 217
National Action Plan on Climate Change (NAPCC), 6, 101, 102, 104
Nationally Determined Contributions (NDC), 42, 55, 58, 82, 102, 108, 127, 137, 169, 189, 191
National Missions for Enhanced Energy Efficiency and Sustainable Habitat, 218
National Policy on Biofuels, 218
Neom, 193
1972 Agreement on Cooperation in the Field of Environmental Protection between the United States of America and the Union of Soviet Socialist Republics, 70, 239

O

O'Neill, Jim, 166
overpopulation, 15, 17

P

Paris Agreement (PA), 6, 12, 42, 45, 55, 81, 82, 84, 87, 98, 108, 121,

122, 127–129, 136, 139, 151, 169, 170, 186, 188, 225
Paris Climate Summit, 122
permafrost, 68, 69
pollution, 4, 14, 17, 87, 106, 107, 122, 123, 127, 129, 139, 151, 157, 208, 221, 223
Putin, Vladimir, 74, 75, 77–82, 85, 88, 90, 91, 179, 235

R

renewable energy, 3–5, 42, 59, 80, 88, 98, 102, 107, 108, 113, 114, 120, 124, 128, 132, 133, 137–141, 151, 152, 154, 156, 157, 173, 177, 187, 197, 214, 215, 217–219, 221, 235, 236
Russia, 12, 13, 28, 68, 69, 72–76, 78–83, 85–89, 130, 131, 175, 178, 179, 234, 237
Russian Academy of Sciences (RAS), 75

S

Sahelian, 205
Salles, Ricardo, 39, 44–46
Saudi Arabia, 1, 7, 8, 75, 166, 167, 177, 179, 185, 186, 188–199, 234, 235, 237, 238
Saudi Green Initiative (SGI), 191, 194, 195
sea level, 37, 42, 207, 222
Secretariat for Climate Change and Forests, 45
solar power, 59, 114, 136, 138, 154, 177
Somalia, 205, 213
South Africa, 4, 12, 13, 150, 154, 156, 166, 169, 171, 218, 240
Special Climate Fund, 177

State Program on Energy Efficiency and Energy Development, 79
State Science and Technology Commission, 121

T

technological innovation, 83, 124, 193, 194, 196, 197
technology transfer, 9, 102, 138, 188, 199, 216
Torosov, Ilya, 87, 88, 178, 236
Trump, Donald, 43, 84, 135
2013 Decree on Greenhouse Gas Emission Reduction, 79

U

Ubuntu, 23, 24, 26–28, 30, 31, 238
Ukraine, 73, 83, 86, 88, 130, 175, 179, 205
Ultra Mega Renewable Parks, 102
United Arab Emirates (UAE), 89, 134, 166, 167, 185, 186
United Nations Conference on Sustainable Development, 42
United Nations Conference on the Human Environment, 40, 99
United Nations Environmental Programme Report, 206
United Nations Framework Convention on Climate Change (UNFCCC), 41, 54, 69, 70, 72, 73, 80, 88, 89, 91, 100–103, 108, 109, 122, 127, 128, 137, 150, 171, 177, 183, 186, 188, 189, 209, 224
UN Security Council, 167
UN Sustainable Development Goals (SDGs), 5, 120, 124, 169, 209, 240

US National Oceanic and Atmospheric Administration (NOAA), 166

W

Washington, 2, 70, 75, 84, 85, 90, 119

Western dominance, 11, 175

wind power, 102, 108, 114, 120, 219, 235

World Bank, 101, 102, 109, 134, 167, 189

World Health Organization (WHO), 71, 165, 221

Y

Yeltsin, Boris, 72, 74

Z

Zimbabwe, 217

Printed in the USA
CPSIA information can be obtained
at www.ICGtesting.com
CBHW050835211024
16148CB00007B/496